KILLING KING

KILLING KING

Racial Terrorists, James Earl Ray,
and the Plot to Assassinate
MARTIN LUTHER KING JR.

STUART WEXLER AND LARRY HANCOCK

COUNTERPOINT
Berkeley, California

KILLING KING

Images on pages 229–38 are reprinted courtesy of the authors.

Library of Congress Cataloging-in-Publication Data
Names: Wexler, Stuart, author. | Hancock, Larry J., author.
Title: Killing King : racial terrorists, James Earl Ray, and the plot to assassinate Martin Luther King Jr. / Stuart Wexler and Larry Hancock.
Description: Berkeley, CA : Counterpoint Press, 2018. | Includes bibliographical references and index.
Identifiers: LCCN 2017054596 | ISBN 9781619029194
Subjects: LCSH: King, Martin Luther, Jr., 1929–1968—Assassination. | Ray, James Earl, 1928–1998. | Conspiracies—United States—History—20th century.
Classification: LCC E185.97.K5 W473 2018 | DDC 323.092—dc23
LC record available at https://lccn.loc.gov/2017054596

Jacket designed by Adrian Morgan
Book designed by Wah-Ming Chang

COUNTERPOINT
2560 Ninth Street, Suite 318
Berkeley, CA 94710
www.counterpointpress.com

Printed in the United States of America
Distributed by Publishers Group West

10 9 8 7 6 5 4 3 2 1

To our families,
who inspire us in our search for truth and answers

CONTENTS

INTRODUCTION

One of the first questions a homicide detective will ask in the wake of a murder, in the absence of direct evidence, is "Did the victim have any enemies?" A follow-up question, less apt to be answered, is "Did those enemies attempt to harm the victim in the past?" Intuitively, in the wake of Dr. Martin Luther King Jr.'s murder on April 4, 1968, many Americans answered that question the same way. Dr. King himself, in his last sermon the night before his killing, foreshadowed the same culprit: "And then I got to Memphis. And some began to say the threats, or talk about the threats that were out. What would happen to me from some of our sick white brothers?"

"Sick white brothers"—entire groups of racists—tried repeatedly to kill Martin Luther King Jr. Our work documents at least nine such attempts between 1958 and 1968. During that time, white supremacists killed civil rights icons like Medgar Evers, Vernon Dahmer, Viola Liuzzo, and dozens of civil rights activists. Dr. King enjoyed little more protection than these men and women. He was not a head of state; he was not protected by the Secret Service, or by the military. That he survived until 1968 is almost entirely a result of good luck and his tendency to change his itinerary at the last minute; occasionally, a government informant volunteered information that saved his life. In that sense, the solution to King's murder is simple: the same kind of racists who had been trying to kill King for years finally succeeded that April 4.

Killing King is not simply the story of a murder; it is the investigation and documentation of a *conspiracy* to murder Dr. Martin Luther King Jr. that began in 1964, and evolved month by month and year by year. The secrecy and convoluted motives of the plotters and the network that bound them together obscured that conspiracy from those investigating Martin Luther King Jr.'s death. Only one man was charged and convicted of the crime.

The murder of Dr. King was not the act of a single man, certainly not one whose motive was never made clear, even in his conviction. The murder was the culmination of a conspiracy involving many characters, many strands, and many twists.

James Earl Ray, the man convicted of King's murder, remains the only person historically associated with the crime. In *Killing King*, we will show that Ray's travels, plans, and contacts from the time of his escape from prison in 1967 to his ultimate appearance in Memphis, in a boardinghouse across from the Lorraine Motel where King and his aides were staying, are an important part of the conspiracy story. But Ray was neither a rabid racist nor an ideological fanatic. His entire criminal career was motivated solely by a desire to make money. And while he asserted, behind prison bars, his absolute innocence for decades until his death in 1997, his protests do not hold up to scrutiny. We will demonstrate that Ray was only one of the people involved and his role is only one strand in the web of the conspiracy. Building on research from the authors' two previous works—*The Awful Grace of God* and *America's Secret Jihad*—we will show how two other men, one a criminal on parole, the other a right-wing terrorist, connect the diverse strands of the conspiracy.

The heart of the conspiracy, which Ray only became aware of in 1967, was a cash bounty on the life of Dr. King, first offered to contract killers in 1964. The first person to take that offer belonged to the "Dixie Mafia," a group we will be exploring in detail. That man, and certain of his associates, first engaged the bounty sponsors, violent white supremacists, in 1964. But these would-be patrons struggled to come up with the cash to make good on the offer. We will trace the connections between the Dixie mafia criminals and white supremacists from the time of the bounty's first appearance in Jackson, Mississippi, in 1964 onward into federal prisons in 1967, then across the nation from California through Mississippi and Georgia—and ultimately to Memphis, Tennessee, and Dr. King's death.

Beyond the King bounty, the Dixie Mafia, and James Earl Ray, we will also follow two other major strands in the web of conspiracy. The first involves members in the White Knights of the Ku Klux Klan of Mississippi, who pursued King's murder and committed other racial and religious terrorist acts over some four years. Ultimately it would be members of this group, under intense FBI pressure and with several members already scheduled to serve prison sentences, who would reach out to career criminals to accomplish what they could not do themselves.

A new ideology came to unite a small subset of the most devoted and influential members of these groups in ways that have not been adequately explored by historians. We explore a set of unsettling apocalyptic religious beliefs, known as Christian Identity, which linked the leaders of the White Knights with fellow religious radicals across the nation, from the home of Christian Identity in Los Angeles through a social network of its followers in the deep South. That racist network enabled the conspiracy in several ways, and ultimately raised and helped transport the money that was needed to draw career criminals into the plot against King. To fully comprehend the King conspiracy, it is necessary to understand the motives, characters, and abilities of the people within that network. That particularly applies to the Christian Identity leaders who used the White Knights for their own covert purpose, one unknown to many within the White Knights and fully understood and appreciated only by a handful within its inner circle.

Congress came close to identifying King's killers in the late 1970s when it formed the House Select Committee on Assassinations (the

HSCA) to uncover and reassess new leads. In 1968 the FBI had asserted that James Earl Ray had acted entirely on his own; the HSCA concluded that the "official version" was insufficient and that Ray likely worked with conspirators. They even investigated several of the key players discussed in this book. But they never fully resolved the crime, in part because they never considered the lead that would have pointed them to the middlemen who recruited the killers, or to the religious fanatics who put the plan in motion. The conspiracy could have been unraveled in 1968. As we will demonstrate, it should have been prevented in 1967.

PART ONE

1

THE WARNING

June 2, 1967, might have gone down in history as a day that
changed history. Donald Nissen, only recently released
from Leavenworth Federal Penitentiary in Kansas, sat
across from Dallas FBI agents in a Sherman, Texas, jail, arrested for
cashing a bad check. But the agents were not there to deal with that
minor charge, one that eventually was dismissed. Nissen had written
to federal law enforcement, insisting he needed to deliver a warning
about a threat to a national political figure.

Nissen shared his story with the agents. In the spring of 1967, a
few weeks before Nissen's release from Leavenworth, a fellow inmate,
Leroy McManaman, approached him about a contract for the murder
of Martin Luther King Jr. Though they were not friends, the two
became acquainted while working alongside each other in Leavenworth's famous shoe factory. Over the course of several months, they
exchanged "war stories" about their criminal histories; Nissen shared
his stories of home robberies and petty theft; McManaman's résumé
included everything from high-stakes bootlegging to the interstate
transportation of stolen cars.[1]

Nissen's intellect likely impressed McManaman. Nissen earned
favor with fellow prisoners as a "jailhouse attorney" who could help

with legal appeals. But two additional facts made the inmate even more attractive to McManaman as a potential co-conspirator: Nissen's sentence was almost over, and the soon-to-be-released inmate had already planned to work in Atlanta, Georgia, hometown of Dr. Martin Luther King Jr.

MacManaman promised Nissen a share of a $100,000 bounty offer if he helped McManaman with King's murder. As the agents recorded in their 1967 report, McManaman outlined two available roles: Nissen could conduct surveillance on King and report his movements to the actual killers, or he could be part of the killing itself. McManaman also asked Nissen to ask his cellmate, John May, a master machinist, whether May could construct a special gun for King's shooting. Additionally, Nissen told the FBI that if he said yes to McManaman, a series of go-betweens would link Nissen into the conspiracy, allowing him to avoid the suspicion of law enforcement. The go-betweens included a female real estate agent in Jackson, Mississippi; someone named "Floyd" whose last name Nissen could not recall for the FBI; and an individual with connections to the U.S. Marshals office. McManaman also told Nissen the money for the assassination was coming through the most violent racist organization in America, the White Knights of the Ku Klux Klan of Mississippi.[2]

Such threats against Dr. King were not unknown to the FBI. Files from FBI field offices around the country contained reports of bounty offers on the life of Martin Luther King Jr. spanning more than a decade. Such occurrences were so common, in fact, that the FBI accidentally stumbled upon another such offer in their first investigation of Nissen's claims. When they interviewed Nissen's cellmate, the machinist John May, he confirmed that Nissen had told him about McManaman's scheme. It had not made any real impression at the time because he had heard of similar offers a few years before, at a bar in North Carolina.[3] In other words, May thought discussions of bounties on King were little more than jailhouse gossip.

That is how the FBI treated Nissen's warning, as simply another of the bounty reports. To be fair, many of the reports lacked specifics that could be corroborated. FBI reports of King bounties often took the form of "he-said/he-said" claims, in which a known racist would be mentioned as offering a contract on King's life. The prominent racist would, as expected, deny said accusation, and federal agents would be left without any basis for further investigation.[4]

However, matters were much different with bounties circulating within federal prisons. The FBI simply did not have the kind of free access to prisoners that they had to civilians. Any prisoner who remained behind bars risked serious and violent payback for talking to law enforcement. There are no pre-assassination records released to date in which an inmate warned the FBI of a King assassination plot as it was forming: none except Nissen's.

But information developed by the FBI, albeit after the assassination, shows that prison bounty offers were circulating and were deadly serious—having filtered into multiple prisons, with dollar offers that were substantial, fronted by socially prominent racists. Notably, the son of a prison guard in Georgia (confirmed, later, by the guard's daughter) told the FBI that his father became aware of meetings between three unidentified Atlanta business leaders and prisoners in Atlanta Federal Penitentiary; in 1967 the businessmen offered large sums of money to any prisoner willing to murder King. The father attempted to provide this information to the Georgia Bureau of Investigation but was rebuffed.[5] By 1968, the FBI asserted: "We have had several instances where persons incarcerated at various times advised that King had a bounty of $100,000 placed on his head."[6]

As will become much clearer in later chapters, the bounty offers against King show a pattern, one that will become important in understanding what happened to Martin Luther King Jr. on April 4, 1968. Wealthy segregationists and white supremacists in the Southeast were becoming increasingly eager to kill King, increasing their dollar offers, from less than $2,000 in 1958 to $100,000 by 1968. Just as important was a change in their tactics, with radical groups turning from plots involving their own members or those of associated groups to those involving professional criminals.

One group of racists had explored contracts with criminals as early as 1964: the White Knights of the Ku Klux Klan of Mississippi, the group Leroy McManaman told Nissen was offering the 1967 bounty. That year the White Knights had offered a contract on King to an increasingly active criminal network—one growing both in its numbers and in its willingness to use brazen, wanton violence—now referred to as the Dixie Mafia.[7] Called "rednecks on steroids," these men (and women) were fundamentally different from their Sicilian counterparts in La Cosa Nostra.

For one thing, they often lacked a formal hierarchy with one godfather calling the shots; rather, the Dixie Mafia comprised several independent and loosely affiliated gangs of more-or-less co-equal members who worked out of two major territories in the Great Plains and in the Southeast. Modern-day desperadoes, members of what were first called the Traveling Criminals or Crossroaders, cut their teeth robbing homes and banks, heisting stolen cars across state lines, running illegal gambling operations, hatching extortion and bribery scams, and running drugs and guns in their theaters of operation. The core of a Dixie Mafia gang might include a bootlegger, a safe cracker, a getaway driver, a strong-arm man (or several), among others, and they would frequently augment their group with additional hoodlums outside of the core group if such expertise or additional manpower was needed.[8]

They were also more avaricious and less scrupulous than the Sicilian Mafia. The Italian mob famously shied away from killing government officials and members of law enforcement. But almost nothing stood between a Dixie Mafia gang and money. In one of the most brazen examples, gangster Donald Sparks, whose base of operations was in eastern Oklahoma, and an associate, William Kenneth Knight, robbed the mayor of Fort Payne, Alabama, in his home, at gunpoint—and then, when caught, stole the victim's car and fled the scene of the crime. (It turned out that members of local law enforcement were "in" on the plot.)[9]

More alarmingly, in 1967, Dixie Mafia members infamously killed the wife of Tennessee sheriff Buford Pusser, lionized in the drive-in movie classic *Walking Tall*; she died in the sheriff's arms, from a rifle bullet that, whether meant for Pusser (and missed) or for his spouse, was no doubt intended to stop the lawman from shutting down Dixie Mafia gambling and liquor schemes at the Tennessee-Mississippi border.[10]

Many in what became known as the State Line mob fled to McNairy and Alcorn Counties (in Tennessee and Mississippi respectively) following a crackdown on Dixie Mafia activity in the vice-infested city of Phoenix, Alabama, in 1954—the year of another bold political assassination. In that instance, a hitman, most believe on orders from local Dixie Mafia lords, killed the law-and-order attorney general elect Albert Patterson. Author Faith Serafin described the horrible encounter:

> Patterson . . . left his office at about 9:00 p.m. As he exited the building, approaching his car that was parked in the alley . . . an assailant approached him and shoved a pistol in his mouth. Without hesitation, the killer fired, shooting Patterson once in the mouth, once in the arm and again in the chest. Albert Patterson fell to the ground bleeding and mortally wounded.[11]

The shocking crime inspired Alabama governor Gordon Persons to call in the National Guard to crack down on the crime-infested metropolis using limited martial law, encouraging the exodus into nearby states. Years later, that led to the Dixie Mafia showdown with Pusser in Tennessee.

More than thirty years after Patterson's killing, Dixie Mafia gangsters murdered Judge Vincent Sherry and his politician wife, Margaret, in their Biloxi, Mississippi, home. The crime was motivated by what turned out to be false suspicions that Sherry was involved in, and skimming money from, a Dixie Mafia extortion scheme. The killing was arranged by Kirksey Nix, a one-time enemy of Pusser, who "maintained tight control over the mob's operations in Louisiana and Mississippi despite spending two decades in prison for killing a grocer."[12]

Not surprisingly, certain Dixie mobsters earned reputations as killers for hire, among them Don Sparks, who some suspect was involved in the still-unsolved murder of Pauline Pusser.[13] Sparks, in fact, earned such a strong reputation as a contract killer that Sicilian crime families hired him for professional murders.[14]

In 1964, the White Knights of the Ku Klux Klan of Mississippi reached out to Sparks and at least one other criminal, in hopes of murdering King when he came to Mississippi. On the run after another string of robberies, Sparks revealed outlines of the plot to a fellow Oklahoma-based gangster, Hermit Eugene Wing, who, within months, revealed the information to the FBI in 1965. When the FBI followed up they approached a Jackson, Mississippi, police officer, John Chamblee, who confirmed hearing rumors that the KKK had "hired a 'killer'; from the State of Oklahoma to murder Martin Luther King Jr. when King was in Jackson. The 'killer'; was known as 'Two Jumps' and came to Jackson, Mississippi to 'case' the layout and while in Jackson, stayed at the Tarrymore Motel was to use a high-powered rifle with telescopic sights. This deal allegedly fell through when the Klansmen could not raise the $13,000 demanded by 'Two Jumps.'"[15]

Donald Sparks earned the nickname "Two Jumps" because of his fondness for rodeo, something the FBI learned, in part, during their 1965 investigation, when a Mississippi Klansman also reported hearing vague rumors of a plot against King. Asked about Sparks, the Klansman, whose name is still hidden in government records, responded, "You mean Two Jumps?" That the Klansman was familiar with Sparks is not surprising given that, according to Klan expert Michael Newton, the Mississippi White Knights used Dixie Mafia men in "strong-arm operations."[16]

But the FBI had dismissed the 1964 White Knights assassination rumor as unreliable—a decision that was to have dire implications for Dr. King. The FBI did so because they could not corroborate another crime mentioned by their Oklahoma informant, implicating Sparks in the murder of a Dixie Mafia drug trafficker. Even though the Oklahoma State Bureau of Investigation gave credit to that claim, the FBI chose to dismiss both it and the allegation that Sparks had been involved in a White Knights plot against King. The FBI chose to dismiss the primary allegations despite the strong corroboration from Detective Chamblee. Those FBI decisions helped seal Martin Luther King Jr.'s fate three years later. In retrospect it appears clear that the threat that Nissen was relaying was simply a second attempt by the White Knights to use Dixie Mafia members to kill Dr. King. In 1967, the White Knights would rely on outsiders to provide the money they could not raise in 1964.

Independent corroboration for Wing's account of the Sparks–White Knights bounty came from another Dixie Mafia member, William Kenneth Knight, who, in the late 1960s, became a valued cooperating witness for federal prosecutors in trials of other hoodlums. Knight participated in criminal activity with both Wing and Sparks, including the aforementioned robbery in Fort Payne. According to post-assassination documents from 1968, Knight told FBI agents that Sparks described the 1964 bounty offer to him (Wing was also present, according to Knight) while they were on the run from law enforcement in 1966; the account closely matched what Wing attributed to Sparks and relayed to the FBI in 1965. Since the conversation between Knight and Sparks occurred in 1966, it had to be an independent discussion of the plot. Knight recalled the dollar figure as $10,000 and he did not remember whom Sparks identified as the sponsor, if he identified anyone at all. The FBI report stated:

> Knight stated that Sparks is perfectly capable of committing a murder and is a known hater of Negroes. According to Knight, Sparks is not known to make jokes and it was believable to Knight that an actual offer was made to Sparks by someone.

When the FBI followed up on Knight's reports and interviewed Sparks, they found him in detention in an Alabama prison. He denied involvement in any King plot, then adamantly refused to answer follow-up questions. The FBI correctly noted that Sparks had been in detention for months and could not have been in Memphis, and used that to dismiss him as a suspect. This ignores the well-established modus operandi of the Dixie Mafia, of organizing crimes from behind prison bars (the murder of Judge Vincent Sherry by Kirksey Nix is only the most famous example.) A more thorough investigation of the aborted effort by the White Knights to pay Sparks to kill King in 1964 would have led to just such an operation. It would have led to Leroy McManaman and the bounty offer he made to Donald Nissen in Leavenworth Penitentiary in 1967.

As will become clear in later chapters, McManaman not only knew Sparks well, he almost definitely worked with Sparks in the unrealized project to kill King in Mississippi in 1964. The second iteration of the White Knights plot, the one revealed by McManaman to Nissen, was a continuation of the effort that had failed to assassinate King in 1964. Only this time, the bounty plot would succeed on April 4, 1968.

The White Knights, and the network of racist zealots who supported them, never wavered in their aim to kill King—engaging in multiple plots until they found their mark, literally and figuratively, in 1968. But in the highly compartmentalized FBI, reports deemed "unreliable" had no currency, so Sparks's account to the informant never reached the agents tasked with investigating Nissen's report of a bounty three years later. It was only revisited in the investigation that followed King's murder.

Nissen himself knew nothing about any connection to the 1964 bounty. The authors developed the connection between the two events by collating and corroborating often minor details in newspaper accounts, interviews, and never-before-released government records. McManaman only relayed the details of the most up-to-date 1967 bounty offer to Nissen. There was no mention of Sparks or "Two

Jumps" and a high-powered rifle at the Tarrymore Motel. Nissen wanted no part of it. He was a career burglar and con man, not a murderer. He had used guns in his crimes, but he had never shot anyone. But saying no to someone like McManaman, while both remained at Leavenworth, was dangerous. Knowing too much already, Nissen could have been killed before his release, before he went to Atlanta and the sales job he had waiting for him. Nissen told his cellmate John May about the offer, but not with any intent to recruit May. Nissen was thinking out loud, debating how to thread the needle between avoiding involvement in a potential capital offense and avoiding being the victim of one at the hands of McManaman. Ultimately, he decided to keep to himself and bide his time until he was released.[17]

This tactic—never saying "yes" or "no" to McManaman—seemed smart at the time, but it would cause Nissen more trouble than he ever expected. On that Friday, June 2, 1967, sitting across from two special agents from the FBI, Nissen thought he had his opportunity to safely extricate himself from future association with the plot against King. Hundreds of miles away from Leavenworth and McManaman, he had no intention of going back to prison on a life sentence, and he gave information to the Dallas FBI as much to protect himself as to save King from being killed.

It now appears likely that Donald Nissen's June 1967 story to federal agents might have preempted King's tragic murder on April 4, 1968—if only the FBI had investigated it more fully. Instead they conducted a superficial investigation in the summer of 1967 that did nothing but expose Nissen to danger.

The FBI did not revisit Nissen's story until April 1968, after Martin Luther King Jr. was assassinated. Nissen, they discovered, had jumped parole and disappeared.[18] Despite his desire to disentangle himself from the plot against King, Nissen's unwilling involvement had only just begun on that summer day in June 1967.

2

THE SPONSORS

The White Knights of the Ku Klux Klan of Mississippi formed in the state's cauldron of anti-integrationist resistance in the early 1960s. No white supremacist group committed more acts of violence in the nation. As one of the few states with a majority nonwhite population, Mississippi's white establishment vigorously opposed efforts to give equal rights to minorities. Yet some white Mississippians did not feel that the reactionary moves made by the wealthy White Citizens Councils and the government-backed Mississippi State Sovereignty Commission went far enough. To some, even the existing Klan regime in Mississippi was too passive, and they abandoned their county-based subgroups (known as Klaverns) in large numbers, coalescing to form the White Knights, led by the devilishly brilliant Samuel Holloway Bowers and eventually becoming the most successfully violent KKK subgroup in the nation.

Law enforcement estimates connected the group to at least "10 murders; to the burnings of an estimated 75 black churches, to at least 300 assaults and beatings and bombings."[1] The violence included the famous Mississippi Burning (abbreviated as MIBURN by the FBI), murders of three civil rights workers in Neshoba County. Klansmen firebombed the home of voting rights activist Vernon Dahmer, in Forrest County, Mississippi, nearly killing his wife and children, who luckily survived.[2] Dahmer died from burns suffered in the attack. Although the group had not officially formed when Mississippi NAACP leader Medgar Evers was assassinated in June 1963—shot in the back by sniper fire, just yards away from his home and his wife and children—many suspect that a budding version of the White Knights had some role in the attack. The man eventually convicted of the Evers murder, Byron de la Beckwith, became a leading member of the White Knights. Like de la Beckwith, who liked to taunt law enforcement with quasi-confessions of the sniper attack, the White Knights were the boldest of any Klan group in the country, certain that a Mississippi jury would never convict them of a crime. They even put local law enforcement and FBI agents on hit lists.[3]

But developments in 1967 brought a new wave of hope for law enforcement. Using federal civil rights laws rather than local murder statutes, the Justice Department finally brought nine Klansmen to account for their roles in the murder of civil rights martyrs Mickey Schwerner, Andrew Goodman, and James Chaney in Neshoba County in 1964. The FBI had devoted a tremendous amount of resources over some three years to establish the facts of the case and, in fact, had developed most of the story by the end of 1964. The sheriff of Neshoba County, Lawrence Rainey, a closet member of the White Knights, arrested the three activists under false pretenses, with the help of his deputy, Cecil Price. While Rainey held the men incommunicado, a posse of Klansmen assembled and traveled to Neshoba, when Rainey obligingly released his prey the evening of June 20. The Klansmen, with Price's help, followed the activists down a dark highway, forced them off the road and out of their vehicle, and killed them in the nearby woods. White Knights Grand Wizard Sam Bowers had set the outlines of the plan in motion more than a month before, and it worked to perfection.

The disappearance of two white men, Schwerner and Goodman, galvanized the nation in ways that most other racial crimes, directed solely at blacks (like Chaney), did not. At the urging of President

Lyndon Johnson, a dogged FBI investigation uncovered the victims' bodies buried under an earthen dam, but a Southern judge dismissed the murder case against Rainey and Price in 1964. In 1967, the FBI developed a high-level informant, Delmar Dennis, inside the White Knights, and the Department of Justice used civil rights statutes to retry the perpetrators. Prized targets among the accused included the infamous brothers Raymond and Alton Wayne Roberts; the latter, according to accounts from those involved in the ambush, shot at least one of the victims. Most importantly, the DOJ set its sights on finally sending the kingpin, Samuel Bowers, to prison.[4]

Born in 1924 to a wealthy New Orleans family, Bowers grew up in Jackson, Mississippi. He enlisted in the navy in World War II and briefly spent time in California before returning to southern Mississippi. He owned a vending machine company, Sambo Amusement Company, but focused his energy on directing the activities of the White Knights. But Bowers was not a typical "redneck," as he called his followers. He had studied engineering at the University of Southern California in Los Angeles, and then at Tulane University in New Orleans. If other Klan leaders played checkers, Bowers played chess, plotting crimes months in advance, using spy-like tradecraft to avoid law enforcement surveillance and always remaining careful—almost paranoid—not to leave his "fingerprints" on his crimes.[5] He would plot crimes in new locations to divert FBI resources away from major investigations and even considered framing rival Klan groups for his own offenses.

Bowers alone had the ability to issue a "code four"—White Knights parlance for a bombing or killing. He did so for both the MIBURN killings and the Dahmer firebombing.[6] But nothing occupied the attention or energy of Bowers like the prospect of killing Martin Luther King Jr. From 1964 on, Bowers attempted to assassinate Dr. King at least four times.

The first attempt, referenced in Chapter 1, involved outsourcing to Dixie Mafia hitmen. Specifically, the White Knights offered a bounty to a bank robber and highly respected contract killer from Oklahoma, Donald Sparks, to eliminate King if he came to Mississippi, as the

minister eventually did in July 1964 in response to the Mississippi
Burning murders. Government files describe Billy Buckles, one of
Bowers's senior lieutenants, telling a group of Klansmen at a summer
meeting that the White Knights were contracting with criminals to
perform an act of violence that would "make the death of Medgar
Evers look sick [by comparison]."[7] Bowers himself told an FBI informant at the end of 1964 that "two men with high powered rifles were
assigned to kill" King when he "last toured the state of Mississippi."
Bowers claimed that the two men continued "working on the matter,"
when in reality the White Knights could not raise a sufficient amount
of money ($13,000) to satisfy Sparks. But this 1964 plot, which we
will refer to from this point forward on as the "Sparks-McManaman
plot," did not die as much as it remained dormant until 1967, when
Leroy McManaman presented it to Donald Nissen in Leavenworth
Penitentiary.

Perhaps realizing that money could be a problem in luring professional killers to kill King, Bowers changed tactics and relied on his
own men. Bowers devised the next plot in 1965, when Dr. King traveled
through Mississippi on his way to Alabama, where civil rights activists pushed the case for voting rights in cities like Selma. The primary
attack was to be by snipers, with a backup plan of exploding a highway bridge if King escaped the shooting. Advanced word of the attack
appears to have come from the deeply placed government informant
Delmar Dennis, a minister who had been close to Klan leader Samuel Bowers. Dennis turned on Bowers because he suspected Bowers's
patriotism and had reservations about the White Knights' excessive
violence. The attack did not occur, but only because King's route was
changed, thanks to Dennis's information, at the last minute.[8]

By this point, Bowers's desire to kill King caught the attention of
the highest levels of American government. President Lyndon Johnson personally ordered the FBI to provide additional protection to
King when he passed through Mississippi in 1964 and 1965.[9] On the
heels of the MIBURN killings, Johnson worried about civil disorder
in Mississippi if the Klan murdered King. Johnson and King worked

closely together to push through landmark civil rights legislation, and as the nation waited for Johnson to sign the Voting Rights Act of 1965 (in August), their working relationship, while contentious, remained relatively close. But Johnson knew that FBI director J. Edgar Hoover enjoyed anything but a close relationship with the civil rights leader.

King, in his capacity as leader of the Southern Christian Leadership Conference (SCLC), made the cardinal mistake of publicly criticizing the FBI for its failures to resolve dozens of civil rights murders throughout the South. Hoover, maniacally protective of his agency's reputation, responded by publicly labeling Dr. King as an enemy of law and order and insinuating that the activist enjoyed close relations with communists. Privately, Hoover pushed his agents to surveil the minister for the purpose of ruining his reputation and even worse. At one point Hoover's agents sent King a letter with the goal of shaming the minister into committing suicide over his alleged extramarital affairs, a letter that arrived concurrently with a tape—sent to King's wife, Coretta—purporting to be a recording of an intimate encounter.[10] More relevant to King's safety, from 1965 on Hoover insisted that his agents discontinue the practice of telling King's advisors about plots against King's life. Instead, Hoover ordered his subordinates to inform relevant police agencies only—a dangerous policy for King because these groups often included large numbers of KKK members and sympathizers. Hoover knew full well the dangers of this policy from his experience providing protection to King on Johnson's orders in 1964. When King went to Mississippi in the wake of the MIBURN murders, Neshoba County sheriff Lawrence Rainey protested the additional FBI security for King. His own men, Rainey insisted, could protect King. At that very moment, Hoover knew, Rainey and his subordinates were being investigated for their role in facilitating the MIBURN killings.[11] Rainey, as noted earlier, belonged to Bowers's group, and detained the three MIBURN victims in his jail on June 21, 1964.

Bowers remained undeterred in his desire to assassinate King, but by 1966, King's own prerogatives created problems for any would-be plotters. Having helped undo legal segregation and discrimination in the South, King increasingly focused his political attention on de facto discrimination in the north, in places like Chicago, Illinois, where King temporarily moved with his family in 1966, to highlight problems with poverty and housing. This brought King out of Bowers's domain. But Bowers crafted an ingenious if unfortunate plan to overcome this logistical problem: he arranged to lure King into an ambush. Bowers approached three men, Ernest Avant, James Lloyd Jones, and Claude Fuller, misfits the White Knights had recently expelled from their ranks, and promised them readmission to the group if they murdered an innocent black man. The first phase of the plan succeeded with the murder of black farmer Ben Chester White in Natchez, Mississippi, on June 10, 1966. The men selected White mostly as a target of opportunity, but also, in part, because he had no substantive connection to the civil rights movement and his death would seem more senseless than politically motivated violence. Having convinced White to help them find their lost dog, the men lured the farmer into their pickup truck and then brought him to a bridge where they abruptly stopped. Using FBI records and court transcripts (the three men were convicted for murder in 1998), Mississippi's *Clarion-Ledger* investigative reporter Jerry Mitchell described the subsequent scene four decades later:

> Claude Fuller got out of the Chevy, grabbed his rifle and loaded it before going around the car and opening the door where White was. Avants stood beside him.
>
> "All right, Pop," Fuller told him. "Get out."
>
> Spotting the rifle, White withered in his seat, bowing his head to pray.
>
> "Get out!" Fuller barked.
>
> "Oh, Lord," White said, "what have I done to deserve this?"
>
> Fuller answered with his automatic rifle, firing two quick bursts that emptied the gun of all 18 shots.
>
> Fuller then turned to Avants and told him to fire, too.[12]

The men heaved White's dead body into the waterway below, and in the days that followed, Sam Bowers waited for the second phase of his plan, once White's body was found on June 12.

King's decisions and movements had confounded the efforts to kill him. If the murderers could dictate King's movements (rather than the other way around), then an ambush would be much more likely to succeed. Anyone studying King's past behavior may have predicted that a murder like White's would elicit an appearance by the SCLC leader. King attended the funeral of Medgar Evers in Jackson in June of 1963; he visited Birmingham to eulogize the four young girls who died after the bombing of the 16th Street Baptist Church; later, he visited Mississippi, more than once, to mourn the Neshoba victims and raise public awareness about the lack of justice in that case. The gruesome nature of White's death could be expected to capture the attention of someone like Dr. King. According to Mitchell:

> There were so many injuries that almost any of the bullets could have killed him. Bullets had pulverized his liver and ripped his diaphragm. At least one had carved a gaping hole in the left side of his heart. The aorta, which carried vital blood to the rest of the body, had been torn in many places. There was no question that he bled to death.[13]

But Bowers miscalculated in believing that White's murder would bring King to Natchez. For one thing, another white man attempted to kill James Meredith on June 6. Meredith, famous for integrating Ole Miss, had begun a one-man 220-mile March Against Fear from Memphis to Jackson, Mississippi, early the previous morning, to inspire African Americans to register to vote. But 30 miles into the march, Meredith sustained serious injuries when Aubrey Norvell, an unemployed hardware store worker, struck him with, as Meredith later described it, "over a hundred pellets" from a 16-gauge shotgun that hit him "in the head, neck, back and legs." King joined several others in taking up Meredith's mantle, a three-week trek that did not include a detour to protest White's murder in Natchez.[14]

This may not have been the first time Bowers considered this kind of a trap. Though more speculative than the White attempt, evidence suggests that Bowers wanted to draw King to Mississippi for the Sparks-McManaman plot. Under this scenario, Bowers had multiple motivations when he ordered a "code four" on James Chaney, Andrew Goodman, and Michael Schwerner in the Mississippi Burning murders. Undoubtedly, the most widely accepted interpretation of the crime—that Bowers wanted to use the murders to scare the hundreds of incoming student activists on their way to Mississippi for Freedom Summer in 1964—is true. But the disappearance of two white men alongside a black man in Neshoba County also generated nationwide attention, and revulsion when federal agents discovered the bodies weeks later. Bowers seemed to anticipate the reaction—one of the largest federal investigations in American history—in a speech given only weeks before in a closely guarded meeting of Klan members.

"The enemy will seek their final push for victory here in Mississippi," he said, referring to the well-publicized Freedom Summer. But he added that open violence between whites and blacks would lead to a "decree from the communist authorities in charge of the national government . . . declaring martial law."[15] The federal intervention in Mississippi did not quite reach the level of martial law, but polls showed that, during the height of the search for the bodies in Mississippi, when Bowers provoked law enforcement by arranging for additional attacks, a large number of Americans favored something like a declaration of martial law if the violence got worse. Such turbulence surely would invite a visit and protests, as it often did, from Dr. King. And this raises questions about something else Bowers told his audience in the speech before the murders. Speaking of guerrilla strike teams who would resist the federal government and respond to outside agitators, Bowers said:

>Any personal attacks on the enemy should be carefully
>planned to include *only* the leaders and prime white
>collaborators of the enemy forces. These attacks against
>these selected individual targets should, of course, be as
>severe as circumstances and conditions will permit. The
>leaders . . . should be our prime targets.[16]

As will become clear in the following chapter, Bowers calibrated
major acts of violence for maximum, public effect. It was part of an
even larger plan to incite violence across the country, not only in Mississippi—one that he kept even from his closest followers; one that he
pursued with a religious devotion.

His failures to kill King from 1964 to 1966 did not deter Bowers.
Instead, he appears to have learned from his mistakes and changed
his tactics. When he could not pay Dixie Mafia killers, he turned "in
house" to fellow Klansmen. When King could no longer be counted
on to follow his announced itinerary in 1965, Bowers attempted to
dictate the time and place of the murder through a trap (White's killing) in 1966. Bowers was not alone in plotting King's assassination;
King escaped numerous times through luck. The minister benefit-
ted from advance warning only once, in 1965, because the informant
Delmar Dennis had become aware of the plot and because President
Johnson took a unique role in protecting King's life. So, to ultimately
succeed in killing King, Bowers relied on a plot that could account for,
and even closely track, King's movements; one that would be flexible,
in place to be activated regardless of time or geography, when the
opportunity presented itself. He turned to a Dixie Mafia hitman who
could follow King, even outside of the domain of Mississippi, and
assassinate him using killers for hire.

But in 1967 and 1968, Bowers faced a major obstacle: the nonstop surveillance and scrutiny of federal law enforcement. Agents in
the Jackson, Mississippi, field office engaged in what amounted to a
virtual war with the Mississippi KKK. Bowers always took extraor-
dinary measures to avoid surveillance. When he gave the aforemen-

tioned 1964 speech about the "enemy's . . . final push for victory" before
the MIBURN killings, Bowers did so in a remote building so that
Piper airplanes could provide aerial warning of any potential law enforcement observers or raids.[17] The audience had been body-searched
upon entry. At one point, he proposed firing the entire leadership of
the White Knights out of concern that some might be informants. In
1967, with his one-time close aide Delmar Dennis prepared to testify
against Bowers and others at trial, Bowers was more cautious than
ever. The FBI's efforts denied him freedom of movement and access to
his lieutenants and foot soldiers.

Bowers responded to this in a familiar way: he turned to outsiders to advance his plans to kill King and engage in white supremacist violence. As described in detail in Chapter 1, the White Knights
floated a high-money bounty offer to the Dixie Mafia to kill King. In
researching Donald Nissen's claims, something became clear: unbeknownst to Nissen, Leroy McManaman, the hoodlum who offered
him the bounty at Leavenworth, very likely participated in the 1964
Sparks-McManaman plot on King. McManaman belonged to the
same cadre of Dixie Mafia gangsters as Don Sparks, a group headquartered in Tulsa, Oklahoma. McManaman knew Sparks personally
according to Robert "Rubie" Charles Jenkins, a fellow member of the
Tulsa gang and Sparks's closest friend. McMamanan, in turn, part-
nered with Jenkins in an interstate car-theft ring that landed both men
in federal prison in 1964.[18] But McManaman, who somehow secured
a commutation from the Kansas governor against the wishes of a state
prosecutor in 1952,[19] also managed to win a rare federal appeals bond
in 1964. This allowed McManaman to temporarily leave Leavenworth
while he challenged his 1963 conviction in the Tenth Federal Circuit
Court of Appeals. The court's jurisdiction included Kansas, where
McManaman and Jenkins were originally convicted, and five other
states.[20] But McManaman not only imperiled his appeal, he risked
adding years to his prison sentence: he spent weeks outside of Kansas, staying with a married real estate broker, Sybil Eure, in Jackson,
Mississippi, in the spring of 1964. Thus McManaman, whose criminal

activity rarely included Mississippi, found his way to the Magnolia State at the same time that his friend, hitman Donald Sparks, took refuge at a Jackson motel, waiting for the money to kill King. There's little doubt he was there to assist Sparks in King's assassination, but the bounty money never arrived, McManaman's appeal failed, and he had to return, before Freedom Summer began, to Leavenworth to serve out his sentence.

It is critical to note that Eure is the woman whose name McManaman provided to Donald Nissen as a go-between if Nissen wanted to join the 1967 King murder conspiracy. She was the first person the FBI interviewed to follow up on Nissen's revelations about the plot in the Sherman, Texas, jail. Eure denied any connection to a King bounty; her explanations for how she knew McManaman defied credulity, including the claim that an unidentified friend recommended McManaman to her as an expert on real estate.[21] Putting aside the dubious notion that a middle-class woman in Jackson would share a mutual connection to a hardened career criminal—and that her friend would encourage Eure to shelter that criminal for weeks— McManaman's only background in real estate was running an illegal gambling operation out of an inn he ran in Colorado. McManaman's prison records reveal a much deeper relationship than Eure admitted: he hoped to marry her when he got out of Leavenworth, and she was his most frequent visitor while he stayed behind bars.[22]

The FBI neglected another important revelation by Eure. Asked if she knew anything about the other two go-betweens that McManaman spoke of to Donald Nissen, Eure provided some interesting answers. She told the agents she knew a Floyd—her own brother, Floyd Gardner. This Floyd, however, was not the Floyd referenced by McManaman, as will become clear in Chapter 5, but the FBI did little to investigate. Eure also identified two men she knew who were connected to the federal marshals office in Mississippi: Charlie Sutherland, a cousin, and Robert C. Thomas, an associate. Neither of them, she asserted, would have anything to do with the Klan or a plot on King's life.

Interviews conducted by the authors with people familiar with

Sutherland and with Sutherland himself confirm Eure's assertions about her cousin. But Robert C. Thomas, as federal authorities would learn soon after the King assassination, did associate with the Ku Klux Klan. Before he began work as a clerk with the southern district court in Mississippi, Thomas was appointed as the chief investigator for the Mississippi State Sovereignty Commission, a state government agency that spied on civil rights groups in Mississippi as part of the state's wider effort to resist federally imposed integration. But as a clerk for the federal courts, Thomas illegally rigged juries on behalf of Sam Bowers. Nissen did tell the authors that McManaman specifically noted that the go-between had recently been appointed as a deputy marshal in Mississippi. This would seem to eliminate Thomas as a candidate (he was only a clerk). But at the time that McManaman stayed with Eure, Thomas had been in the news for having been deputized as a marshal *temporarily*, to help law enforcement as needed, if civil rights protests got out of hand. And, as a clerk in the court, Thomas was in a unique position to cover for McManaman as he violated his appeal bond and visited Mississippi. He could have, for instance, provided false documentation to show that McManaman was in Jackson to provide information to authorities there. No record indicates that the FBI investigated either Sutherland or Thomas as the potential go-between Nissen cited in his July 2 warning about the King plot.

This is because the FBI accepted Eure's claims of innocence and ignorance without a qualm. They arranged a cursory follow-up investigation at Leavenworth, and did not even bother to interview McManaman until months after the King assassination, even after John May corroborated parts of Donald Nissen's story. A respectable Southern woman like Eure, they reasoned, would not involve herself in anything like a KKK murder conspiracy. On one level this observation dovetailed with history: women played an important support role for the KKK but they almost never participated in acts of terrorism or assumed positions of leadership. But the FBI, once again, underestimated Sam Bowers. At the very moment the FBI visited Sybil Eure,[23] Sam Bowers was planning yet another way around the FBI's nonstop surveillance, and it included employing a Jackson woman, Kathy Ainsworth, among a team of terrorists.

The choice to use Ainsworth as a terrorist starting in 1967 was a stroke of evil genius. An attractive young elementary schoolteacher, she did not fit any of the stereotypes usually assigned to Klan members, allowing her to keep her terrorist activities hidden even from a vigilant FBI. But Ainsworth embraced racial and ethnic resentment as stridently as anyone who ever burnt down a black church or attacked a civil rights protestor. Raised by a virulently racist single mother, Margaret Capomacchia, Ainsworth was mentored in white supremacy by Sidney Crockett Barnes, a vile bigot who fled Florida to Mobile, Alabama, after a law enforcement crackdown on racial violence. Barnes did not stop his support for terrorism, becoming part of a failed 1963–1964 plot against Martin Luther King Jr.'s life that will be detailed in the next chapter. Both Barnes and Margaret Capomacchia enjoyed close connections to Klansmen in Mississippi, and Barnes sent his daughter to college there, with Kathy as her roommate.[24] Kathy later joined the Americans for the Preservation of the White Race in Mississippi, a front group for the Mississippi White Knights, but privately worked closely with both the White Knights and the United Klans of America. She even kept her militant associations secret from her husband, a man Sidney Barnes, the surrogate father who gave her away at her wedding, did not approve of as her spouse. Barnes wished Kathy had married someone else: a like-minded extremist, Thomas Albert Tarrants III.[25]

Barnes introduced Kathy to Tarrants, a tall, lanky, and bright twenty-year-old, at the Barnes residence in Mobile. He indoctrinated both Tarrants and Ainsworth in a version of racist ideology embraced by Sam Bowers and a network of fanatics that stretched across the United States. Tarrants went searching for Bowers in the summer of 1967, and Bowers would use both him and Ainsworth to launch a series of attacks on black and Jewish targets that bewildered the Jackson office of the FBI for months. But that wave of violence was just a prelude for the grand finale, the assassination of Martin Luther King Jr.

3

THE MOTIVE

In the summer of 1967, Sam Bowers routinely met secretly in the woods with Tommy Tarrants. Oftentimes, they met only after Bowers changed vehicles several times. When they communicated in person, Bowers often insisted that they exchange messages on paper rather than verbally, and that the papers then be burnt. Sam Bowers had great plans for Tarrants, plans of which the young radical may not have been fully aware, and Bowers had no intention of letting local or federal law enforcement disrupt his agenda.

In using Tarrants and Ainsworth, Bowers was not using outsiders simply to avoid legal scrutiny and engage in terrorism. Bowers was showing his true colors for the first time since he became the Grand Wizard of the White Knights in 1964. Bowers ran the White Knights with two agendas. One, defending the so-called Southern Way of Life, was obvious both to his members and to the general public. The other, a religious vision of a holy race war, he kept even from his top lieutenants. But not from Tarrants. Sidney Barnes, the Mobile painter who mentored Tarrants and Ainsworth, had already inculcated both of his charges in the same religious worldview as Bowers. All of them—Bowers, Barnes, Tarrants, and Ainsworth—followed the teachings of Wesley Albert Swift. One of the few White Knights

who knew about this new, secret cadre of terrorists was Laud E.
(L. E.) Matthews. He even referred to the Tarrants/Ainsworth group
as Swift's "underground hit squad."[1]

From his pulpit in Southern California, Swift stood, literally and
figuratively, as the focal point in a religious movement that wedded
together fundamentalist, apocalyptic Christian ideas with white supremacist ideology. Known today as Christian Identity, its roots
could be traced to Victorian-era pseudo-anthropology. A small set
of amateur anthropologists with theological interest began speculating about the lost tribes of Israel, the subgroups of Hebrews who
in Old Testament lore settled the northern half of the Kingdom of
Israel in 722 B.C., only to be exiled by an Assyrian king, never to
be seen again. These Victorians argued that some of these lost tribes
ultimately resettled in Europe, becoming the progenitors of white Europeans. In this telling, white Christian Europeans then had partial
claim, alongside Jews, to being God's chosen people.[2]

When these ideas spread to the United States, they became popularized by William Cameron, the editor for automobile tycoon Henry
Ford's *Dearborn Independent*. Ford and Cameron infamously used their
periodical, with a distribution in the hundreds of thousands, to spread
anti-Jewish conspiracy theories throughout North America and the
world (Adolf Hitler had copies). The appeal of the paper dovetailed
with the resurgence of the Ku Klux Klan, whose membership in the
1920s reached into the millions across the United States. The pro-
Confederacy Lost Cause narrative celebrated in the critically acclaimed
film *The Birth of a Nation* (1915), and the nativist and xenophobic animus directed at the wave of immigrants—Jewish and Catholic—who
flooded the United States between 1880 and 1920, helped revitalize the
Klan. Thus in the United States, and in North America as a whole, the
Anglocentric interpretation of the Lost Tribe narrative became mixed
with racism and anti-Semitism. Before long, racist scholars began arguing that white Europeans had exclusive claims as the Chosen People
and that those calling themselves Jews in the contemporary world were
something akin to imposters. But it took young theologians like Wesley

Swift to develop ideas rooted in an idiosyncratic and "creative" reinterpretation of the book of Genesis into a full-fledged school of thought.[3]

Swift and a handful of other seminarians attending Bible school in Southern California focused their attention on the story of Adam and Eve in the Garden of Eden. As World War II raged, their thoughts paralleled the worst racist dogma of Hitler's Third Reich. According to Swift and his friends, conventional understandings of the story of the forbidden fruit missed a key element. Swift agreed with some conventional religious scholars that the account is a metaphor for a sexual relationship between Adam and Eve; this is the great (original) Sin that leads to the Fall of Man after the serpent, Satan in reptilian form, tempts Eve to disobey God and eat from the Tree of Knowledge. But Christian Identity's originators believed that the book of Genesis alludes to a second intimate relationship—one between Eve and the serpent/Satan. The first act of intercourse produces one seed-line of humanity, through the person of Seth. This seed-line produces the people who will reach a covenant with God through Abraham, and settle the Kingdom of Israel to fulfil God's promise to Abraham's descendants—the "Chosen People." Consistent with the earlier, if speculative, scholarship, these are the "Chosen People" who are exiled from Israel and migrate to Europe. But the second act of intercourse, between Eve and the serpent, produces a demonic seed-line, through the person of Cain. Cain is the offspring of Satan in this rendering, and "so-called Jews" belong to Cain's bloodline. So, according to Christian Identity scholars, the people who call themselves Jews today are really imposters, falsely asserting their status as Chosen People while really operating on Satan's behalf. As for people of color—they are subhuman descendants of the "beasts of the fields" described in Genesis as created before God formed Adam from dust and Eve from Adam's rib. The essence of Christian Identity theology thus becomes this: the satanic, imposter Jews manipulate people of color in a two-thousand-year *cosmic conspiracy* against the true Chosen People, white Europeans.[4]

Embraced at first by a very small group of people, this radical theological interpretation had far-reaching consequences—ultimately producing a unique motive for Martin Luther King Jr.'s assassination. The motive grew out of Christian Identity devotion to their own view of End Times—God's final judgment on humanity, before the righteous are saved and Jesus returns to earth in a thousand-year reign in a paradise on Earth. Like other fundamentalist Christians, Identity believers look for guidance from the final book of the New Testament, the Book of Revelation, to understand what God has in store for the world. They share a belief that the prophecies in the Book of Revelation will signal the pending End Times. Notably, Identity Christians, like many fundamentalist Christians, believe that God will impose a series of enormous calamities on the Earth, during a period known as the Tribulation. A false prophet—the antichrist—will seemingly solve the world's problems but, in reality, he is Satan's minion. The forces of Satan will amass an army and terrorize humanity until Jesus, and the army of God, vanquish them at the final battle—the Battle of Armageddon. God will then bless his faithful followers with a thousand-year reign, with Jesus as king.

But Swift and his devout followers interpret the End Times differently than do conventional Christians, differences largely rooted in their reinterpretation of the origins of mankind. The antichrist, in their telling, is not just one man, but the entirety of world Jewry. Moreover, since the birth of Cain, these minions of Satan have been working against mankind. Swift's sermons frequently asserted that Jews, using international communism as their tool, manipulated everything from the American government to the United Nations to the civil rights movement for satanic ends; he referred to this as "the Beast system," a description of what other Christian Identity followers (and other fundamentalist Christians) believe is the rule of the antichrist implied in the Book of Revelation. The End Times is simply an accelerated period where their true intentions are exposed, and where God ultimately saves his Chosen People, white Europeans. The foot soldiers for the army of Satan, in this scenario, are the subhuman people of color who operate at the whims of the imposter Jews. And the Battle of Armageddon, in essence, is a holy race war.

Another distinctive feature of Christian Identity theology explains why so many of its members, as it will become clear, engaged in provocative acts of violence to incite this holy race war. A large number of conventional fundamentalists believe that faithful Christians will be spared the Tribulation through something known as the Rapture. Devout Christians will literally vanish before the world experiences plagues, earthquakes, and related horrors. But Christian Identity believers reject the Rapture. To the contrary, they believe that good Christians—for example, white Europeans—will have to fight the forces of Satan during the Tribulation. Christian Identity zealots stockpiled weapons at alarming rates throughout the 1960s (and beyond) in part because of this understanding. And when they began to see signs of End Times, in the social upheaval that marked the mid- to late 1960s, they increasingly became willing to use them.[5]

And it fell to Swift, from his pulpit at the Church of Jesus Christ Christian, to interpret and convey those beliefs to Christian Identity followers, a group that included some of the most well-known and violent racists in the country, several of whom had already conspired to assassinate King in multiple plots. The charismatic Swift's influence derived from his radio ministry. Swift began his racist and anti-Semitic sermons in the 1950s; estimates suggest that by 1967 he reached tens of thousands of listeners on the West Coast. Those who could not get Swift's signal could hear his sermons on tape, via an informal distribution network that included his most devoted followers. And Swift ordained a number of ministers in his Church of Jesus Christ Christian; they relayed his ideas to audiences across the country while Swift preached to a mostly female audience in Hollywood.[6]

In his sermons, Swift used a combination of astrology, current events analysis, biblical exegesis, and even ufology to divine evidence that the End Times were approaching. A key moment came in February 1962. An alignment of astrological and real-world international events convinced Swift that the world was entering the "zero hour," the final period before the onset of the Tribulation. Swift told his parishioners:

Zero hour has come . . . We will watch the signs as they
develop and we will watch the measures as they follow
in the course of this year.

Do not forget the sign of the "son of man" in the
heavens. It will only end when the skies are filled with
the crafts of heaven to make your experiments of rock-
etry look like amateur experiments, when all the hosts
of heaven join you in the greatest show of power, of
glory in all the earth. When your race shall be elevated
to its position with the smiling face of our Father in all
His majesty and glory saying—these are my children
with whom I am well pleased.[7]

Events in Mississippi that September convinced Swift his prog-
nostication was accurate. Black air force veteran James Meredith
challenged the University of Mississippi's racial exclusion policy by
enrolling in the institution, a court-supported action that nonetheless
inflamed the citizens of Mississippi and provoked white supremacists
from across the country who flocked to Mississippi to protest. Governor Ross Barnett personally and physically blocked Meredith's entry
into Ole Miss with the help of state troopers, forcing President John F.
Kennedy to send National Guard troops to impose the court order and
protect Meredith. Havoc ensued. Protestors and college students bat-
tled the federal troops, using everything from rocks to rifles. Several
participants on both sides sustained injuries; a local man and a foreign
reporter died in the melee. Things only settled after JFK sent hundreds of additional troops to Oxford, Mississippi, to impose order.[8]

The Ole Miss race riot inspired Swift, whose fellow Christian
Identity minister, Oren Potito, helped incite the crowds to violence.
In the immediate aftermath Swift told his audience:

I want you to know that you are in the latter days.
"And as it was in the days of Noah" [refers to] a massive program of Satan's kingdom which is to mongrel-

ize your race. They want to implement this program with troops. They want to back it by every conspiratorial measure that Satan can dream up. And some of these brainwashed people lifting up a standard of self-righteousness which is Satan's own lie—behind this shield they march to destroy . . .

. . . I am going to tell you this. [The Lord] is coming in with a long sword and a sharp sickle. And He is coming in to reap the Grapes of Wrath. And to trample the Wine Press of Judgement. I want you to know tonight, that you are a part of this battle. So don't surrender. Don't give in. If they are going to try to force your Race with violence, then we shall meet them in like token. Let me assure you of this. That in this occupation, have no fear. For He said:—"I shall be like a wall of fire about you." "No weapon formed against you shall prosper." . . .

Again, I say that we are not alone. As I said this afternoon, He said—"I shall never leave nor forsake you even until the end of the age."[9]

Just as importantly, the events at Ole Miss appeared to confirm an important element of the Christian Identity worldview: that rank-and-file whites could be energized into violence against the federal government, whose leaders, as Swift indicated in his sermon, "worked" at the behest of their antichrist Jewish puppet masters. Before 1962, Christian Identity believers found little sympathy, even among aggressive racists, for their vitriolic anti-Jewish message. Raised on a very different version of Christianity from their youth, and focused on resisting integration, most Southern racists could not understand the call for genocidal violence against Jews. The Klan employed anti-Semitic rhetoric since its second revival in the 1920s, but actual violence against Southern Jews and Jewish targets was rare in part because Southern Jews had largely assimilated into the modern American South.[10] But if they could keep their anti-Semitic message to a whisper, Christian Identity ministers could find natural allies in the Jim Crow South among conventional racists looking to preserve the so-called Southern Way of Life. Reverend Potito, a Christian Identity minister, helped rile up the white crowd at Ole Miss into a violent frenzy without mentioning Jews.

Potito belonged to a group whose name deliberately obscured its extremist and Christian Identity disposition: the National States Rights Party (NSRP). The NSRP was formed in 1957 by white supremacists J. B. Stoner, a limp-legged Georgia lawyer, and his friend and fellow Georgian Ed Fields, a chiropractor. The group did run people for elected office, as their name implies, including for president and vice president of the United States in 1960 and 1964.[11] But they also were among the most violent white supremacist groups in the country, earning a place on California attorney general Thomas Lynch's list of the most dangerous terrorist groups in his state by 1965.[12] The group's periodical, *The Thunderbolt*, did frequently feature blatantly anti-Semitic articles, but in public, the group chose not to feature the racist elements of its platform. Stoner's history illustrates why.

Having openly supported the Nazis as a teenager during World War II, Stoner likely became familiar with Identity ideas as early as the late 1940s, as they filtered to Georgia from Western Canada. He soon moved to Tennessee and began to write books that echoed the Christian Identity message that Jesus was not Jewish, that Jews were imposters and literally Satan's spawn. He also started his white supremacist career by calling for the mass extermination of Jews. Hitler, in Stoner's view, did not go far enough. His public focus on condemning Jews, even above blacks, led the Tennessee Ku Klux Klan to expel Stoner from their ranks. Other Klan organizations shunned him, forcing Stoner and Fields to form the Christian Anti-Jewish Party in the 1950s, but that group failed to attract enough members.[13]

Ultimately the two men chose to form the NSRP in large part to disguise their ideological and violent intentions. Stoner attempted to awaken the white masses to his cause by orchestrating a wave of Jewish temple bombings across the country in 1957 and 1958. But this only confirmed his frustrations and those of his followers. White Citizens Councils, which included some Jewish members, condemned the bombings. President Dwight Eisenhower publicly denounced the bombings and formed a task force that helped identify the immediate perpetrators but failed to develop a case against Stoner. To Stoner's chagrin, although Klan groups deployed anti-Semitic rhetoric, they directed their violence almost exclusively against blacks. Antiblack violence satisfied only part of the Christian Identity agenda; it struck at the symptoms rather than the disease. For the Christian Identity End Times prophecy to be fulfilled, "everyday" whites would have to join in the holy race war against Jews and people of color. The Ole Miss riots showed this was at least possible.[14]

The Ole Miss riots helped galvanize racists across the country; thousands joined the KKK and similar organizations to resist federally mandated integration. Others saw the government's intervention in the South as a sign that they should join militant antigovernment groups, like the Minutemen. This presented opportunities for Christian Identity fanatics but also risks. If the upheaval in the American South illustrated signs of the End Times, then these radicalized whites could become the foot soldiers people like Swift needed to wage war against the Beast system.

But the Christian Identity believer's concurrent anti-Semitism and advocacy of egregious violence ran the risk of turning off even hardcore Klan sympathizers. Christian Identity believers had to walk a fine line between their religious imperatives and their need for a widespread following. If they did not form their own organizations, followers of Swift assumed roles in the upper echelons of conventional racist groups while hiding their violent, race-war agenda from rank-and-file segregationists until their God "demonstrated" his message. Swift, with his second in charge Lieutenant Colonel William Potter Gale, was no exception to this balancing act. He used the Church of Jesus Christ Christian as the first "front" in a four-front structure later referred to as the Christian Defense League. Researcher David Boylan describes the system:

Faithful members of the CJCC were recruited for the "Second Front" . . . the AWAKE movement. The more militant members were then recruited in to the "Third Front" which was the Christian Knights of the Invisible Empire "which will have the outward impression of a political-religious group not interested in violence." It was from this group that the most militant members were recruited for the "Inner Den." These recruits were the ones that committed acts of violence. Gale stated that "leaders in our country might have to be eliminated to further the goals of the CKIE" and that "God will take care of those who must be eliminated."[15]

Several Swift devotees assumed key positions in other supremacist groups. Gale, who enjoyed a hot-and-cold relationship with Swift, worked within the California Rangers, an overtly antigovernment and anticommunist group but one, with Gale in charge, that could also serve a religious agenda. The Minutemen were like a national version of the Rangers. Again, under the auspices of antigovernment and anticommunist militancy, the group attracted hundreds, if not thousands, of members across the United States, people who might have been turned off by talk about astrological signs and the two seedlines of Adam. But several of the most important leaders also were key figures in Swift's church. Walter Peyson, the right-hand man to Minuteman founder Robert DePugh, was a Christian Identity fanatic.[16] Dennis Mower, the West Coast leader of the Minutemen, was Swift's personal aide;[17] Kenneth Goff, leader of the largest Minutemen subgroup out of Colorado, wrote Christian Identity books.[18]

It was an easy sell for men like Peyson, Mower, and Goff to get rank-and-file Minutemen to prepare as an army in a future civil war, using the fear of communist subversion of the U.S. government as the pretext. Minutemen collected an enormous arsenal of weapons. In the raid of just one Minutemen compound in New York, federal authorities discovered

1,000,000 rounds of rifle and small-arms ammunition, chemicals for preparing bomb detonators, considerable radio equipment—including 30 walkie-talkies and shortwave sets tuned to police bands—125 single-shot and automatic rifles, 10 dynamite bombs, 5 mortars, 12 .30-caliber machine guns, 25 pistols, 240 knives (hunting, throwing, cleaver and machete), 1 bazooka, 3 grenade launchers, 6 hand grenades and 50 80-millimeter mortar shells. For good measure, there was even a crossbow replete with curare-tipped arrows.[19]

Another raid of one Minuteman's ranch in California uncovered "eight machine guns, and one hundred rifles, shotguns and pistols. When they searched his barn they found an ammunition dump for heavy caliber rockets, bombs, and thousands of rounds of ammunition."[20]

At a secret Minuteman compound, senior Minuteman leader Roy Frankhouser (another Christian Identity follower) showed a reporter thirty four-foot-long rockets he claimed could strike targets several miles away. Of course, such over-the-top weapons hoarding was also consistent with the religious prophecy of Swift, one in which the forces of God must do battle with the antichrist when the Tribulation begins.

As racial unrest intensified in the long hot summers of 1966 and 1967, Swift encouraged his followers to see the prophetic implications. "No wonder there is confusion in the land," Swift told his audience in the aftermath of the summer's rioting. "This confusion comes from the mind of Lucifer whom Jesus said was from the Netherworld while the Children of God came down from above. Thus out of the Netherworld comes a constant revolution and ferment into your society, and this continues until it is destroyed." But to destroy it, white Europeans would have to start their own "great uprising . . . against the evil in [the nation.]"[21]

The record shows that Swift's most devout followers did more than sit idly as tensions mounted, waiting passively for God's plan to unfold. They became provocateurs, using incendiary rhetoric and even violence to drop a match in a lake of gasoline. Rev. Potito, as mentioned earlier, stoked racial resentment at Ole Miss. Christian Identity Minister Connie Lynch toured the country to attend counter-rallies with his friend J. B. Stoner. Together, the men formed what Klan expert Patty Sims called a "two-man riot squad." Sims describes their escapades in her book *The Klan*:

> Lynch once told a Baltimore rally crowd: "I represent God, the white race and constitutional government, and everyone who doesn't like that can go straight to hell. I'm not inciting you to riot—I'm inciting you to victory!" His audience responded by chanting, "Kill the niggers! Kill! Kill!" After the rally, stirred-up white youths headed for the city's slums, attacking blacks with fists and bottles. At another rally in Berea, Kentucky, Lynch's diatribe was followed by two fatal shootings. Again, in Anniston, Alabama, he goaded his audience: "If it takes killing to get the Negroes out of the white man's streets and to protect our constitutional rights, I say, 'Yes, kill them!'" A carload of men left the rally and gunned down a black man on a stretch of highway.[22]

The Minutemen planned several acts of violence, including placing poisonous gas in the ventilation system at the United Nations and attacking Jewish summer camps. Only poor planning prevented what could have been highly provocative actions in the cauldron of the 1960s. As one New York investigator noted: "Kooks they are, harmless they are not. . . . It's only due to their incompetence, and not any lack of motivation, that they haven't left a trail of corpses in their wake."[23]

But the Minutemen did attempt to inflame racial tensions between blacks and whites during the peak of civil disorder in the 1960s. They prepared fake pamphlets, designed to look like black nationalist propaganda, urging blacks to riot. "Kill the white devils and have the women for your pleasure,"[24] they read. At one point, Minutemen sped through black neighborhoods tossing these pamphlets out the window.

Swift devotee and Minuteman acolyte Thomas Tarrants described the entire phenomenon thusly: "Part of the strategy was to create fear in the black community—but it was more important to produce racial polarization and eventual retaliation. This retaliation would then swell the ranks of whites who would be willing to condone or employ violence as a viable response to the racial problem . . . Our hope and dream was that a race war would come."[25]

Ultimately killing Martin Luther King Jr. came to be seen by Samuel Bowers and certain of his associates as the one act that could indeed foment a national holy race war. For years King had been a target of these radicals; he would become the only target. Nearly every serious attempt to kill King from 1958 to 1967 involved Christian Identity zealots or groups who were led by them.

As early as 1958, Stoner had offered to "bring his boys from Atlanta" to Alabama to kill King for a "discounted rate" of $1,500. Stoner directed the offer to members of the United Klans of America, as part of a larger package of violent activity that included bombings targeting other Alabama civil rights activists. Stoner managed to carry out some of the ancillary attacks, but his more brazen plans were thwarted by authorities who knew about them in advance. Stoner was the target of an operation organized by Alabama law enforcement authorities, including arch-segregationist Bull Connor. Interesting that someone as bigoted and barbaric as Connor—he famously arranged with Klan members to let them violently beat the Freedom Riders at Birmingham bus terminals in 1961—would be far outside the mainstream Stoner when it came to violent extremism. In 1958, Connor arranged with a KKK member to coax Stoner into talking about potential acts of violence in Alabama. Prosecutors believed that the effort came too close to entrapment, and did not prosecute Stoner. Stoner did not get a chance to have "his boys" kill King, but as usual, he did not go to prison for his antics, either.[26]

In 1963, Alabama was home to two additional murder plots against Dr. King. In the early morning hours of May 12, 1963, in Birmingham, a bomb destroyed King's room at the A. G. Gaston Motel. This came hours after another bomb detonated at the home of his brother, Rev. A. D. King, the night of May 11. The two men had been working with other civil rights leaders began to secure integrationist concessions from Birmingham's white elites after weeks of protests. That both men survived the attacks can only be attributed to luck. The motel bombers, as King later noted, "placed [the explosives] as to kill or seriously wound anyone who might have been in Room 30—my room. Evidently the would-be assassins did not know I was in Atlanta that night."[27] No one was ever arrested, but internal police investigations show the FBI strongly suspected members of the NSRP, who had held a segregationist rally that night, of participating in the attack. The timing of the attack suggests an additional motive—inflaming the black community. King himself suggested this. "The bombing had been well-timed," the civil rights leader asserted. "The bars in the Negro district close at midnight, and the bombs exploded just as some of Birmingham's Saturday night drinkers came out of the bars. Thousands of Negroes poured into the streets."[28] If this was the goal, it had its intended effect. The coordinated bombings triggered the first major race riot in the history of Birmingham, one that almost forced President John F. Kennedy to use federal troops to quell it.

The second major riot occurred four months later, when members of a Klavern blew up the 16th Street Baptist Church in Birmingham, killing four young girls. The leaders of the United Klans of America, the nation's largest Klan group, had recently shunned Eastview Klavern #13 for its connections to the over-the-top-violent NSRP, the church bombers associated with Fields and Stoner.[29] No one would have expected King to be in the Birmingham church, but King had used the building as a headquarters for his May protest campaign. Rev. King acted as everyone would have predicted in the wake of the horrifying violence—he returned to Birmingham to deliver the girls' eulogy. He also came, with other civil rights leaders, to help calm Birmingham as tensions remained high following the bombing and large-scale riots. Birmingham was a city on the brink of horrific urban combat, according to civil rights activist Rev. Ed King (no relation to Martin Luther King), who joined the push for nonviolence following the bombing. Ed King saw law enforcement officers with heavy-caliber machine guns on the streets. He is convinced, to this day, that any additional rioting would have resulted in a large-scale bloodbath. "All it would have taken was a bottle breaking, sounding like a gun," he said.[30]

This is likely what Christian Identity believers had intended when they spent the days following the bombing looking for an opportunity to shoot King with a high-powered rifle. The "honor" fell to Noah Carden, a member of the Mobile White Citizens Council and a Swift devotee who was once discharged from the military on suspicion he was psychotic. According to Sidney Barnes, whose description months later of the assassination plot was surreptitiously recorded by informant Willie Somersett, Carden could never get a clear shot on King, who was constantly surrounded by aides. Barnes also revealed that he, Carden, and three other Christian Identity radicals—William Potter Gale, Admiral John Crommelin, and Bob Smith—all met in Birmingham the day *before* the bombing of the church.[31] None were Birmingham natives, and Gale came hundreds of miles from California. This raises the possibility that these men knew about the church bombing in advance. Many suspected Stoner helped mastermind the bombing; he enjoyed close relationships with all five men. Crommelin ran for political office, including, in 1960, vice president of the United States, under the banner of the NSRP. Had Carden succeeded in assassinating the leader of the civil rights movement on the heels of the murderous bombing, Ed King believes it would have triggered massive riots and violence not only in Birmingham, but across the South.[32]

Barnes and company continued to plot against Martin Luther King Jr.'s life in 1964, according to information Barnes conveyed to Somersett and recorded on tape without his knowledge. Somersett even provided Barnes with a rifle for the task, one that Miami police had secretly marked. King's unpredictable changes in itinerary continued to keep him alive.[33]

Records indicate Stoner joined a close friend of his, James Venable, a fellow attorney from Georgia and longtime leader of the oldest national Klan organization, in an attempt to kill King in 1965, one that also involved the goal of triggering race riots. The plot was exposed when a young radical, Daniel Wagner, got caught transporting explosives from Georgia to Ohio. Wagner told Columbus, Ohio, police— and later Congress—about a King assassination plan revealed to him by a bleach-blonde Klan empress, Eloise Witte, one the few female Klan leaders in the country. Witte, who ran a Midwest chapter of Venable's National Knights of the Ku Klux Klan, told Wagner that the Klan planned to gun down King and his family after King delivered a commencement speech at his wife Coretta's alma mater, Antioch College in Ohio. The plot failed when Witte could not organize enough men in time to participate in the ambush, despite a $25,000 bounty offered by Venable's Klan. A second witness, a young member of the NSRP, confirmed this account to Congress even as Witte, predictably, denied it. Such an egregious act of violence certainly would have triggered massive violence in Ohio, and possibly across the country.[34] But Wagner added something else—the explosives he brought to Ohio, given to him by Venable's Klansmen, were to be used to blow up buildings belonging to civil rights groups and to the Nation of Islam, a militant, black separatist group. The goal, Wagner said, was to ignite a race war.[35]

A second 1965 King assassination plot in Swift's native state of California would have been just as if not more inflammatory had it succeeded. Police arrested a Swift acolyte, Keith Gilbert, with 1,400 pounds of dynamite; the intended target: the Palladium theater in Los Angeles, as the city honored King for recently winning the Nobel Peace Prize.[36] In recent years, Gilbert has opened up about the plot, minimizing his own role (and his connection to Swift) but highlighting the part played by Dennis Mower, Swift's chauffeur. Gilbert described being pressured into the Palladium bombing plot against his will by Christian Identity fanatic Mower. Gilbert even claims that he gave the anonymous tip to the police that led to his own arrest—a way of avoiding mass murder while also avoiding the wrath of Mower.

Either way, killing King and hundreds of his supporters in one blast certainly would have triggered violent outrage.[37]

Because these plots routinely failed, they generally left little concrete evidence to back a prosecution for potential murder. Only Gilbert, who was caught red-handed with explosives, went to prison for his role in a King plot. The FBI, when it had jurisdiction to investigate these crimes, often risked exposing informants at a potential trial, with little or no guarantee that such a leap of faith would be rewarded with a prosecution. It was hard enough to convict someone in the South for actual acts of racial violence, much less potential acts of violence. In other instances the FBI failed to piece together the contours of the plots, questioning their very existence. This was true, notably, of the original plot involving McManaman and Sparks. More than anything, law enforcement agencies at all levels of government failed to see the ideological framework that connected these plots, the two degrees of separation, so to speak, from every serious MLK murder plot and Wesley Swift's teachings. Christian Identity did not become a commonly understood phenomenon in counterterrorism circles for at least another decade, in part because Swift's devotees were so good at blending in with more conventional white supremacist groups. No one was better at this game than Sam Bowers.

Bowers faced the same issues confronting other Christian Identity activists—the lack of enthusiasm from rank-and-file racists for anti-Jewish terrorism, the resistance to excessive violence in general, the lack of openness to Identity teachings. Bowers, like the senior members of the NSRP and the Minutemen, had to hide his extremist religious beliefs from his rank-and-file members. He did a good enough job of this that few scholars recognize the impact of Swift's teachings on the leader of the White Knights of Mississippi. Bowers self-identified as a "warrior priest" in interviews he gave at the end of his life. He also described a spiritual moment in the 1950s, when, in grave condition from an automobile accident, a heavenly power "visited him" and convinced him to serve God. But Bowers's idea of serving God may well have been influenced by his time in Southern

California studying engineering at USC. Bowers attended the school after serving in the navy in World War II. He would have been in Southern California at exactly the moment that men like Swift began to systematize Christian Identity teachings.[38]

How he first became acquainted with Christian Identity is unknown. But no close student of Bowers's career doubts his affinity for Swift by 1967. He discussed Swift's sermons with newly arrived Tommy Tarrants, who idolized Swift, and with Burris Dunn, one of Bowers's closest lieutenants. Dunn helped distribute Swift's taped sermons, and his fanaticism for Swift ultimately drove away his wife and children. What even the most avid scholars of Bowers's career, such as Charles Marsh, fail to recognize is that the Grand Wizard embraced Swift's ideas from the moment he assumed leadership of the White Knights, in 1964. Dunn, for instance, was on Swift's mailing list at least as of 1965, and no one who knew the pair would believe that Bowers followed Dunn's lead rather than the other way around. Informants describe Bowers trying to convince his other Klan members to be an anti–"Jew Klan" rather than a solely anti–"N***R Klan" in 1964, but with little success. But the most obvious signs of Christian Identity influence come via Bowers's own writings.

In the October 1964 *Klan Ledger*, the periodical Bowers wrote for the Ku Klux Klan, Bowers protested against the widespread FBI intrusion into Mississippi to investigate the Mississippi Burning murders. But in the back pages, literally in fine print, Bowers shifted from secular to religious writing. The biblical passages he cited include those that are almost never mentioned outside of Christian Identity polemics, even by conventional pastors who used the Bible to justify segregation. Bowers, predictably, railed against "today's so-called Jews" who "persecute Christians, seeking to deceive, claiming Judea as their homeland and [that] they are 'God's Chosen' . . . They 'do Lie,' for they are not Judeans, but Are the Synagogue of Satan!" He adds: "If a Jew is not capable of functioning as an individual, and must take part in Conspiracies to exist on this earth, that is his problem." Passages also reference "Jew consulting anti-Christs" and assert that "Satan and the Anti-Christ stalk the land."[39]

The early influence of Swift on Bowers helps explain why Bowers became obsessed with killing Mickey Schwerner, the Jewish activist who was among the three activists targeted by Bowers's goons in Neshoba County. Schwerner's enthusiasm for civil rights was enough to motivate the men, like Sheriff Lawrence Rainey, who arranged the Mississippi Burning murders. But Bowers chose to highlight something else after the three deaths. It was "the first time that Christians had planned and carried out the execution of a Jew," he gloated.

The Christian Identity component of Bowers's thinking also explains the grand predictions he made on the eve of the killing and the actions he took immediately after. Recall that in a speech given two weeks before the Neshoba murders, Bowers prognosticated that soon-to-pass events in Mississippi would bring forth martial law, that they would create conditions for an internal rebellion in the state, and a cycle of violence involving white Southerners and black militants. Many see that speech as anticipating the violence that would greet the wave of student activists set to "invade" Mississippi during Freedom Summer. But through the lens of Christian Identity, the warning makes much more sense as a prediction of the beginnings of a race war, one that Bowers hoped to stoke with the Mississippi Burning murders. In killing whites as well as blacks, then carefully hiding their bodies, Bowers invited the very federal interference he railed against in his public speech. This was especially true as Bowers continued to arrange for violent acts for weeks as federal agents searched for the three missing activists. It is important to recognize that Bowers was exploring an assassination attempt on King, using criminals like Donald Sparks, in 1964. He spoke about targeting the leaders of the civil rights movement in the same speech in which he warned of the (supposedly) coming insurrection in Mississippi. Polls show that Bowers almost got his wish, with the majority of the country favoring placing Mississippi under martial law if the violence in Mississippi became more serious in the summer of 1964.[40] Had the country witnessed the killing of Martin Luther King Jr., and the rioting it surely would have provoked, that easily would have qualified as "more serious."

But Bowers could not publicly disclose his true intentions—to provoke federal intervention—to his audience of white Southerners raised for decades to resent federal interference during Reconstruction. Christian Identity beliefs did not hold sway with rank-and-file Klansmen who, if anything, wanted less federal intrusion in their state's affairs. Bowers's aide Delmar Dennis in fact described Bowers telling him privately that "the typical Mississippi redneck doesn't have sense enough to know what he is doing . . . I have to use him for my own cause and direct his every action to fit my plan."[41]

He also described that plan to Dennis:

> Bowers outlined on a blackboard the overall strategy of which the White Knights were merely a part. He said he was trying to create a race war, and open violence on the part of white Mississippians against native Negro citizens and civil rights agitators. He predicted that Secretary of Defense Robert McNamara would be required to send troops into Mississippi to restore order. Martial law would be declared and the state would be under full dictatorial control from Washington. The excuse for the control would be the race war he was helping to create by engendering hatred among whites in the same manner as it was being fomented by leftist radicals among blacks.[42]

Delmar Dennis specifically tied Bowers's plan to foment a "race war" to the Grand Wizard's 1965 assassination plan to murder King when the civil rights leader passed through Mississippi, over a bridge, on his way to protests in Selma, Alabama. As previously discussed, Option A in that plan involved a shooting ambush, while Option B involved blowing up the bridge. Only Dennis's intervention as an informant averted the plot.

Ben Chester White was murdered on June 10, 1966. Bowers had arranged the murder in hopes of luring King into an ambush zone. Four days earlier, a racist shot and wounded James Meredith during his nonviolent March Against Fear, to encourage Mississippi's black population to vote. Several civil rights leaders, including King, descended on Mississippi to continue Meredith's mission. But the schisms over tactics, between King and more militant leaders like newly elected Student Nonviolent Coordinating Committee (SNCC) chairman Stokely Carmichael, became obvious and open. In fact, Carmichael used the closing of the march to deliver his famous Black Power speech on June 16. One can imagine what would have happened if Bowers had succeeded in luring King to a more controlled kill zone, just days after an icon like Meredith nearly died from racial violence with Carmichael on hand.

By 1967, Swift's prophecies about the conditions in America continued to focus on the End Times. The taped sermons Bowers and Tarrants "discussed" in the woods spoke of a nation "in great tribulation. And . . . you will see more of this tribulation. [God said] 'As you see these things coming to pass, then look up . . . For you are my battle axe and weapons of war. And I am going to stir my people up and I will call for my people to stand upon their feet.' And eventually the Children of the kingdom, the nations of the kingdom, the powers of God, are going to destroy the powers of the Antichrist."[43]

To a Swift devotee, the antichrist was not one man, as mainstream fundamentalist Christians believe, but the entire race of demonic, imposter Jews, as Bowers indicated in his comments after the Neshoba murders. Professor Neil Hamilton, in his study of right-wing terrorist groups, noted that white supremacist groups viewed King as an agent of the Satanic-Jewish conspiracy; killing him became a top priority. King's successes in pushing for integration in America only reinforced that perception.[44] But King became, literally and figuratively, the victim of his own success. By 1967, for reasons that will become clear, he was an even more inviting target for those hoping to ignite a holy race war. To fulfill Christian Identity prophecy, men like Bowers became more determined to kill a prophet.

4

THE TARGET

More than just basic racism and money motivated the people trying to kill Martin Luther King Jr. during his lifetime.[1] Prophecy also played an important role—prophecy in both senses of the term. Laymen hear the word *prophecy* and imagine a religious visionary channeling a higher power to predict the future. King's antagonists, a network of racial terrorists, were convinced they could accelerate God's final days of judgment on Earth as predicted in the Book of Revelation. Inciting a holy race war became their chief objective, and murdering Martin Luther King Jr. became the linchpin in that strategy. This is because of the unique role King played in American society in the changing social contours of the 1960s. King exemplified a different, far less supernatural, understanding of the concept of prophecy. Some biblical prophets are tasked by God to warn a wayward community of believers that they are deviating from God's expectations, to remind them of the noble calling from which they strayed, lest they receive God's wrath. But as Jesus told his congregants at Nazareth, "No prophet is accepted in his own country." If he did not realize this before 1965, Martin Luther King Jr. certainly came to understand it firsthand as his mission began to evolve in the years immediately preceding his death.

No one represented the prophetic tradition, in the American context, better than Martin Luther King Jr. Fusing ideas of salvation with concepts like liberty and equality, King called on America to repent from the sins of segregation and Jim Crow, and, as he famously told a crowd in Washington, D.C.: "Now is the time to make real the promises of democracy. Now is the time to rise from the dark and desolate valley of segregation to the sunlit path of racial justice . . . Now is the time to make justice a reality for all of God's children."[2]

His efforts, combined with sacrifices and grassroots political activity from thousands of others, helped push forth the Civil Rights Act of 1964, outlawing legal discrimination, and the Voting Rights Act of 1965, tearing down most conventional barriers to the franchise for black Americans. The country inched its way toward King's dream of an egalitarian nation and King won the Nobel Peace Prize in 1964 and a place among Gallup's most admired Americans.[3]

But by 1967, King's optimism for America's future began to temper. The Civil Rights Act and the Voting Rights Act represented major blows to legal racism, but the impact was limited largely to the American South. Since World War I, millions of blacks had migrated out of the South to America's urban areas in the North and on the West Coast. Jim Crow and poll taxes did not limit their opportunities. Simple but profound prejudice, manifested in limited social mobility, economic and housing discrimination, concentrated poverty, and police brutality, posed the biggest obstacles to blacks outside Dixie. King did not rest on his laurels as of 1965; he simply shifted his priorities to issues of social and economic justice that had always animated part of his mission. And he began to shift his geographic attention as well, to northern cities. In 1966 he uprooted his family from their middle-class Atlanta existence to live, for six months, in a Chicago ghetto, to highlight patterns of housing discrimination and poverty.[4]

But northern racial prejudice proved to be a daunting challenge for King, and the people he championed became increasingly frustrated, throughout the country, with the lack of justice and opportunity in their everyday lives. The beginnings of capital flight and deindustrialization only exasperated people of color even more. Higher-paying jobs in unskilled factory labor, often the best and only chance for a middle-class lifestyle for blacks denied widespread access to higher education, slowly began to disappear. As the black community's hope for King's vision began to waver, so too did its faith in his approach of nonviolent resistance.

King viewed nonviolent resistance as a philosophical idea informed by Jesus Christ as much as Mahatma Gandhi. "*Nonviolence* is a powerful and just weapon, which cuts without wounding and ennobles the man who wields it," King argued in his Nobel Prize acceptance speech.[5] But to others, nonviolence was simply a means to an end: at best a strategy, and otherwise simply a tactic to be used for black liberation. So long as it helped publicize the civil rights conflict to indifferent audiences in Montana and North Dakota, and even to the unaligned world in the midst of a cold war, many activists could turn the other cheek. But as many contemporary historians pointed out, even at the peak of King's influence not everyone embraced nonviolence. In 1963, Malcolm X, the spokesman for the Nation of Islam, comparing his religion's ideas of violence to King's, said, "Our religion teaches us to be intelligent. Be peaceful, be courteous, obey the law, respect everyone; but if someone puts his hand on you, send him to the cemetery."[6]

Malcolm X referred specifically to acts of violent unrest earlier that year as signs of growing frustration within the black community. The murder of Medgar Evers in June 1963 and the bombing the 16th Street Baptist Church in September of the same year, ignited riots in Jackson, Mississippi, and Birmingham, Alabama, respectively. That said, each of these uprisings occurred in response to acts of outrageous violence. The May 1963 riots followed a failed attempt to kill King and his brother, A.D.

Another act of racial violence triggered a major urban riot in Harlem in July 1964, after a controversial police shooting resulted in the death of fifteen-year-old James Powell. "Bottles, rocks and Molotov cocktails rained down from tenement rooftops and smashed in the littered streets," the *International Herald Tribune* reported.[7] It went on to note 116 civilian injuries (revised by historians to 118) and at least forty-five stores "broken into . . . looted or damaged." The Harlem riot triggered a wave of similar uprisings in American cities over the next few weeks: first in Brooklyn, New York, then Rochester, New York, then several cities in New Jersey, and finally in Philadelphia, Pennsylvania. That these events occurred after the signing of the Civil Rights Act of 1964, and in northern cities, foreshadowed the dynamic that would plague the country in the years that followed: incidents of police or even suspected police abuse sparking powder kegs of socio-economic frustrations, first in one city, then in adjacent cities. Rev. King, commenting on the Harlem riots, spoke of the need to eliminate "conditions of injustice that still pervade our nation and all of the other things which can only deepen the racial crisis."[8]

Yet another wave of riots struck in 1965, the most notable coming after the passage of the Voting Rights Act, in the Watts section of Los Angeles. Another incident of police misconduct unleashed literal and figurative fires in one of the worst urban riots in American history. Over six days of violence, thirty-four people died, more than one thousand people were injured, and over six hundred buildings were damaged. "People said that we burned down our community," Tommy Jacquette, then a twenty-one-year-old resident of South Central Los Angeles, recalled. "No, we didn't. We had a revolt in our community against those people who were in here trying to exploit and oppress us."[9] King faced a difficult audience in young men like Jacquette when the reverend visited Watts, hoping to negotiate a "peace" between the residents and local leaders. At one point he addressed a crowd:

> However much we don't like to hear it, and I must tell the truth. I'm known to tell the truth. While we have legitimate gripes, while we have legitimate discontent, we must not hate all white people, because I know white people now . . . Don't forget that when we marched from Selma to Montgomery, it was a white woman who died on that highway 80, Viola Liuzzo. We

want to know what we can do to create right here in
Los Angeles a better city, and a beloved community. So
speak out of your hearts and speak frankly.[10]

The response Dr. King received symbolized what would become
a growing schism within the civil rights movement. An unidentified
attendee from the crowd insisted:

The only way we can ever get anybody to listen to us is
to start a riot. We got sense enough to know that this
is not the final answer, but it's a beginning. We know it
has to stop, we know it's going to stop. We don't want
any more of our people killed, but how many have been
killed for nothing? At least those who died died doing
something. No, I'm not for a riot. But who wants to lay
down while somebody kicks em to death? As long as we
lay down we know we're gonna get kicked. It's a beginning; it may be the wrong beginning but at least we got
em listening. And they know that if they start killing us
off, it's not gonna be a riot it's gonna be a war.[11]

Dr. King did not see this warning as hyperbole. Having received
a less-than-warm response in his Watts visit, and having failed to
negotiate a truce between local black leaders and the white political
establishment in Los Angeles, King briefed his political ally President
Lyndon B. Johnson about the situation on the ground. In a private
conversation, the Reverend King worried, "Now what is frightening
is to hear all of these tones of violence from people in the Watts area
and the minute that happens, there will be retaliation from the white
community." He added, ominously, "People have bought up guns so
that I am fearful that if something isn't done to give a new sense of
hope to people in that area, that a full-scale race war can develop."[12]

King said this in 1965, a year that saw only eleven urban riots.
The Watts eruption accounted for the vast majority of the injuries,
deaths, and arrests that year. In 1966, the number of riots shot up

to fifty-three. None came close to matching the intensity of Watts, but Americans spent five times as many days rebelling against oppressive conditions.[13] By 1966, King's one-time supporters increasingly began to support Black Nationalist and militant groups, such as the Black Panthers. Dedicating a good deal of their activities to community uplift programs, such as free breakfasts, the Panthers' ten-point platform appropriated the language of the late Malcolm X (assassinated in 1965), saying, "We will protect ourselves from the force and violence of the racist police and the racist military, by whatever means necessary." They asserted their constitutionally protected Second Amendment rights and urged "all Black people . . . [to] arm themselves for self-defense."[14] One-time pacifist groups such as the SNCC, who previously enjoyed close if sometimes rocky relationships with King, placed violent resistance into their charters. Rejecting the practice of civil disobedience King popularized, SNCC spokesperson Stokely Carmichael asserted, in June 1966: "The only way we gonna stop them white men from whuppin' us is to take over. What we gonna start sayin' now is Black Power."[15] Carmichael clarified his position later: "When you talk about black power you talk about bringing this country to its knees any time it messes with the black man . . . any white man in this country knows about power. He knows what white power is and he ought to know what black power is."[16] H. Rap Brown, the leader of SNCC, famously asserted that "violence is as American as cherry pie."[17]

Martin Luther King Jr. increasingly had to gear his prophetic mission toward calling his own community back to nonviolence. Black power, as defined by activists like Carmichael, he argued, implied something too exclusionary and too threatening. "Black supremacy or aggressive black violence is as invested with evil as white supremacy or white violence," Rev. King asserted in October 1966. But he ultimately placed the blame for the growing stridency among his flock on a "new mood" rooted in "real, not imaginary causes." He added:

> The mood expresses angry frustration which is not limited to the few who use it to justify violence. Millions

of Negroes are frustrated and angered because extrava-
gant promises made less than a year ago are a shattered
mockery today . . . In the northern ghettos, unemploy-
ment, housing discrimination and slum schools consti-
tuted a towering torture chamber to mock the Negro
who tries to hope . . . Many Negroes have given up faith
in the white majority because "white power" with total
control has left them empty handed.[18]

King's willingness to speak truth to power, and to challenge a national, rather than strictly Southern, audience, hurt his esteem among
white audiences. He fell off Gallup's list of America's most admired
people, and a poll showed his disapproval ratings among white Americans increasing from 46 percent in 1963 to 68 percent by 1966. He
remained enormously popular with black Americans, but polls also
began to highlight the schism among black Americans about how to
best achieve social justice. Fifteen percent of black Americans told
pollsters in 1966 that they would be willing to join a riot. Another poll
reported that twice as many blacks said the recent riots improved their
political position as said the riots undermined it.[19]

The factionalism and violence grew much deeper in 1967. It started
that April in North Omaha, Nebraska. "Police in Omaha, Nebraska,
said they could not pinpoint what started the trouble. But bottles and
rocks were flying once again in the same part of town, mainly Negro,
where 2 riots broke out last summer," one Omaha newspaper reported.
"An estimated 200 people took part—pelting cars, smashing windows, and looting stores."[20] The paper wondered "whether we're facing
another 'long hot summer' of racial violence—the 4th one in a row."
Many cities would, indeed, experience another year of social upheaval,
and many more would experience it for the first time. *The Congressional
Quarterly* composed a list of instances of civil unrest for 1967:

Nashville, Tenn., April 8–10—Several hundred Negro
students from Fisk University and Tennessee A. and I.
State University rioted on three nights after a Negro

student at Fisk was arrested by a white policeman; at least 17 persons were injured and 94 arrested; the disturbance started a few hours after Stokely Carmichael spoke to Vanderbilt University students; two of his aides were arrested.

Cleveland, Ohio, April 16—Violence erupted in the predominantly Negro Hough area, with rock throwing, window breaking and looting.

Louisville, Ky., April 20—Police fired tear gas into a crowd of more than 1,000 whites taunting open housing demonstrators; the mob threw bricks and bottles.[21]

On May 8, in a public and honest moment, Dr. King told the journalist Sander Vanocur:

I must confess that that dream that I had that day has in many points turned into a nightmare. Now I'm not one to lose hope. I keep on hoping. I still have faith in the future. But I've had to analyze many things over the last few years and I would say over the last few months.

I've gone through a lot of soul-searching and agonizing moments. And I've come to see that we have many more difficulties ahead and some of the old optimism was a little superficial and now it must be tempered with a solid realism. And I think the realistic fact is that we still have a long, long way to go . . .

But King would not abandon the cause of nonviolence. He ended by telling Vanocur:

I feel that nonviolence is really the only way that we can follow, cause violence is just so self-defeating. A riot ends up creating many more problems for the Ne-

gro community than it solves. You can through violence burn down a building, but you can't establish
justice. You can murder a murderer, but you can't murder murder through violence. You can murder a hater,
but you can't murder hate. And what we're trying to
get rid of is hate and injustice and all of these other
things that continue the long night of man's inhuman-
ity to man.[22]

King's deepest convictions could not contain the unrest and discord.

> Jackson, Miss., May 12–14—About 1,000 Negroes at
> Jackson State College protested the arrest of a Negro
> student; the National Guard quelled the disturbance in
> which one Negro was killed; Willie Ricks of SNCC
> told the crowd: "An eye for an eye, an arm for an arm, a
> head for a head, and a life for a life."

> Houston, Texas, May 16–17—Hundreds of students at
> predominantly Negro Texas Southern University rioted
> after clashing with police while protesting the arrests
> of student demonstrators; 487 were arrested; one police-
> man was killed and two others were shot . . .

> Boston, Mass., June 2–4—More than 1,000 persons
> in a predominantly Negro neighborhood rioted after a
> group of mothers staged a sit-in to urge reforms in wel-
> fare and contended they were beaten by police; at least
> 60 were injured, 90 were arrested and property damage
> was estimated at $1 million . . .

> Tampa, Fla., June 11–13—Negroes rioted in a 60-block
> area after a white policeman shot and killed a Negro
> burglary suspect who refused to halt; 16 persons were

injured and more than 100 arrested; property damage was estimated at $95,000.

Cincinnati, Ohio, June 12–18—Negroes rioted in three predominantly Negro sections, hurling Molotov cocktails, smashing store windows and looting; one person was killed, 63 were injured and 276 were arrested; property damage was estimated at $2 million; on June 15, the third night of rioting, [SNCC leader] H. Rap Brown arrived and said that the city "will be in flames until the honkie cops (National Guardsmen) get out." In another speech that day he said that "SNCC has declared war."

Dayton, Ohio, June 14–15—Negro youths threw rocks and smashed store windows; four persons reported injured and 23 arrested; on the night of June 14, Brown urged a crowd to "take the pressure off Cincinnati." The same day, he had told a crowd in Dayton: "How can you be nonviolent in America, the most violent country in the world. You better shoot the man to death; that's what he's doing to you."

Atlanta, Ga., June 18–21—Rioting in the predominantly Negro Dixie Hills section followed a speech by Stokely Carmichael at a rally held to protest the shooting of a Negro by a Negro policeman; Carmichael and SNCC aides were active throughout the riot; Carmichael said: "The only way these hunkies and hunky-lovers can understand is when they're met by resistance" and he told a rally: "We need to be beating heads." One person was killed, three were injured and at least five were arrested.[23]

As violent as some of these incidents were, they would be eclipsed by two of the worst urban riots in American history in the middle of

July. In Newark, false rumors that a black cab driver had died in police custody sparked four days of rioting from July 12 to July 17, requiring massive intervention by local and state police as well by the National Guard. The urban combat that commenced resulted in 23 dead and 750 injured. Follow-up studies indicated that law enforcement, including the National Guard, had expended 13,319 rounds of ammunition in pursuit of snipers who may not have existed.[24] A week later, Detroit, Michigan, experienced the single worst urban riot in the history of the nation: after five days of rioting, 43 people were dead, 1,189 were injured, and over 7,000 were arrested. Sandra West, a UPI reporter who lived her whole life in Detroit, described the chaos:

> Sunday I saw sights I never dreamed possible . . . Raging fires burned out of control for blocks and blocks. Thick black smoke and cinders rained down at times so heavily they blocked out homes as close as 20 feet away.
>
> Looters drove pickup trucks loaded with everything from floor mops to new furniture. Price tags still dangled from the merchandise.[25]

Riots also struck Birmingham, Chicago, and Milwaukee, among other major cities. In sum, during the "long hot summer" of 1967, the United States experienced 158 different riots, resulting in 83 deaths, 2,801 injuries, and 4,627 incidents of arson.[26]

With national press reports that "guns—hand guns, rifles, shotguns—are selling as though they were about to close down the gun factories,"[27] King continued to insist on nonviolence. But in August of 1967, he told a crowd of frustrated young civil rights activists that blacks "still live in the basement of the Great Society" and observed, some months later, that a "riot is the language of the unheard. And what is it America has failed to hear? It has failed to hear that the plight of the Negro poor has worsened over the last twelve or fifteen years. It has failed to hear that the promises of freedom and justice have not been met. And it has failed to hear that large segments of white society are more concerned about tranquility and the status quo than about justice and humanity."[28]

The urban violence and King's dissatisfaction with the "plight" of not just the "Negro poor" but America's lowest economic strata as a whole would, by December of 1967, become the basis for the Poor People's Campaign, a planned mass march from Mississippi to Washington, D.C., to call for a massive expansion in social spending. It became King's last mission, but one that, in continuing to cling to nonviolence as a principle, would struggle for grassroots support. It was King's murder on the eve of the march, unfortunately, that galvanized support for the effort in ways that King could not by moral suasion and charisma.

Civil unrest came from more than just disaffected, poor urban youth. Increasingly, Americans became more and more disturbed by America's involvement in the war in Vietnam. Most of the protests in 1967 dealt with the quagmire in Southeast Asia. King saw the war as perhaps the chief contributing factor in the social upheaval plaguing the nation. It not only diverted resources away from President Lyndon Johnson's social uplift programs under the Great Society, it "poisoned the soul" of America with violence, in King's mind. He did not find it surprising that domestic America could be so violent when, as the minister famously announced in his landmark antiwar speech in April 1967, the American government was "the greatest purveyor of violence" in the world.

But his outspokenness against both the Vietnam War and the lackluster government commitment to social spending alienated King from Lyndon Johnson. This had implications not only for King's political influence but also for his life. Johnson, at times, insisted that FBI director J. Edgar Hoover provide additional protection for King, something Hoover chose not to do, on his own initiative, after 1965. As was detailed earlier, Hoover resented King for, among other things, publicly criticizing the FBI's efforts at solving civil rights–related murders. King's opposition to the war certainly did nothing to encourage Hoover to reverse his policy of keeping threats on King's life from reaching the ears of King's entourage. (Hoover, instead, told his agents to inform local police agencies.) Government attention did increasingly turn to issues of civil unrest, but not with the aim of providing social programs to pacify the urban poor. The FBI, CIA, and military increasingly—and covertly—pushed back against the black power and antiwar movements that they feared could inspire a domestic revolution; a homegrown "Tet Offensive," as historian Gerald McKnight put it.

Developed in response to the 1967 riots, the army's "Civil Disturbance Plan," known as Operation Garden Plot, allowed for "Federal forces to assist local authorities in the restoration and maintenance of law and order in the 50 states," and, until 1971, as many as two army brigades remained on call specifically for this purpose.[29] The official plans observe that:

> Civil Disturbances which are beyond the control of the municipal or state authorities may occur at any time. Dissatisfaction with the environmental conditions contributing to racial unrest and civil disturbances and dissatisfaction with national policy as manifested in the anti-draft and anti-Vietnam demonstrations are recognized factors within the political and social structure. As such, they might provide a preconditioned base for a steadily deteriorating situation leading to demonstrations and violent attacks upon the social order. The consistency and intensity of these preconditions could lead in time to a situation of insurgency should external subversive forces develop successful control of the situation. Federal military intervention may be required to preserve life and property and maintain normal processes of government.[30]

The prospect of an American insurgency was not limited to planners in the Pentagon. By the end of 1967, the fear found a voice in the mainstream media. *U.S. News & World Report* ran an interview with Richard Stanger, a career State Department officer who specialized in studying foreign insurrections. Asked if an "open insurrection [in the United States] is within the realm of possibility," Stanger answered:

> Yes, it is well within the realm of possibility. The evidence is that we are now in a transition. We are passing from mere nuisance demonstrations over civil rights and the Vietnam War to something much more violent and dangerous . . . I fear we have witnessed only a beginning. The demonstrations may well become more violent and the rioting [may] get worse, unless something drastic is done. Invariably violence feeds on itself—and it is habit-forming."[31]

Like the biblical prophets he quoted so often in his sermons, King occupied a unique position in a country that seemed on the brink of some kind of sectarian civil war in 1967. His country increasingly turned its back on him the more he called on it to repent of its ways. Appeals to "law and order," from the likes of presidential candidate Richard Nixon, resonated more with white America than King's calls for equality and justice. He called on black Americans to remember the philosophy and tactics that won them hard-earned gains in the first half of the decade, even as frustration boiled into violence in their hometowns.

But even as King's message of nonviolence lost its appeal, and even as white Americans condemned King as an agitator, he retained his esteem as a person within the black community. He remained, by a large margin, the most revered figure in the black community, according to polls. As such he became an almost perfect target of opportunity. The assassination of Dr. King—in as public and dramatic a fashion as possible—could well represent what we now refer to as a tipping point, a single act that could move the nation into widespread rioting and a full-scale white-on-black, black-on-white race war.

5

THE MONEY

Not long after his encounter with the Dallas FBI on June 2, 1967, Donald Nissen resolved the mistaken charges filed against him in Sherman, Texas, and was released from jail. After picking up a car that his future boss had left him, Nissen made his way to Atlanta and began working as a book salesman at one of the country's largest book distributors. When not lured by the criminal lifestyle, Nissen was an excellent salesman. At least for the moment, he looked to avoid criminal behavior. Atlanta offered a chance to make legitimate money.

In July, not long after his arrival in Atlanta, Nissen thought nothing of it when Floyd Ayers, a fellow salesman, approached him with a request. Ayers wanted Nissen to deliver a package to a real estate office in Jackson, Mississippi. Nissen barely knew Ayers, but in the field of traveling sales, such favors among colleagues were common and, as it was on his trade route, Nissen agreed. Nissen was surprised to find that the address was a private residence that functioned as a business. He delivered the package to a tall, blonde, middle-aged woman, barely talking to her and not exchanging names.

Nissen never asked Ayers about the contents of the package, but after he returned to Atlanta, Ayers revealed something shocking to

Nissen. An eccentric who stood out even in a field known for strong personalities, Ayers divulged its contents and purpose: the package contained money for the murder of Martin Luther King Jr.

Nissen had not been thinking about the King bounty offer since his meeting with the FBI. And at the time he failed to understand a number of things that were going on around him. Most importantly, he failed to consider the possibility that he did not realize that the Floyd—Ayers—who had approached him in Atlanta could be the same Floyd mentioned as a go-between for McManaman. For one thing, he did not know the last name of the "Floyd" he referenced to the FBI in Dallas in June. More to the point, both Nissen and the FBI assumed that the Floyd referenced by McManaman lived in Mississippi because of the context of the bounty.[1] The others mentioned in the bounty, notably the White Knights, all operated in Mississippi. But McManaman never specified where "Floyd" was from. In retrospect Nissen's experience makes it obvious that McManaman's Floyd was Floyd Ayers, someone who, unbeknownst to Nissen until after King's murder, did enjoy close associations with the Ku Klux Klan. Nissen did tell the FBI the full name of a woman in Jackson, Mississippi—another go-between—but he did not get a name from Ayers, only an address. And only now, with the benefit of released documents and follow-up research, is it apparent that the woman whose name he divulged to the FBI that June, Sybil Eure, lived in and sold real estate in Jackson—operating her business out of her home.[2]

Ironically, Nissen had unknowingly involved himself in the exact plot he had worked to avoid, having gone so far as to warn the FBI about it. He had delivered a package with money from one of McManaman's go-betweens, Floyd Ayers, to another, Sybil Eure, in Mississippi. This accident of fate owed itself to the most important and faulty assumption Nissen made: that because he had not said yes when McManaman asked him to join a King murder conspiracy in Leavenworth, he was "in the clear." But Nissen also had not said no to the bounty offer, and apparently McManaman took this as tacit consent. Having revealed the plot to the FBI, Nissen put it in the back of his mind. Hence, he saw nothing sinister when Ayers gave him a nondescript package to deliver on a normal route.[3] Ayers likely took Nissen's agreement to deliver the package as final confirmation that the ex-convict had, in fact, willingly joined the conspiracy. These mutual misunderstandings would be why Ayers would feel safe in discussing the content's package with Nissen.

Having already reported the plot to the FBI, Nissen decided not to risk a second contact with the Bureau in Atlanta, trusting that they would be following his lead. His faith was misplaced.

Shortly after Nissen delivered the package to a real estate office at 423 Raymond Road, in Jackson, Mississippi, the FBI knocked on the same door. As noted earlier, the FBI prematurely dismissed Sybil Eure as a potential suspect in the King murder plot; a respectable Southern businesswoman, they reasoned, could not possibly have anything to do with criminals or the Ku Klux Klan. But it appears using someone of Eure's gender and social status was as much a conscious decision to misdirect a potential investigation as the decision to use someone as self-aggrandizing and as eccentric as Floyd Ayers.

Ayers's revelations about the package spooked Nissen. If, before, he feared possible retribution from someone in law enforcement—recall that the third go-between, per McManaman, was connected to the U.S. Marshals office—now Nissen worried about criminal repercussions. However unwitting it may have been, in delivering the package, he helped advance a murder plot. A jury might not be sympathetic to his pleas of ignorance. He could now add a possible return to prison to physical reprisals if he said anything more. He simply buried himself in his sales job, hoping that the FBI would unravel the King plot. It appears that the FBI's visit to Eure did force the plotters to lay low. But the Dixie Mafia was a brazen group who would do anything for money, and Sam Bowers and his network of Christian Identity colleagues were just as zealous for a race war. When it became evident that the FBI investigation died after agents visited Eure, the plot resumed. Only now, as it became clear that Nissen was a snitch rather than a participant in the plot, the conspirators had to find someone else to assume one of the two roles described by McManaman. The "caser" who could stalk King. Or a shooter.

The transfer of money from Georgia to Mississippi becomes a very important part of understanding the machinations that eventually led to King's murder. As noted in an earlier chapter, the White Knights did not have the resources to front a $100,000 bounty. But Sam Bowers asserted that the White Knights belonged to a larger network of racists. It is worth remembering that several unsuccessful bounties had originated in the Southeast, specifically in the Atlanta area. At least one was specifically connected to James Venable, the leader of the National Knights of the Ku Klux Klan, the second largest Klan organization in America, with chapters in states across the nation. Venable headquartered his group in Stone Mountain, Georgia, the site of a famous cross burning that literally and figuratively ignited what historians call the second Klan revival. Largely dormant since the end of Reconstruction, a combination of nativism and nostalgia for the values of the Old South (inspired by the release of the popular and racist film *Birth of a Nation*), relaunched a new Klan that attracted millions of followers across the nation in the 1920s. By the 1950s and 1960s, Stone Mountain remained a mecca of sorts for the Klan, and Venable was one of the longest-serving KKK leaders in the country.

In some ways, Atlanta also became the spiritual center for the civil rights movement. Martin Luther King Jr. made his home there, and the organization he led in his fight to end segregation, the Southern Christian Leadership Council (SCLC), was headquartered in Atlanta. The white citizenry in the city that was supposedly "too busy to hate" vociferously opposed the civil rights movement, publicly harassing nonviolent protestors and sometimes resorting to acts of violence and terrorism. Civil rights protestors were opposed not only by the Klan, but also by more "respectable" hate groups—White Citizens Councils.

Following the 1954 *Brown v. Board of Education* decision by the U.S. Supreme Court, a decision whose implications for the end of

Jim Crow stunned Southern leaders, groups of influential and wealthy whites formed Citizens Councils to fight desegregation in almost every major Southern city, Atlanta included. Claiming to support legal and political challenges to integration, the Citizens Councils nonetheless were known to privately back Klan activities, even as they publicly eschewed violence. As Professor Chester Quarles noted:

> The Citizens Council was well known among law enforcement officers as a "rich man's Klan." Many meetings of the White Citizens Council were dismissed with fervent prayer; then the Klan leaders went back into a smaller room and had a real meeting.[4]

Quarles adds that several notable Klan leaders belonged to Citizens Councils, among them Byron de la Beckwith, the racist who assassinated Medgar Evers. According to investigative reporter Jerry Mitchell, de la Beckwith's son intimated that the Mississippi White Citizens Council ultimately encouraged Evers's assassination. Clearly murder did not fall outside the moral boundaries of elite racists. They simply needed others to do the dirty work for them.[5]

Evidence first revealed by researcher Lamar Waldron, and corroborated with new data uncovered by the authors, now strongly suggests that Southeastern businessmen raised the money to kill King, then transferred it to Venable, who then turned to the most reliably violent and determined racist group in the country, Sam Bowers's White Knights, to finish the deed in 1967 and 1968. The transfer of "the package" by Nissen became the catalyst for this plot.

A key figure in understanding the Atlanta connection is Joseph Milteer, someone who bridged the worlds of the elite Citizens Councils and the less august Ku Klux Klan. Milteer, a stridently racist sixty-six-year-old former traveling salesman from Quitman, Georgia, described himself as a "non-dues paying member" of Atlanta's White Citizens Council. While he officially helped run the racist Constitution Party, he also enjoyed close ties to more violent groups and individuals. Notably, he commingled with members of the National States Rights Party (whose chief spokesperson, J. B. Stoner, shared a friendship and a law office with James Venable) and also with the National Knights and specifically with Venable and his close aid, Calvin Craig.

Like Venable and Stoner, Milteer had a history with assassination plots against national figures. Weeks before November 22, 1963, he famously told a friend, Willie Somersett, that John F. Kennedy would be killed. Like fellow racist Sidney Barnes, Milteer did not know that Somersett was an FBI informant secretly taping the conversation. On the same tape, Milteer described an ongoing effort by a leader in the Tennessee-based Dixie Klans to kill Dr. King. Milteer was in a position to know about such plots. Government records show that he attended at least two national meetings in 1963, ostensibly for racists trying to coordinate anti-integration activity, where assassination plots were discussed.[6]

Milteer never stopped pursuing the King murder, and Waldron's research reveals that Milteer worked with a crew of southeastern businessmen to raise a much larger bounty on King. Waldron developed an anonymous source who described how the plotters raised a pool of money without having to commit too much of their own, conceivably traceable dollars to the cause. According to this source, Milteer and two other unnamed Atlanta businessmen secretly siphoned off union dues from factory workers at the Lakeland General Motors auto plant in Atlanta, creating a nest egg for a major King bounty. With the help of Hugh Spake, a factory manager, the three men convinced those in control of the fund that the money was being used for general anti-integration activities. Meanwhile, they quietly redirected portions of it to fund a plot against Dr. King. Over several years, the total amount raised became quite substantial.[7]

This Atlanta bounty scenario also fits with the bounty offer referenced in earlier chapters connecting criminals to businessmen in Atlanta. Here again, unidentified Atlanta businessmen reached out to prisoners in Atlanta's Fulton County jail with a $100,000 bounty to kill Martin Luther King Jr. A jailer's son, an officer at MacDill Air

Force Base, reported this to the FBI in 1975. His sister, Janet Upshaw, later confirmed the story to the authors. This is consistent with another story revealed in the 1970s, of an Atlanta-sponsored bounty offer on King's life. Two brothers, Claude and Leon Powell, house painters who had a reputation for violence, claimed to have been approached by a friend in an Atlanta bar who told them that an acquaintance could put them in touch with someone with a serious cash offer for killing Dr. King. A few days later the brothers were approached by a man in the bar who showed them a briefcase full of cash (as much as $25,000) and promised that amount up front plus an equal amount after the murder. The brothers declined the offer and later passed a lie detector test on their story. However, they eventually refused to give testimony to Congress in the late 1970s, even under subpoena, and replied to threatened contempt charges by saying it was not worth risking their lives.[8] The FBI had not learned about the Atlanta offer until 1976, and upon investigation they were "unable to . . . discredit the story."[9] The offer of such large bounties in a bar is also not unusual in the King case. When the FBI interviewed Nissen's cellmate, John May, about the McManaman offer, May casually relayed that he overheard talk about a $100,000 bounty offer on King at a bar in North Carolina in 1965, before he was convicted for the crime that ultimately sent him to Leavenworth.

Milteer had close relationships with people both in North Carolina and in Georgia, including in Atlanta. He emerges as a logical bagman for those in elite circles hoping to raise cash to kill King. Notably he had connections with many white supremacists around the entire country and could move freely without suspicion as someone who continued to sell items, notably guns, around the nation. But Milteer's connection to Venable ultimately closes the circle on the bounty that found its way to Mississippi. According to newspaper and magazine articles[10] and interviews with Floyd Ayers's brother,[11] Venable personally employed Ayers. Ayers's biography, in fact, suggests a man who desperately wanted to be important, to be considered a mover and a shaker. He earned a reputation for exaggerating his own accomplishments and connections.[12] He may have suffered from some form of mental illness or personality disorder; he spent time in mental institutions. Together this made him a perfect conduit for the bounty money. On the one hand, Ayers would be desperate to earn favor with a prominent person like Venable. On the other hand, anything he said after King's murder could be passed off as yet one more crazy assertion by an eccentric. This is not idle speculation. As the timeline to King's murder advances, it will become clear that this is exactly what happened.

IN JULY OF 1967, at approximately the same time Donald Nissen was establishing himself in Atlanta, John L. Rayns, a dishwasher at the Indian Trail Restaurant in Winnetka, Illinois, purchased a 1959 Chrysler from a private owner. Fellow employees described him as "nice . . . efficient and dependable." He was quiet, too, and kept to himself—for good reason. "John L. Rayns" was an alias for James Earl Ray, and Ray was a fugitive from justice.[13]

Three months before, in April, about the same time that Leroy McManaman offered Donald Nissen a role in the King assassination, Ray escaped from Missouri State Penitentiary (MSP) in Jefferson City. A career criminal who, like Nissen, was known for robberies, Ray was serving twenty years as a habitual offender, his career in crime marked by well-planned offenses foiled by poorly executed escapes. In 1954, Ray stole from a cleaning business and escaped through a broken window. But police discovered his shoes literally stuck in the mud, where Ray had lost them before he made it to his getaway vehicle. They found a tired, muddy, and stocking-footed Ray heading out of town along the railroad tracks. Neither law enforcement nor the jury believed Ray's claim that he was simply out on an early morning walk.

Things improved by his next major crime—a series of armed robberies. But at one store, a brave employee followed Ray as he escaped with his partner in crime, and observed the two men cleverly changing cars. Ray was easily traced to their rooming house and, when faced with his pursuers, admitted, "I cannot deny, and I won't admit it." A jury convicted him in twenty minutes, and Ray found his way to MSP.[14]

But on April 23, 1967, his luck improved: he slipped out of the prison in a truck that delivered bread from the prison bread factory, where he worked, to another part of the "farm." He hid himself in a bread box.

Ray escaped MSP with more than just the scent of yeast on his prison clothing. One inmate, James Brown, recalled that as far back as 1963 Ray had expressed displeasure with King's marches; Ray had insisted that he "would get Martin Luther King when I get out" of MSP. Ray then mentioned that a prison group called the Cooleys "would pay $10,000 to have King dead." Asked years later to revisit his claims, Brown confirmed Ray's promise to get King, but claimed ignorance of the Cooley group. The partial retraction likely was motivated by fear. Another former MSP inmate, Thomas Britton, independently confirmed the existence of the "Cooley Club," a small group of "old cons" who would provide protection for prisoners against other prisoners. He also, independently of Brown, connected Ray to the group.[15] But Britton refused to accept or even be associated with any reward for information on King's murder for fear of retaliation by the Cooleys, *even though Britton was out of prison at the time*. His fears may have been well warranted, as an FBI investigation not only confirmed the existence of the group in MSP, but raised the possibility that the group existed across the federal prison system.[16]

Britton did not even specifically associate the Cooley Club with an assassination bounty, but he did provide important corroboration for the idea that Ray was aware of and intrigued by bounties on King's life. According to Britton, Ray discussed a $100,000 offer to kill King from a "businessman's association." Expressing an interest in pursuing such a bounty if he ever got out of prison, Ray added: "There is more than one way to make money than by robbing banks."

Further confirmation of Ray's knowledge of a high-dollar prison offer comes from former inmate Donald Lee Mitchell. In an affidavit to the Shelby County prosecutors in May of 1968, Mitchell stated:

In 1961, I had the opportunity to meet one James Earl
Ray. I was introduced by a friend of mine by the name of
Hawks, who was doing twenty four (24) years . . . Ray
showed great contempt for the colored convicts, as he
very seldom talked to them except on business deals
for dope or money. He was always telling me how the
boys from St. Louis and K.C. always kissed their ass.
He said he never would, because if it hadn't been for
Lincoln they would still be shining his shoes.

When he first mentioned escape I thought he
wanted me to leave with him, but I quickly explained
that I got out on June 1, 1966, that year. He said no, I
want you to help me . . . Then after I make it I'll wait
on you in St. Louis . . . [Ray said] some people (friends
in St. Louis) fixed it with someone in Philadelphia, for
him to kill Dr. Martin Luther King . . .[17]

One is justified in wondering if Ray exaggerated his role in and
knowledge of a plot to Mitchell. Ray had no bona fides as a killer
himself and no background in assisting in capital crimes. It is possible
that Ray could have volunteered to help track King's movements, but
the conspirators would be counting on someone whose participation
in any plot would require that he escape from a federal prison—not
a promising contingency. Indeed, Ray's immediate activities after his
escape point away from him leaving with a King bounty as his top
priority.

Once out of MSP, Ray made no immediate effort to engage any
would-be plotters. Instead, he burglarized a trailer for a blanket and
food, took a train to his hometown of St. Louis, and then fled by bus to
Chicago, until May of 1967, when he found work at the Indian Trails
restaurant for eight weeks under the Rayns alias. Ray wanted to make
enough money to flee North America. Fellow MSP prisoners confirmed that a widely known criminal network in Montreal could help
obtain fake Canadian identification; with that in hand, Ray could exit

to a country without extradition treaties with the United States. In
the early summer of 1967, Ray began to write the Canadian consul in
Chicago about its immigration procedures. He would soon be on his
way north of the border.[18]

His immediate efforts to escape the law also undermine the idea
that Ray was some kind of violent bigot, fixated on killing Martin
Luther King Jr. Ray may have harbored racial animus toward blacks,
as evidenced by the statements of people like Brown. But other prisoners did not describe Ray as someone stewing with deep prejudice.
He asked to work in a segregated prison environment, but Ray also
worked amicably with people of color at places like Indian Trails after
he escaped. It is not surprising that Ray, who grew up in Jim Crow
Missouri, would share the same bigoted worldview (and a distaste for
those, like King, who challenged it) as millions of others who lived
below the Mason-Dixon line. But few people, outside of Klan members and their core sympathizers, directly participated in violence in
the name of racism. None of those who knew Ray best described him
as being politically motivated, much less a KKK member. What they
did describe, almost to a person, and what is borne out by Ray's life,
is a man motivated by the love of money. Mitchell said Ray promised
him $50,000 for help in killing King.

This dollar figure and other aspects of Mitchell's account later
intrigued congressional investigators when they reinvestigated King's
murder in the late 1970s as part of the House Select Committee on
Assassinations (HSCA). Mitchell's reference to St. Louis and Britton's to a "businessman's association" dovetailed with new leads suggesting that two St. Louis businessmen, Jack Sutherland and John
Kauffman, arch-segregationists with documented connections to racist groups, fronted a King assassination bounty to criminals. The lead
developed almost by accident when FBI agents investigating a 1978 St.
Louis jewelry heist unearthed a report, submitted by an informant in
1974, claiming that Russell Byers, a career hoodlum, told two attorneys, Lawrence Weenick and Murray Randall, that he had received
a high-money offer from the two businessmen to kill King. Byers did

this in the informant's presence. The FBI disclosed this information during the congressional investigation, and it became one of the most important leads explored by the HSCA. Byers, a career criminal who may have had motive to fabricate the account, was not without his skeptics. But Congress did locate a corroborating witness, someone who had infiltrated a criminal conspiracy outside of prison in the late 1960s, and heard relevant individuals discussing a bounty on King's life in the course of his work.[19]

Something else tantalized congressional investigators even more about this St. Louis plot: it allegedly reached into Missouri Penitentiary through a prisoner, John Spica, who lived in the same cell block as James Earl Ray. Spica, like some other associates of Ray's inside MSP, belonged to St. Louis's criminal underworld. When interviewed by Congress, Spica distanced himself from any association with Ray: a claim contradicted by two other prisoners. Making matters more mysterious: Spica died shortly after his interview, from a car bomb, in 1979. Congress also discovered that Sutherland engaged in political activity—in support of segregationist George Wallace's 1968 presidential candidacy—in and immediately around the Grapevine Tavern, owned by James Earl Ray's brothers, John and Jerry.[20] All three Ray brothers partook of the criminal lifestyle, and at least one author contends that they named the pub the Grapevine to telegraph its other purpose, that of an "underground communications network criminals use to commission and solicit new crimes."[21] As noted earlier, bounty offers circulated in similar haunts.

But the timeline of these associations presents further problems for the idea that James Earl Ray left prison with killing King as his top priority. The American Independent Party did not form until July of 1967, and the Grapevine Tavern did not officially open for business until January 1968.[22] In other words, Ray did not have the means to engage the plotters once he escaped MSP in April 1967, and again, his documented actions comport with Ray's account: his number one goal that summer was escaping North America. Absent specific knowledge of whom to contact, lacking any bona fides in white supremacist circles, Ray would be taking tremendous risks waiting and hoping to "make good" on a bounty offer. He knew that, as an escaped fugitive, law enforcement agencies across the United States soon would be looking for him.

A figure of $100,000—almost $800,000 in today's money— certainly would be attractive to a con like Ray. This would be the total amount if one interprets Ray's account to Mitchell as reflecting a bounty reward of $50,000 *each* for a King hit. The bounty total of $100,000 also echoes the dollar figure offered to Donald Nissen in Leavenworth by Leroy McManaman. But Mitchell's statements go even further in associating the Leavenworth bounty with the boun- ties circulating in MSP. Ray told Mitchell that "someone in Phila- delphia . . . fixed" the King murder. Mitchell never clarified (or Ray never clarified to Mitchell) what he meant with that reference. An observer's first inclination is to associate the label with the City of Brotherly Love in Pennsylvania. But Philadelphia is also a city in Ne- shoba County, Mississippi, the scene of the famous Mississippi Burn- ing murders of three civil rights activists in 1964, one of many crimes orchestrated by the Mississippi White Knights. This is the same group who promised $100,000 to outside criminals, like McManaman, if they would assassinate Martin Luther King Jr.

Many suspect that, as Ray evaded the law, he monitored the plots through his brothers Jerry and John. The three men were close, and all had criminal backgrounds. Such speculation tends to lead inves- tigators in the direction of the St. Louis bounty rather than a bounty emanating from Atlanta and working its way to Sam Bowers's Mis- sissippi. But Ray also had developed a few relationships with prison- ers inside MSP, including people who were out before he escaped. Such men could also have forwarded information they heard about any potential King plot to Ray. New information suggests one such candidate, and provides very strong corroboration for the details of the bounty described in the first half of this chapter.

Louis Raymond Dowda developed a relationship with James Earl Ray when the two worked together in the MSP mess hall. On the surface, Dowda is not a likely candidate to have helped Ray access the men sponsoring the King bounty for a simple reason: he was one of the only people close to Ray—there were not many to begin with— who stridently insisted that Ray could have killed King and would have done so for money. In his first interview, Dowda told investigators that his one-time friend harbored extremely racist sentiments and that Ray "made several statements to the effect" that he would "kill Martin Luther King" if "the price was right."[23]

But a closer examination of Dowda's statements suggest that he may have been outspoken to avoid having to answer follow-up questions that could expose his deeper knowledge of a conspiracy. In follow-up interviews with the FBI, Dowda developed a habit of admitting potentially incriminating information only after they pressed him for more information on Ray. Dowda, for instance, neglected to tell the FBI, until later interviews, that he made a suspicious trip to California at the same time Ray settled in Los Angeles in November of 1967, a matter that will be discussed in more depth in later chapters.[24] Dowda also at first failed to mention to the FBI that he worked at a drugstore in Atlanta that was very near where Ray set up shop the month before King was assassinated. Dowda himself then raised the possibility that Ray may have been seeking him out when Ray briefly settled in Atlanta two weeks before King's murder; he insisted they never met. Dowda correctly noted that he stopped working at the drug store months before Ray came to town, but that, of course, raised the question of where Dowda worked during the relevant period. It is on that issue that Dowda appeared to have the most to conceal, for reasons that will become obvious.

Dowda told FBI agents that he worked at the Bonanza Sirloin Pit in Marietta, Georgia, during the relevant period. He then, quite randomly and without explanation, felt the need to tell the agents about one solitary long-distance phone call that came into his place of work in 1967. The timing of the call, in November, it is worth noting, dovetailed with Dowda's trip to California.[25] The origin of the call, as Dowda best remembered, was Oklahoma. Tulsa, Oklahoma, is the headquarters of the Dixie Mafia gang that included Sparks, McManaman, Rubie Jenkins, and others. But what made this revelation even odder is that

Dowda did not even answer the call he randomly remembered for the FBI agents. The employee who did bears a familiar last name: Ayers.[26]

Dan Ayers, the teenage employee, is, in fact, the nephew of Floyd Ayers, the courier of the bounty money. His father (Rev. John Ayers, Floyd's brother) recently confirmed this to the authors, before he was made aware of the significance of the connection. It is unlikely, given Dan's age at the time, that he had any direct connection to a King conspiracy (he has not contacted the authors, despite a request through his father). But he could have been used as an unwitting conduit to Floyd. It also should be noted that the owner and manager of the Bonanza Sirloin Pit acted suspiciously in the months following the King assassination.

According to Dowda, the two men became oddly interested in Dowda's problems with the criminal justice system. E. R. Collins, the owner, and Lloyd Jernigan, the manager of the Bonanza, went out of their way to provide Dowda with help after he was convicted for a larceny charge some time after King's murder. Most striking to Dowda, Collins's bail company not only fronted Dowda's bond, it made full payment of the $1,400 in restitution the court required Dowda to pay to his victims. Jernigan then advised Dowda that he did not have to pay Collins back.

Dowda told the FBI that he thought Collins and Jernigan were patronizing him because they believed Dowda had inside information about the King assassination. Dowda, as he always did, asserted that, if that were the case, his bosses were simply misinformed about what he did and did not know. But the FBI failed to press Dowda about why these men would be so concerned in the first place if they had nothing to hide. And even here, Dowda may have been coy with the FBI. He did not volunteer this information or in a timely manner. Rather, the FBI approached Dowda yet again in 1974 after a jailmate, whose name is redacted in FBI documents, provided the Bureau with details of a conversation he had with Dowda. Dowda, according to this source, told the jailmate that he never fully revealed all he knew about the King assassination to investigators. Specifically, Dowda, per the jailmate, claimed to know that the King murder resulted from a conspiracy funded by Atlanta-based businessmen. One of these sponsors, notably, was a senior officer for General Motors[27] (who ran the Lakeland auto factory where union dues were secretly diverted for a King bounty). It was only when confronted with this story that Dowda told investigators his tales about his bosses at the Bonanza Sirloin Pit. While his story predictably minimized any involvement Dowda may have had in the King murder, it is worthwhile to note that he was implying guilty knowledge on the part of two other Atlanta-based businessmen, who happened to have employed the nephew of someone who, per Donald Nissen, helped transport bounty money from Atlanta to Jackson.

It is unlikely that Dowda, if he was directly involved in the King assassination, would have associated James Earl Ray with racism and a price tag on King's life; but he may have been a conduit to Ray for information on the bounty if he heard about it in Atlanta. He may have hoped that by quickly condemning Ray, the FBI would not explore Dowda's connection to the story any further. We are unfortunately left to speculate, as Dowda is now deceased.

However, as this book went to print, brand-new information reached the authors that has the potential to fundamentally add to what we know about the King bounty's origins in Atlanta, and it relates to Louis Dowda. The authors finally reached a relative of Dowda's—his nephew—who confirmed what Dowda's ex-wife had told us: Dowda had written down what he knew about the MLK assassination. Unlike Dowda's ex-wife, who simply speculated on the matter, the nephew had actually read some of the material. The nephew had only a fuzzy memory of what it said, but he told the authors that it showed his uncle had been involved in scouting King's movements in Atlanta in connection with the assassination, but that his uncle had nothing to do with what eventually transpired in Memphis on April 4. Again, the nephew did not remember much detail and may not have given the material a thorough reading. We are presently trying to acquire any material written by Dowda, but the nephew is not sure where it is currently stored.

The nephew provides another very tantalizing connection to events related to a bounty's genesis in Georgia. The authors had previously mentioned a jailer who became aware of a $100,000 bounty offer on MLK circulated by unnamed businessmen within the Atlanta prison system. This jailer happens to share the same last name as the nephew, and, more saliently, to his mother (and Louis Dowda's sister), Ramona. She passed away as Ramona Price, but the mother was known as Ramona Wehunt in 1968. Some public-records searches suggest a relationship between Ramona Wehunt and Robert Wehunt Sr., the jailer in question. But we have not been able to fully uncover the nature of this relationship, and it is one that the nephew is not certain about—but does not dismiss. This raises the distinct possibility that Robert Wehunt had passed the bounty information on to his family and it reached Ramona's brother and Ray's friend Louis Dowda. If this information included the names of the businessmen who were floating King assassination offers in Atlanta's prisons, and one or more happened to be connected to the Bonanza Sirloin Pit, Louis Dowda may have obtained a job there for the express purpose of learning more about the King bounty, information that he would later at least attempt to pass on to his former prison buddy, James Earl Ray. Hopefully, Dowda's written material will be unearthed and can clarify this matter.

Ray could have heard of the White Knights bounty in prison or in the bars he frequented while he evaded law enforcement—or from former prisoners who had their ears to the ground. In many ways, the particulars of which bounty reached Ray's ears and how do not matter. In MSP, Ray himself did not appear to have a firm grasp of exactly who sponsored these bounties and why. Byers's account suggests that the conspiracy itself had not yet fully formed by 1967. When he asked Sutherland how the racist intended to raise money for the crime, Sutherland said "a secret southern organization" would easily raise the money. Ray himself seemed to have only rough outlines of a plot when he discussed it with Britton. Pressed by Britton for details on the "businessman's association" and the $100,000 bounty on King's life, Ray insisted "I don't know but I intend to find out."

PART TWO

6

DETOUR

In the summer of 1967, the man who would one day be accused and convicted of killing Martin Luther King Jr. was still focused on his primary goal of leaving North America. James Earl Ray finally had his opportunity to make a run for it. Having purchased yet another car under the John L. Rayns alias, Ray quit his job in Illinois and made his way to Montreal by way of Indianapolis and Detroit.

By July 17, Ray arrived in Montreal and registered at the Motel La Bourgade under the Rayns alias. The following day, he rented an apartment using the name Eric Starvo Galt, telling the manager he was employed at Expo 67, the International and Universal Exposition being held in Montreal.[1] While Ray insisted that he developed his aliases himself, his explanations suggest that his choices were not nearly as simple as he represented. Of course, the use of fake identities and aliases is common among criminals. Ray did drive past road signs for the Canadian town of Galt on his way to Montreal. The record suggests that if Ray did have help developing the Galt alias, it was from individuals who did not know how to work the Canadian passport system.[2]

Investigation did locate an Eric S. Galt (the man's full name was

Eric St. Vincent Galt). He lived in Toronto and worked for Union Carbide as a manufacturing inspector for proximity fuses. The FBI further determined that Eric Galt was listed in the 1967 Toronto telephone directory. But there was no "Eric Starvo Galt" who was a legal Canadian citizen. Because of that, Ray could not steal the "real" identity of Eric Starvo Galt. Ray was not unfamiliar with the techniques involved in identity theft, as he would demonstrate after the King assassination.[3] But in 1967, Ray would have had a problem if he had tried to steal the identity of the real Eric St. Vincent Galt to obtain a passport, as St. Vincent Galt traveled internationally and already had a passport. There is no evidence that Ray ever held any sort of Canadian identification for either Eric S. Galt or Eric Starvo Galt. Certainly he had none for Eric St. Vincent Galt. It seems logical to view Ray's first use of the name "Eric S. Galt" or "Eric Starvo Galt" as a simple alias of convenience. It is noteworthy only because Ray would use that alias again back in the United States when obtaining a driver's license in Alabama.

It is clear that Ray's first goal in Canada was simply to acquire what he needed to leave for a foreign country—according to various sources and Ray's own inquiries, a country in Africa, most likely one whose practice of racial segregation fit his own prejudices. But Ray misunderstood the legal requirements for obtaining a Canadian passport, which he would need for international travel out of Canada. His understanding, as illustrated by his actions after the King murder, indicated that he believed that he would need a Canadian citizen to vouch for him to get the required paperwork. During his escape after the King murder (but only after taking considerable pains to steal a real identity), an employee at a Canadian travel agency informed him that a sponsor was not a requirement and that the travel agency could sign off on a form which, with a birth certificate, would be all he needed for a Canadian passport. If he had known that, it is highly likely that Ray would have been long gone back in 1967 and never returned to the United States at the time of the assassination.

Because he thought he needed a Canadian sponsor, Ray spent

most of his six weeks there in 1967 planning and looking for such a person, in particular, a female sponsor. Ray seems to have had no notable interest in women other than his routine use of prostitutes. At the time of his escape from prison, he had no women friends and his relationships with women were limited. But Ray had no problem using women for his own selfish ends.

While in Canada in 1967, Ray went to great lengths to create a new and respectable image in what would be a failed effort to recruit a female patron. He spent hundreds of dollars on new clothes, including a tailored suit. The money for this and other expenses, he claimed, came from robbing a Montreal brothel; Ray refused to identify the establishment, and investigations failed to corroborate his claims, of this and other explanations he gave of his sources of money and the reasons for certain of his travels. Next, Ray (as Galt) booked a stay at a premier Canadian resort, Gray Rocks Inn. At Gray Rocks he met and impressed an attractive Canadian lady. She lived in Ottawa, but she and a girlfriend planned to go to Montreal to visit Expo 67, and so they followed him there, spending a couple of days. He told her he needed to talk to her about something very serious and would come to visit her in Ottawa. Ray would eventually admit that his interest in her was as a potential sponsor for the passport he would need to leave Canada, but for some reason Ray did not follow her to Ottawa for another eleven days.

They maintained an ongoing romance while she commuted back and forth from Ottawa. But Ray became paranoid when the woman revealed that she was an employee for the Canadian government. He no longer wanted her as his potential sponsor and ended the relationship abruptly. From Ray's future actions, he also appears to have changed his mind about finding a new country—instead he headed back into the United States, risking recapture.

It is this change of mind that led many to think that Montreal represented Ray's first "entry" into a conspiracy against Martin Luther King Jr. Ray claimed that while his lady friend was in Ottawa, he frequented bars in Montreal and came to know a man named "Raul."

According to Ray, it was Raul who became his guiding force, convincing Ray to become a courier in a drug- and gun-running operation back in the United States, first for money, but ultimately for the necessary papers to leave North America. In most renditions of the story, Ray and his attorneys imply that Raul worked, in some way, for the United States national security apparatus, although Raul never directly said this to Ray.

From the time of his conviction for King's murder, until the day that he died, Ray maintained that this Raul figure manipulated him into the movements and activities that would incriminate him, unwittingly, as the perpetrator of King's murder. Raul thus became the centerpiece in Ray's efforts to paint himself as a complete (and innocent) dupe in the King murder. But each time Ray inserted Raul into his self-serving counternarrative, he raised doubts about his claim. Ray, for instance, could not keep his descriptions of Raul straight, depicting Raul as a "blond Latin," a "red haired French Canadian," an "auburn-haired Latin," and a "sandy haired Latin."[4] In the 1990s, Ray finally made a positive identification of Raul from a passport photo of a Portuguese immigrant. But there was a big problem with that identification. In the early 1970s, Ray asserted that another picture bore a "striking resemblance" to Raul, and this person looked nothing like the Portuguese immigrant Ray insisted was Raul in the 1990s.[5] In addition, the immigrant was still alive, and his employment records conclusively showed that he could not have been at the places where Ray and Raul allegedly met.

Ray's claims about Raul have engendered two camps: those who believe Raul was a complete fiction, invented by Ray after the fact to hide his guilt in the King murder, and those who contend that Raul was a composite character, reflecting separate individuals who pushed Ray into a conspiracy to kill King. They speculate that Ray used this ruse to protect the real culprits from law enforcement scrutiny, possibly to avoid retaliation in prison, and many who embrace this scenario still believe these separate individuals framed Ray for King's murder. The authors do not dismiss this possibility that Raul is a composite of some sort, but we ultimately believe that no one person named Raul ever existed, that Ray used the fictional gunrunner mainly to hide his own complicity in a King murder conspiracy. In fact, Ray had done this in a previous crime, fabricating, with his partner in crime Walter Terry Rife, an individual named Walter McBride, whom Ray blamed for the various offenses. Ray did not convince a jury, but the FBI nonetheless went searching for McBride after King's murder with no success (obviously). Ray's actual one-time partner in crime told the FBI that they had "fabricated" McBride (and others) to pass blame and mitigate charges.

But Raul may also be a composite of real people who helped Ray identify would-be conspirators and who, eventually, helped him join the plot and escape from authorities in the immediate wake of King's murder. Ray, in this scenario, used one fictional character to explain away a series of incriminating movements and interactions with different individuals.

While the character of Raul is most likely a fictional creation of Ray's, there is one figure associated with Ray's time in Canada whom Ray may have used to derive his Raul character.

In investigating Ray's movements in Montreal in the summer of 1967, Canadian reporter Andre Salwyn made a diligent search for potential Ray associates near the Neptune Bar, a hangout in the neighborhood of Ray's Montreal apartment. Ray claimed he met "Raul" there. Salwyn located a young lady who said that during that summer she had a boyfriend who hung out at that bar. He was from New Orleans (a place Ray later visited twice) and he used the names Rollie and Rolland—and the alias Max Lindsay. The girlfriend told Salwyn that Rollie was an interesting fellow. He had a special radio in his ivory Camaro (which he used to monitor police calls), carried guns in the car's trunk, and made a lot of long-distance calls from her apartment. Salwyn's investigation would show those calls were to New Orleans and Texas.[6] A second Canadian girlfriend told Salwyn that Rollie had been working at Montreal General Hospital and that she had also telephoned him at a hospital in New Orleans.[7]

"Rollie" was Jules Ricco Kimble, a native of Louisiana who had contacts in the criminal underworld and to the Ku Klux Klan. Kimble led a very colorful life, beyond having a wife in New Orleans and two concurrent girlfriends in Montreal. Kimble's background included Klan activities, suspected drug dealing, and assault. He was also under investigation for attacking black labor leaders targeted by the Klan. The HSCA confirmed that Royal Canadian Mounted Police files showed Kimble had called New Orleans daily, listened to police broadcasts, carried guns, and made racist comments.[8] Kimble had told one of his Canadian girlfriends that he had been involved with narcotics, and she stated that he would sometime disappear for an hour and return with plenty of cash.

The HSCA also confirmed that beyond his tendency to spin tales, Kimble had been arrested in Louisiana for impersonating an officer, aggravated assault, and possession of illegal weapons. His wife told investigators that Kimble used fake medical degrees and other documents to gain employment at a New Orleans hospital and thereby obtain access to controlled drugs.[9] Kimble also had significant Klan contacts. In July 1967 he met with four Grand Dragons of the Klan at his home; afterward he disappeared for several days. Other meetings with Klan leaders occurred earlier in February and March 1967. Kimble was also a suspect in the bombings of union officers and other labor-related violence; he ended up serving a federal sentence for those crimes.

There is no certain proof that Kimble and Ray met each other, but if they did, Kimble's connections could have proven useful to Ray. And in several ways Kimble would have been a good match for Ray's "Raul." If Ray did meet Kimble, even casually, Kimble may have served as a model for the Raul figure Ray would ultimately develop to explain away so many of his suspicious movements, and his eventual, timely appearance—with a rifle—at a certain Memphis boarding-house on April 4, 1968.

Whatever or whoever Ray met in in Montreal, his movements suggest that something and someone fundamentally changed his mind about what to do next. Having failed to get a woman to endorse his application for a passport, conventional accounts suggest he soon went straight back into the United States. Ray, of course, attributed his apparently spontaneous return to the machinations of the mysterious Raul, who sent him onward from Montreal to run drugs back into the United States. But if this is false, something else must account for Ray's willingness to risk recapture by returning to America. Without Ray as a reliable source, we are left with speculation.

Ray may have heard loose gossip in bars, perhaps from someone like Kimble, about where one would go to find out more about the kind of bounty offers that circulated in Missouri State Penitentiary. Someone like Kimble, whether he had direct knowledge of a bounty or not, could certainly have suggested white supremacist connections. John Nicol, an investigative reporter for the Canadian Broadcasting Corporation, using never-before-seen Royal Canadian Mounted Police files as well as HSCA documents, suggests that Ray may have stayed in Toronto before reentering the United States.[10] Previously, Ray was believed to have spent time in Toronto only after the King assassination, during his escape.

Canada, and Toronto in particular, had its own burgeoning white supremacist movement by the late 1960s, with Christian Identity influences going back as far as the 1940s. At least one Klan expert speculated that Ray may have made contact with individuals connected to these groups.[11] Nicol's investigation went further, showing that the HSCA identified specific individuals with white supremacist backgrounds who relocated to Canada in the 1960s. A seal on the records prevents us from knowing exactly why these men were persons of interest to Congress. We do know that these men became the vanguard for J. B. Stoner's NSRP after 1963, creating franchises throughout North America. Stoner trained these individuals and nourished their racism in a city that saw as much segregationist violence as any other city in the Deep South: Birmingham, Alabama. It was a place James Earl Ray had never been before. It was also a place where white supremacists plotted as many as three different assassination attempts on Martin Luther King Jr., in 1958 and 1963.

Ray arrived in Birmingham on Sunday, August 25, 1967, still using the name Rayns when checking into the Grenada Hotel. The following day, he would take the first step in establishing a new U.S.
identity as Eric Galt, by checking into a rooming house under that
name. According to the manager at the rooming house, Ray claimed
that he was taking a long vacation from his recent employment at the
Ingalls shipyard in Pascagoula, Mississippi, possibly staying several
months. Ray's immediate priority seems to have been to establish a
basic "Galt" identity. Two days after checking in as Galt at the rooming house, he rented a safe deposit box. Apparently one use of the box
was to stash his other identity documents; he was very sensitive to the
risk of having conflicting sets of identification papers in his possession. That would prove to be a reasonable concern, since in June 1968,
this discrepancy led to Ray's capture in London.

These actions, though seemingly trivial, may be the start of a
pattern of activity to establish a false background as an extreme racist, someone whom white supremacists could trust to partake in an
assassination of Martin Luther King Jr. if Ray could find the sponsors. In the world of spy craft, this is known as building a legend;
anyone who infiltrates a country or an organization needs to have
some kind of record, as close to genuine as possible, to make themselves attractive and believable to their associates and employers.
Charles Faulkner, in his excellent microanalysis of Ray's behavior,
added that the bank Ray used for his safety deposit box was the go-to
branch for the United Klans of America; research by the authors
establish that the specific branch Ray used was also used by the National States Rights Party.[12] Additionally, Pascagoula, Mississippi,
and Ingalls shipyard in particular, was a hotbed for Klan activity.[13]
Faulkner (citing additional examples of legend-building that will be
discussed in later chapters) argues that Ray, lacking any legitimate
connection to extremist groups, felt the need to plant bread crumbs
to entice racists to involve him in a conspiracy, and to ultimately
collect a share of a bounty.

Ray's next move was to purchase a sporty used Mustang, get it

registered, and then obtain an Alabama driver's license for himself
in the name of Eric S. Galt. Ray was not required to present birth or
other identification to get the license; he stated on his application that
he had been previously licensed in 1962 in Louisiana. Within approximately a week of his arrival in Birmingham, James Earl Ray, also
known as John Rayns, was able to present at least minimal paperwork
to legally identify himself as Eric S. Galt. That would be the identity
he would use for the next several months, during his time in Birmingham, through Atlanta, and all the way to Memphis. Eventually, his
continuing use of the Galt alias allowed the FBI to quickly track and
identify him, based on the registration of the Alabama-tagged Mustang that he abandoned in Atlanta after the assassination.

With his first priority met, Ray was mobile with enough identification to get through a traffic stop, book a motel room, or cross
a border. Then, for the next several weeks, Eric Galt did nothing—
well, nothing much that we know of. The rooming house manager
in Birmingham told the FBI that he was a quiet fellow, spent time
alone in the lounge during the day watching television, ate breakfast
late to avoid mingling with the other tenants, and otherwise spent a
lot of time in his room. Later, there would be a number of witnesses
to Ray's activities in Mexico and in Los Angeles; he frequented bars
there, as he had in Canada. But if he frequented bars in Birmingham,
nobody talked about it. He did go out for one known activity: dance
lessons; he also enrolled in correspondence courses in locksmithing,
a useful skill for someone still pursuing a career in crime. By themselves the dance lessons seem very much out of character for Ray
(and he would enroll for another dance course in Los Angeles a few
months later), but in combination with another of his options, they
make much more sense.

Ray reportedly sold sex magazines in prison, ordered sex manuals
while in Canada, asked his brother about joining him in the pornography business, and in Birmingham, as Eric Galt, ordered a complete
filmmaking system from a company in Chicago. The system included
a Super 8 camera, a dual projector, a combination splicing machine,

and a twenty-foot remote control—everything one would need to make sex movies, including the ability to film in slow motion and under different types of lighting. While in Montreal, he had sent a money order to a manufacturer in California for a compound that would turn regular glass into a two-way mirror. Clearly, with the right subjects, Ray could parlay photography into a less risky income source than armed robbery or, under the right circumstances, use it to blackmail victims to raise money in his quest for a Canadian passport and ultimate emigration to Africa.

While in Birmingham, Ray seems to have spent time establishing a Galt identity and focusing on his filmmaking pursuits and his dance and locksmith classes. But does that account for all of Ray's time in Birmingham? We simply don't know. We do know that his rooming house was very close to NSRP national headquarters. The Canadian white supremacists investigated by the HSCA, for reasons still unknown, all once worked in that building as far back as 1963. Ed Fields was coy when asked, decades later, if Ray paid the group a visit during his stay in Birmingham in 1967. While Fields denied having any direct and personal interactions with the future accused assassin, he also would not dismiss the possibility that Ray met with others from the NSRP.[14]

Ray needn't have visited the NSRP headquarters to pursue rumors of a King bounty. If he had gone to a local bar, as was his custom, he would have found that Birmingham bars were still frequented by the old hard-core racists who had been involved in years of racist violence. Ray might have seen coverage of the convictions and pending jail sentences for the White Knights in Mississippi. If he turned up any particular information about a bounty related to the White Knights, he most likely also came across newspaper and television coverage of the FBI's massive effort in Mississippi, the trials, and the testimony of informants. If so, that might have raised some flags for the ever-cautious Ray, turning him back to other options.

Ray apparently became restless in Birmingham; he didn't seem to be having much fun—at least according to the folks at the dance studio. But his car tags and driver's license now proved that "Eric S. Galt" was an "Alabama boy" (reinforced with a Confederate sticker on his Mustang). He had figured out what he needed to proceed with his plans to produce pornographic movies. The movie equipment had arrived from Chicago on October 4. He was not satisfied with the movie camera that had been substituted and wrote to request a replacement. But Ray was not willing to wait and that same day went out, bought a Polaroid instant camera, and wrote a letter to the dance studio canceling the rest of his lessons. The Polaroid would just have to do for starters. By October 6, he was on the road again. His rooming house manager, Mr. Cherpes, related that just before Ray left, he made a telephone call to Pascagoula, Mississippi, supposedly to verify employment, stating that he was headed there to take a job on a boat. Ray later denied saying that and claimed instead that he had headed to Baton Rouge to try to contact Raul about a smuggling job. If nothing else, this does support the idea that Ray was informing someone about his moves, in anticipation of future contact.

What Ray really did on his way from Birmingham to Mexico, who Ray really saw, or where he really stopped, remains uncertain. Perhaps he didn't need to stop anywhere at all, since his known activities in Birmingham and his next stops in Mexico demonstrate that he was still pursuing other options. He might have gone to Birmingham in pusuit of a King bounty, but he now was going on to Mexico with something entirely different in mind. And in Mexico, Ray's social life was about to dramatically improve—at least for a few months.

7

ON HOLD

There are a variety of views of Ray's departure from Birmingham, his subsequent sojourn in Mexico in October 1967, and his move to Los Angeles by the end of that year. According to Ray, the trip was the result of "Raul" giving him a little smuggling work to keep him busy while holding him in reserve for some future use.[1] Others have written that Ray's sojourn in Mexico ties in with his recruitment by organized crime as a low-level drug smuggler.[2] Still others present it as one more interlude in his decades-long role as an asset for the CIA.[3] Our view is that Mexico tells us a great deal about Ray's personal agenda in 1967: Ray still had an interest in collecting a bounty on King, but it was only one option, not the final one. That stage would not happen until after all the easier options began to run out at the end of 1967 in Los Angeles.

Ray appears to have made a quick and relatively direct trip to Mexico from Alabama, crossing into Mexico on October 7. He was issued a tourist card as Eric S. Galt when he crossed the border at Nuevo Laredo, New Mexico. Apparently he drove straight on to Acapulco, staying for four days in the same hotel as on his first trip there in 1959.

There is sufficient reason to speculate that Ray, in fact, did engage in some cross-border smuggling, both going to and coming back from Mexico. Journalist William Bradford Huie, who worked closely with Ray on a series for *Look* magazine while Ray faced trial, discovered evidence that a Mexican federal police officer had trailed Ray to his hotel in Acapulco. Huie also discovered that the hotel registration page that should have contained Ray's name suspiciously had a section cut out of it. There was a handwritten explanation at the bottom of the page, suggesting that on October 14 (a week after Ray had entered Mexico), a federal police officer named Ramon del Rio had taken and examined the page. Huie interpreted this as an indication that there had been some suspicion that Ray was involved in smuggling and that he had been the subject of at least a minimal investigation.[4] That might also explain why Ray moved on after only four days; Ray himself said he left because Acapulco was just too expensive. It would be no surprise to find Ray smuggling drugs into Mexico, since he admitted that he had done so on his first trip there years before.

Still, it appears that Ray's primary goals in Mexico were getting into the pornographic film business and exploring options for staying outside the United States. He had obtained the equipment, and with the right subjects, Ray would have everything he needed to make sex movies.

As Eric S. Galt, Ray moved from Acapulco to Puerto Vallarta, which was still undeveloped and not the tourist haven it would become in future years. He spent three weeks there, first at the Hotel Rio and then at a more expensive beach hotel, the Tropicana. As he had at Gray Rocks in Canada, Ray cultivated an upscale image. He was well-dressed, drove a flashy sports car, spent money, and presented himself as an American writer, complete with cameras and a portable typewriter.

Ray himself discussed visiting a local brothel repeatedly "on business."[5] He also visited other brothels, establishing relationships with two prostitutes: first, a girl calling herself La Chilindrina and then another woman who went by Irma La Douce. Ray spent an extended period with Irma, drinking, having sex, sleeping late, and visiting the beach—all a total change in behavior from his previous stops since his prison escape. Ray used Irma as his first photographic test subject. Following a trip to the beach, he asked her to sit in his car, exposing herself with her skirts up. The Polaroid photo turned out poorly, and Ray tore it up; he stopped a few miles later and made a second attempt, but it, too, turned out badly. This seemed to upset Ray, and the next day Irma described him as irritable, complaining of a headache and ready to get into a fight in one of the local bars.[6]

A few days later, Ray showed up drunk at the bar where Irma worked, and she refused to sleep with him that night. She also refused his offer of marriage a day or so later. Ray threatened that he would begin to see the other women again. That didn't change her mind, so he tried making out with the first woman he met, but that didn't work either. Eventually Ray moved to a more upscale hotel and began visiting a new hotel bar, becoming friends with the bartender there. While out one night hitting the clubs and bars, Ray and his bartender friend met a young woman who caught Ray's fancy. She doubled as a cigarette girl and club photographer and was much more attractive than the prostitutes Ray had first approached. The two men picked up the woman, and Ray began dating her, taking her to the beach, each photographing the other. They spent nights together.

Ray was clearly taken with the woman and eventually confided to her that he was making good money with marijuana sales. He was buying it on weekends at the nearby Yelapa resort and smuggling it back to sell to tourists on the local beaches. Ray wanted her to go with him on his next trip, probably as cover. It turned out that telling her that was a mistake; the woman had a young child and wanted nothing to do with marijuana. She made a clean break with Ray, telling him she could not see him anymore.[7]

His dual rejections and failure to produce any substantial pornography seem to have had a bad effect on Ray, despite his drug-peddling successes. That Ray had thought it was possible to become a Mexican citizen may explain his bad mood; he did remark in later testimony that one of his reasons for leaving Mexico was that he had concluded he couldn't secure permanent residence.[8] That the requirements for citizenship involved more than simply marrying a Mexican citizen seemed to be lost on Ray. His attempts to establish some long-term female relationships, including a marriage proposal, would have been for naught.

Ray also might have thought that he could obtain citizenship by getting into business in Mexico. He spent considerable time with a couple of different bartenders and expressed interest in investing in some sort of business. But the best offer he could get was to trade a plot of land for his Mustang; he refused that offer. One of the options Ray more seriously considered was getting into the bar business, which might have kept him in Mexico. Bartending was a very portable skill, much like locksmithing. Both were skills that Ray seriously pursued after his escape from Missouri State Penitentiary; they would have served him well if he had made it overseas. During 1967, Ray appears to have had much more interest in his locksmithing, dance, and bartending courses and porno filmmaking than in a King bounty. Known to be extremely tightfisted with money, he spent a good deal of what he had on lessons and equipment for these options, hauling the film equipment all the way from Birmingham to Memphis and continuing the locksmithing course even after his arrival in Atlanta. We feel that this is a good indication that Ray was operating as his own man, with his own goals and plans, and was not being run by any other parties during 1967.

It's also worthwhile to note that while reading *U.S. News & World Report* in Mexico, Ray happened across an advertisement for immigrants wanted in Rhodesia. Ray wrote them for information but had not received an answer by the time he left Mexico.[9] James Earl Ray's Mexican jaunt and his initial porno film efforts ended in the middle of November 1967. Ray moved directly to Los Angeles, and his stay there became the springboard for his substantive involvement in the King murder.

•

CLEARLY THINGS HAD not gone as Ray had hoped in Mexico; he had no path to Mexican citizenship and could not stay forever as a tourist. So, it was back to the United States and to a city that he had first visited many years before. Ray's initial time in Los Angeles was similar in some ways to his Mexican interlude. At first he seemed to be unconcerned about money and continued to spend at an uncharacteristically high level. He arrived in L.A. on November 19, 1967, and moved into an apartment on North Serrano Avenue. It wasn't a great neighborhood, but it was right off Hollywood Boulevard, a good place to pick up a prostitute or to sell drugs to the hippies. It also provided a number of the all-day bars that seemed to be standard hangouts for Ray.

If the neighborhood sounds like a familiar one for Ray, one of his first acts was extremely uncharacteristic: he had a telephone installed. Ray would testify that he wanted it for job hunting, which he surprisingly did. At first it seemed there would be a delay with the telephone installation, but Ray told the telephone company that he was working with Governor Wallace's American Independent Party and that there was limited time to work at getting Wallace on the ballot. In fact Ray had already called the local Wallace headquarters for information. This new interest in politics was also uncharacteristic for James Earl Ray. We can only speculate whether Ray's newfound interest in politics was merely a cover to prospect the rumored King bounty among Wallace supporters. How much contact Ray may have had with members of the American Independent Party and with Wallace supporters is also a matter of speculation. We do know that he took people to the office to register them to vote, and, when questioned, these registrants stated that Ray appeared to be quite familiar with, and at home in, the office. Ray later denied that.[10]

At first, Ray's known activities in Los Angeles consisted of spending money, not making it. He booked a series of seven sessions with a Beverly Hills clinical psychologist; the sessions involved hypnosis, and Ray used his real name during the sessions. Later the specialist commented on Ray's shyness, noted his dislike for blacks, and highlighted Ray's belief that one could use hypnosis simply to look someone in the eye and make them do what he wanted them to.[11] Ray also spent a good deal of time in bars and engaged in a variety of activities, enrolling in both bartending classes and another series of dance lessons. The dance lessons were at an exclusive and expensive dance school. He also took up with Marie Martin, a cocktail waitress and go-go dancer whom he had met in a club; Ray seems to have gone to some lengths to establish a relationship with her. He still had his camera equipment and perhaps still had hopes of getting into pornography. Ray knew that Marie had a boyfriend in prison for possession of marijuana and that she had some sort of criminal record of her own back in New Orleans. He met her cousin Charlie Stein, who also had quite a colorful past involving criminal possession of narcotics.

Ray and Charlie Stein would make a much-discussed cross-country round trip to New Orleans in December 1967. It's possible that Ray agreed to the trip under a misconception. Marie Martin said that it began with her telling Ray that her cousin Rita Stein had a serious problem: she urgently needed to get her two children out of New Orleans before they were placed in a children's home. It seems plausible that Ray accepted the trip because he thought it would involve going off to New Orleans with Rita Stein, or possibly both women. Apparently Marie had asked Ray, "You wouldn't want to drive me down to pick them up, would you?"[12] Marie went on to say that Ray became extremely unhappy when he realized that, rather than heading east with the two women, he was going to be making the trip with Rita's brother Charlie.

As will become clear, Ray's reluctance to join a joyride with someone like Charlie Stein was likely due to his other agenda. By December, before the trip, Ray began to run low on money. His previous efforts at raising money seemed to provide him with temporary reprieve at best until he could find his next con. Perhaps New Orleans would provide yet another opportunity for Ray to buy and sell drugs. Or perhaps Ray understood that New Orleans was just the right place to find a nexus between criminals and violent racists, one that could finally bring him into a criminal conspiracy.

•

TO AN OUTSIDER, the fall and winter of 1967 should have looked like
Sam Bowers's lowest moment, not the time when he would be plan-
ning his most provocative acts of violence. In September 1967, Tommy
Tarrants joined Kathy Ainsworth and a handful of other hardcore
White Knights to begin a series of terrorist attacks that caught law
enforcement completely off guard for months. Sam Bowers finally put
Swift's "underground hit squad" to use.

On September 18, 1967, two dynamite bombs caused $25,000
worth of damage to Temple Beth Israel in Jackson, the Mississippi
capital's only synagogue, one of the oldest temples in the American
South. Dozens of black churches had been bombed or set ablaze for
over a decade in Mississippi and in the rest of the South. But Jewish
houses of worship had largely been spared since J. B. Stoner's wave of
attacks in the late 1950s. The timing of the attacks baffled law enforcement as much as the target. Without question, Perry Nussbaum, the
temple's rabbi, had been an outspoken advocate for civil rights reform.
But Nussbaum had taken those courageous and unpopular stances for
years without eliciting a violent response. What's more, with the federal trial for the 1964 Neshoba killings set to start—three years after
state charges had been dropped—Bowers and his followers remained
under constant law enforcement and media scrutiny. Someone outside
the watchful eye of federal law enforcement had made an unprecedented and brazen statement.

Behind the scenes, Tarrants was pursuing a goal that had long
eluded Sam Bowers: targeting Jews alongside blacks. Whereas the
membership of the Mississippi White Knights had dwindled after
the passage of civil rights legislation mid-decade, a growing number
of the remaining members were becoming sympathetic to that goal.
Some racists held listening parties where tapes of Swift's sermons
were played. Bowers was able to augment Tarrants and Ainsworth's
secret team with men like Danny Joe Hawkins, whose entire fam-

ily devoted themselves to the Klan, and Bennie Waldrup, Hawkins's hard-drinking friend.

Sometime in October 1967, as James Earl Ray made his way to Mexico, Tommy Tarrants reached out to Wesley Swift. It is unclear if this was by mail or by phone. But Tarrants impressed Swift enough that Swift invited Tarrants to come to California and become his understudy. Tarrants did not make his pilgrimage to Swift for several months.[13] In the meantime, Swift's sermons continued to beckon men like Bowers and Tarrants to action.

Swift's October 9 sermon, "Confusion Throughout the Land," reflected the past summer's urban rioting and general social upheaval. The minister told his audience that the chaos "comes from the mind of Lucifer"—world "Jewry," as Swift called it—who are using the "the processes of integration today of your society to gain . . . complete control of the instructions in your nation." From the "the Netherworld comes a constant revolution and ferment into your society, and this continues until it is destroyed." As to the "revolutionists," they included black activists—"the Carmichaels, and the Rap Browns" all of whom were "communists." But Swift gave special attention to Martin Luther King Jr., whom he rarely referenced by name in hundreds of sermons. "And the government has those records but you cannot get them for they know that Martin Luther King is a communist. And they are willing to cover this up of Martin Luther King being a communist." On King he added, "But I think that he is about ready to come to an end anyhow."[14]

On October 18, federal judge William H. Cox forced a deadlocked jury to re-deliberate; two days later the jury offered a compromise decision, convicting seven men while acquitting seven other defendants for violating the civil rights of Mickey Schwerner, Andrew Goodman, and James Chaney. The jury failed to reach a decision for three defendants. Sheriff Lawrence Rainey, who had held the three activists like bait in his jail, was among the "not guilty," but his deputy Cecil Price received five years and triggerman Alton Wayne Roberts received ten. Most important to federal prosecutors, Judge Cox sentenced the mastermind, White Knights Grand Wizard Sam Bowers, to ten years in prison.

The White Knights already had been making plans to shift leadership in the event of a conviction. L. E. Matthews, an electrician from Jackson who made bombs for the Mississippi White Knights, was next in line.

But appeal bonds meant that most of those convicted would have months before they set foot in a federal prison. A new lawyer arrived in town to help with those appeals: J. B. Stoner. Stoner developed strong relationships with several of the Mississippi KKK members, including Danny Joe Hawkins and his father, Joe Denver. For the first time, the NSRP began to make a major push to develop chapters in Mississippi. The nationwide cross-affiliations between white supremacists had grown deeper by 1967, in part because of the glue of Christian Identity ideology.

And Christian Identity ideology meant that Sam Bowers would not sit still, even when facing impending prison time. The attacks by Tarrants and his elite group intensified in November. Two months after bombing his synagogue, terrorists bombed Rabbi Perri Nussbaum's home, destroying "the kitchen, living room, kitchen, and part of the bedroom."[15] No one was killed. That November, Tarrants and company also bombed a church rectory, the home of a civil rights activist, and the home of the dean of Tougaloo College, Mississippi's historically black institution.

Stoner did not lose his lust for violence, or his morbid sense of humor. Seeing that no one had died in these attacks, he advised a White Knight that the group should go from using one or two sticks to a "whole case of dynamite."[16]

The FBI was not laughing. They increased their surveillance of the Klan. The White Knights countered the FBI with a level of bravado not seen in other Klan-FBI rivalries throughout the nation. The White Knights even placed FBI agents on hit lists. Shortly after the Nussbaum bombing, a caravan of KKK members forced a team of FBI agents, who had been following other Klansmen as part of a surveillance operation, off the road. The Klan members held the FBI agents at gunpoint while the target of their surveillance mission, Danny Joe Hawkins, exited his vehicle and confronted the agents. A young precocious racist whose entire family, including his father and mother, dedicated their lives to the White Knights, Hawkins proceeded to smack one of the FBI agents, Sam Jennings. Later, Tarrants and his cadre would place Jennings on a hit list.[17]

But Bowers's biggest plan, to assassinate King, appears to have been on hold. By this time, it is likely that the Dixie Mafia gangsters, like McManaman, finally realized the full extent of the problems caused by Donald Nissen's actions that summer. Additionally, McManaman's close ally, Donald Sparks, was on the run, having been placed on the FBI's Most Wanted list that August. Plans would have to be reconstituted and reconsidered if these criminals wanted to collect their money, and if Bowers wanted to ignite his race war. Anyone on the outside looking in for the bounty would have to wait.

8

BACK IN BUSINESS

By December 1967 life had stabilized for Donald Nissen. He was making a good living selling books, he had remarried, and his wife was pregnant. He dutifully maintained his parole requirements and avoided criminal activity. The concern he had over the McManaman plot, and his package delivery for Floyd Ayers, registered as a distant memory. Or so it seemed.

Everything changed when Nissen visited his probation officer. Nissen cannot recall if it was the first or second of December, but when he left his parole officer at the Atlanta Federal Building, a man accosted him outside, asking, "Are you Donald Nissen?" When Nissen answered in the affirmative, the man made a vague reference to Leroy McManaman, then issued a veiled threat to Nissen about "talking too much." At that moment his friend who'd dropped Nissen off at the parole office called for him, and the other man quickly left. Nissen was convinced the incident arose from his decision to tell the FBI about the White Knight bounty offer on King.[1]

As Nissen related to the authors in 2009, his fears intensified significantly when someone shot out the windows of his car in the days that followed. Equally frightening was something he remembered from McManaman's initial offer: a federal marshal was one of the go-betweens in the plot. To Nissen, this opened the possibility that his own probation officer, or someone connected to him, could be involved in the King plot. Paranoid, Nissen resolved that he could not go to federal law enforcement again. Even with a new marriage, a pregnant wife, and a well-paying job, Nissen jumped parole—a crime that would send him back to federal prison if caught.[2]

The threat against Nissen suggests that, whatever chilling effect the visit to Sybil Eure may have had on their murder conspiracy, the Dixie Mafia still wanted to collect the enormous bounty on Martin Luther King Jr.'s head. This is implied in the exact nature of the threat. Rather than tell Nissen that they were going to get even with him for having snitched on them to the FBI, they warned Nissen against saying anything *further* about the bounty in the future. In the time it would have taken for ideas to spread from Eure to McManaman and from McManaman to the other participants in the plot, nothing happened. The FBI did not even bother to interview McManaman himself. While McManaman's partner in the 1964 King plot, Donald Sparks, was finally caught in December 1967, Dixie Mafia gangs were known for reconstituting themselves with new criminals from crime to crime, often using prison contacts to do so. And for the kind of money being fronted by the White Knights to kill King in 1967, it is unlikely that Dixie Mafia members would have been deterred by a single FBI visit to Sybil Eure's home that did not result in any follow-up investigation. But the December threat to Nissen in Atlanta is just one indication that the King bounty was back in play.

With his knowledge of the King assassination bounty placing his life in danger, Donald Nissen approached his boss, Harold Fitzgerald, with his predicament. With a pregnant wife and no real desire to return to a life of crime, Nissen wanted to continue selling books. With Fitzgerald's blessing, they decided that Nissen should assume the name of another employee, William Edward Gibson, and move to nearby Florida.

As close as he was to danger in Georgia, Nissen took every opportunity to sell materials on the road. This first led him to New Hamp-

shire, where a sales associate brought unwanted attention to him. Bill
Gordon took the company car, registered to Nissen, on a drunken
joyride. Arrested for DUI, Gordon finagled his way out of trouble.
Matters became even tenser for Nissen when he went to Portsmouth,
New Hampshire. Two FBI agents came looking for Nissen, and even
approached the hotel clerk asking about him. Another company car,
also last registered in Nissen's name, disappeared in New York. But
the agents had only Nissen's real name, and no picture to allow them
to distinguish between Nissen and the real William Gibson. The incident encouraged Nissen to leave New England and head to Ohio,
where he stayed for a while before heading back down south.[3]

Nissen's excursion south took him through Oklahoma and then to
Central and West Texas. In San Antonio, he once again faced a close
call. At Lackland Air Force Base, Nissen resumed his established
sales operation, which included a friendly and long-standing relationship with a non-commissioned officer, Sergeant Hesten Kelly. But the
officer knew him under his real name, not the fake name (Gibson) he
provided to officials at Lackland. Realizing this, Nissen convinced
the sergeant that he was ducking an alimony problem from a divorce.

His quick thinking saved him in San Antonio, but he faced a
much graver danger just a few weeks later, in Del Rio, Texas. Nissen
frequently stayed at a local motel where he enjoyed an intimate relationship with the manager. Nissen began to notice odd things at the
hotel. Most alarmingly, he saw a large contingent of law enforcement
officers around the premises on a regular basis. When someone broke
into his car one evening, Nissen became convinced these officers were
suspicious of him. Having broken his parole requirements for months,
he became worried his days were numbered. But it turned out that a
separate set of people attempted the robbery—fellow criminals. The
government arranged for almost twenty individuals, charged with interstate prostitution and bank robberies, to be housed at the hotel while
they awaited a federal trial. The motel was almost evenly divided between alleged lawbreakers and the lawmen, marshals, prosecutors, and
others, biding their time until trials could start in April.[4]

Nissen did not realize how dangerous the situation was. The men and women awaiting trial belonged to a Dixie Mafia group, commonly referred to as the Overton Gang, with close ties to the Tulsa-based Dixie Mafia gang that included Donald Sparks, Leroy MacManaman, and Rubie Jenkins—men who, as noted many times previously, had connections to a King assassination bounty both in 1964 and (in the case of McManaman) 1967. One of the leaders of the Overton Gang, Jerry Ray "Fat Jerry" James, also was a leader in the Tulsa gang. In fact, law enforcement officers arrested Fat Jerry with Donald Sparks when the latter finally was brought into custody after a string of robberies the previous December.[5] For several days, Nissen slept just feet away from men who could easily kill him—and would have had no qualms about doing so—had they known about his interactions with the FBI.

But in March of 1968, Nissen continued to avoid both law enforcement and the Dixie Mafia gangsters looking for retribution. In fact, federal law enforcement did not even realize Nissen violated his parole and left Atlanta until April 2, two days before King's murder in Memphis.[6] As will become clear, the coincidental timing of that discovery would prompt a reexamination of Nissen's June 1967 revelations.

AN ADDITIONAL DEVELOPMENT pointing to a renewed bounty plot against King also occurred in December of 1967. Informants for the FBI revealed that James Venable, Grand Wizard of the National Knights of the Ku Klux Klan, officially established himself as Grand Dragon of the California Knights of the Ku Klux Klan (CKKKK).[7] Still living in Stone Mountain, Georgia, Venable allowed William V. Fowler to continue to manage the group's day-to-day operations. While symbolic, it was nonetheless unusual, and significant, as it tied Venable to Swift's network. Fowler ministered in Swift's Church of Jesus Christ Christian. Indeed, he required that CKKKK members regularly attend Swift's services. Swift's FBI file indicates that Fowler was even a proxy for Swift, while he was running the CKKKK.[8]

Like his support for violent activity, Venable's allegiance to Christian Identity theology is often obscured by his "good ol' boy" image. His most public anti-Jewish behavior was almost comical—an effort to establish a national boycott on kosher food. But Venable's ties to Christian Identity were more substantial than this. His legal strategy in defending a group of men, who, under his friend J. B. Stoner's conspiracy, blew up the Hebrew Benevolent Congregation in Atlanta in 1958, was to argue for a Jewish conspiracy. He would pen a book on the thinking of the KKK that celebrated those who persecuted Jews throughout Western history, including "Saint Adolf, of Bavaria, the greatest anti-Jew since Jesus Christ and the Greatest White Champion," an obvious reference to Hitler.[9]

The idea that Jesus Christ despised Jews is a major motif in Christian Identity teaching; Christian Identity scholars employ selectively quoted passages in which Jesus berates a subset of Jews, the Pharisees for instance, as a condemnation of the entire bloodline of Jews for all of eternity. One can find those ideas, for example, in the work of Thomas O'Brien, a rabid Christian Identity believer who, by 1967, became the editor of *The Imperial Night-hawk*, the periodical for Venable's group.

As with Bowers, the obvious changes in the Christian Identity direction by 1967 push one to wonder if the Christian Identity influence on Venable stretches back further, and perhaps even inspired Venable's attempts at killing King. Venable's failed effort to kill King in 1965 coincided with a foiled bombing plot against Black Nationalist targets with the goal of creating a race war. Venable had long sought to kill King, saying to an informant as far back as 1961, that "Martin Luther King Jr. should have been dead long ago" and that "he had to be killed."[10] But the 1965 plot had a different flavor to it. It closely echoed Bowers's scheme in 1965: to polarize the races until they waged war with each other, fulfilling Christian Identity prophecy.

Thus what is noteworthy is not Venable's affinity for someone like Rev. Swift, but the coincidental timing of his outreach to Swift's followers in California. Like his good friend Stoner, who first made major inroads into Mississippi via senior members of the White Knights, during the summer of 1967, Venable's unprecedented relationship with Swift began at the same time Swift followers like Bowers were fronting a bounty on King's life. Indeed, Venable's first obvious connection to Fowler began in April of 1967, when the bounty was offered to Donald Nissen in Leavenworth; Venable even visited California to deliver speeches to the CKKKK on multiple occasions that month.[11]

It is worth nothing again that the King bounty money had been given to Nissen by Venable's employee, Floyd Ayers. In late June, Nissen then brought the bounty money, unwittingly, to go-between Sybil Eure in Mississippi, placing it in the domain of Bowers and the White Knights. If Lamar Waldron's source is right, it was Joseph Milteer, a close associate of Venable's, who likely raised the money for this bounty. As it happens, Milteer devoutly followed the teachings of Wesley Swift. In his cross-country visits, Milteer even attended meetings where Swift spoke.[12]

All this activity seems too suspicious to be a coincidence. Rather, it appears as if a group of radicals who worked independently— sometimes even as rivals—to advance the cause of white supremacy had finally coalesced with the goal to murder Martin Luther King Jr. As the leading advocate of nonviolence, King was seen as the last buffer between right-wing whites and a growing number of militant blacks, between an "ungodly" world of race mixing and the ethnic cleansing of Armageddon that would bring the Second Coming of Jesus Christ. A different kind of resurrection, of a once-dormant bounty plot, would be in order.

SOMEONE ELSE WAS coming to California from Georgia in the winter of 1967, and he likely was looking for James Earl Ray. Having failed to mention it in his first interview with investigators after the King assassination, Louis Dowda, Ray's friend from Missouri State Penitentiary, finally told investigators that he traveled with his family by car from Atlanta to the Los Angeles area in the last week of November 1967. Dowda admitted that he stopped along the way to visit several former associates from MSP but that his ultimate destination was his brother-in-law for the Thanksgiving holiday. Dowda claimed that his trip had nothing to do with James Earl Ray, that he did not even know about Ray's escape from MSP until some time after the trip. This is hard to believe.

The men Dowda visited included a former prison guard at MSP and the man who once ran the prison kitchen, where Dowda had befriended Ray. Dowda also neglected to mention that he had visited the MSP. The guard who revealed this did not know Dowda's reason for the visit, but he did suggest Dowda as a possible co-conspirator in a King plot with Ray, based on Dowda's bigotry when he was incarcerated. Even more suspicious was Dowda's activity when he got to his brother-in-law's home in California. Dowda stayed only for dinner and then left for several days with his family. Dowda admitted having visited Jewell Rigger, the wife of another MSP prisoner who worked in a psychiatrist's office in Beverly Hills. In a previous interview, Dowda identified that prisoner, Donald Rigger, as one of Ray's closest friends at MSP.

It would be amazing if none of these people bothered to mention Ray's escape to Dowda. It seems more likely that Dowda visited these people for information about Ray's escape and where he might be located. It is worth noting that Dowda made this visit from Atlanta just after someone from Oklahoma made a suspicious long-distance phone call to Dowda's place of work at the Bonanza Sirloin Pit in Marietta, Georgia. The individual who received that call was the nephew of Floyd Ayers, identified by Donald Nissen as a go-between/bagman in the King assassination. Dowda, as noted in Chapter 5, told authorities years after King's murder that he believed the manager and the owner of the Bonanza were somehow connected to King's assassination. Dowda of course did everything he could to minimize his own role and knowledge of a plot. It may well be that he attempted to find Ray to relay information or rumors about a King bounty. There is no evidence that he found his former prison colleague, but given how little we know of Ray's day-to-day activities in Los Angeles, it is certainly possible the two met.

At approximately the same time as Dowda's visit, Ray began to make phone calls to the headquarters for Alabama governor George Wallace's presidential campaign. But Ray took no other suspicious steps that suggested he had obtained concrete information that could link him to the King bounty. Instead, James Earl Ray began to look for legitimate work in L.A. He answered classified ads in the *Los Angeles Times*, applied for a job as a vacuum cleaner salesman, and tried to get a job as a maintenance man. He placed two ads in the paper, one for restaurant work and one for general labor. Apparently, these efforts were frustrated because he had no social security card for Eric Galt and was afraid to use his long-established false identity of Rayns and its legitimate identification. His relatively energetic job-seeking (compared to earlier stops in Birmingham and Mexico) gives the impression that Ray was beginning to run short of money and that he was looking for any opportunity to generate cash.

This may partly explain Ray's decision to go on the road trip to New Orleans in mid-December 1967, ostensibly to take Charlie Stein to New Orleans so he could bring Rita Stein's children back to California. Of course, it would be no surprise to find Ray using the trip to New Orleans as an opportunity to generate some money based on contacts there. It was not Ray's first exposure to the city; in 1955, he had stopped there during a multistate escape following theft of postal money orders. In 1958, he had spent time there following the armed robbery of a bar. Ray admitted he had done some minor cross-border smuggling after the New Orleans sojourn in 1958, as he passed through Texas and crossed the border at Matamoros into Mexico. On December 15, Ray departed for New Orleans in his white Ford Mustang, with Rita's brother, the eccentric Charlie Stein, riding shotgun.

With its libertine culture and its easy access to imported contraband through its ports, New Orleans always was a haven for criminals. But it was also a city in America's Deep South, one whose reputation for cultural exchange often fell short when it came to genuine

racial integration. In 1958, the same year Ray passed through New
Orleans, black enrollees at the University of New Orleans (a newly
formed branch of Louisiana State University) faced daily chants of
"two, four, six, eight, we don't want to integrate." Just two years later, a
mob of angry whites shouted epithets and threats at six-year-old Ruby
Bridges as she integrated an all-white public school; federal marshals
had to provide her with a security escort. As nexus for both criminal
activity and anti-integrationist resistance, New Orleans offered James
Earl Ray several possible access points into a King bounty plot.

Even before leaving for the Big Easy, Ray dragged his traveling
companion, Charlie Stein, to the presidential campaign headquarters
for Alabama governor and arch-segregationist George Wallace, insisting that Stein register to vote. Ray also called Wallace headquarters more than once. This may have been in keeping with Charles
Faulkner's assertion that Ray was developing a background legend as
an extreme racist, either to attract people with knowledge of a bounty
plot and/or to legitimize his own interest in such a plot if he found the
sponsors. It could also be that Ray was looking for a specific person.[13]
A Swift follower and one-time member of the NSRP, James Paul
Thornton, worked out of the same Wallace campaign office. Thornton
was a one-time high-level official for the NSRP in Birmingham before
1965, and he developed relationships with several of the NSRP members who went to Canada, and who were investigated by Congress in
the late 1970s, for their possible connection to King's assassination.
After he returned to his home state of California, Thornton became
active in the California Rangers, the antigovernment group founded
by Christian Identity minister William Potter Gale. If Ray sought out
Thornton in person, he would have just missed him, as Thornton was
fired from his job for his extremist connections.[14]

Stein told investigators that Ray made frequent stops on his trip
from Los Angeles to New Orleans and on at least a couple of occasions used pay phones for unknown reasons. Ray himself would admit
to making two calls, but only to his brother Jerry. The FBI rightly
assumed that Ray, who was out of Stein's sight on a number of occa-

sions, could have made far more than two calls. Bureau agents canvassed the route Ray and Stein took to New Orleans and attempted to trace all calls from pay phones during the relevant period.[15] The available FBI "MURKIN" (MURder of KINg) records lists dozens of numbers that were eventually traced to people who were then interviewed and cleared. But there are some interesting gaps in the Bureau's call accounting that were not accounted for and, unfortunately, are unable to be traced today.

Ray stayed in New Orleans for two days, from December 16 to 17. With Charlie Stein, he dropped off the materials Marie Martin had asked them to deliver to her family and, on the recommendation of the Steins' relatives, registered at the Provincial Motel. Charlie Stein stayed with his relatives, and both men affirmed that Ray spent most of his time outside of Stein's company. Much of what we know of Ray's activities comes from Stein's secondhand account of what Ray told him and Ray's firsthand account in books and interviews—both of which have question marks as to their reliability. Stein clearly attempted to profit and make a name for himself based on his limited association with Ray, and Ray attempted to, as always, use the New Orleans trip to paint a picture of himself as an innocent dupe in King's eventual murder. But both men gave indications that the trip had some conspiratorial purpose. Ray, of course, claimed the visit to New Orleans coincided with yet another meeting with Raul, where once again Raul continued to promise Ray he would eventually provide the fugitive with fake identification and a passport out of North America if he continued to assist Raul in his various gun- and drug-smuggling schemes.

Stein never mentioned the name Raul in any of his numerous early post-assassination interviews with either the press or the FBI. But Stein did tell both the press and law enforcement that Ray expressed a goal of meeting someone in the Industrial Canal area of New Orleans; Stein recalled Ray describing this man as an "engineer" or an "industrialist" but he could not remember his name.[16] After the assassination, Ray played coy with his own investigators on these leads, convincing researcher Harold Weisberg that the accused assassin had far more intimate knowledge of New Orleans than he ever let on or wanted to share.[17]

Weisberg never found any engineer or industrialist, but he did investigate New Orleans addresses that Ray provided to one of his attorneys after the assassination. Weisberg's follow-up investigation revealed one of the addresses as a site for criminal activity, but he could never get James Earl Ray to discuss it. Weisberg came to believe that Ray was covering for whatever criminals he met in New Orleans. Still sympathetic to Ray, Weisberg nonetheless wrote: "He is the only link to the conspirators of which I know with certainty. That is the area in which he held out from me and he was frank about it, in his own way, saying he would not do the FBI's work for it."[18]

Other authors, such as William Bradford Huie, have noted, like Weisberg, that Ray was excessively concerned about investigations into his time in New Orleans and refused to talk when confronted about his time there. Some, like Lamar Waldron, have speculated that Ray must have met with organized crime elements working for New Orleans Mafia kingpin Carlos Marcello. Waldron makes much of the fact that Ray and Stein were involved with procuring drugs and that this would certainly place Ray in Marcello's domain. While the likely (but not definitive) reason for Ray's New Orleans venture included the procurement of some quantity of drugs, it is equally likely that these could have come from criminals, such as Louis "The Mechanic" Smith, who were shifting allegiances to the rapidly expanding Dixie Mafia. This network was very much at odds with the old-line Marcello organization. Certainly low-level drug sales would not necessarily catch Marcello's eye, as he was making hundreds of thousands of dollars a year from shipping literal barges full of heroin into the ports of New Orleans. It seems more likely that other members of the Dixie Mafia, as the proverbial second fiddles in New Orleans, interacted with Ray.

Criminal elements in New Orleans enjoyed particularly close relationships with the White Knights of the Ku Klux Klan, unsurprising, given their geographic proximity to southern Mississippi. A 1970s informant report relayed a conversation with White Knights terrorist Danny Joe Hawkins (and close friend of Tommy Tarrants) in which Hawkins told the informant that contacts in New Orleans were the primary weapons providers to the Mississippi Klan.[19] Sam Bowers had attended college and had deep family contacts in New Orleans, and Deavours Nix, the White Knights' intelligence chief, previously worked in New Orleans publishing racist tracts. When in 1973 police arrested White Knights member Byron de la Beckwith, he was reportedly carrying a bomb for an attack in New Orleans, intended for the home of Adolph Botnick, a Jewish attorney.

Publicly, of course, Ray would claim that everything he did was part of some kind of puppet show engineered by the mysterious Raul to frame him for the crime. In later years, he introduced leads from Louisiana that threw off investigators, including Weisberg.[20] Raul, again, could indeed be a composite character that includes references to real criminals Ray met in New Orleans. But Ray was not an ignorant dupe, mindlessly moved around as a pawn to set him up in the King murder. Indeed, the plotters did not even turn to Ray for another couple of months. They had a real patsy to begin framing in the meanwhile.

ON DECEMBER 22, 1967, Sam Bowers did something highly unusual: he convinced Tommy Tarrants to join him on a trip to Collins, Mississippi. The purpose: to machine-gun the home of Ancie McLaurin, a black man accused of shooting a white police officer.[21] This represented a major departure from Bowers's usual cautious behavior. This was a man who ordered crimes and rarely participated in them. Indeed, he employed tradecraft worthy of James Bond to avoid government scrutiny. What's more, two months earlier, federal prosecutors had convicted Bowers for his role in ordering the Mississippi Burning killings; he escaped with a relatively minor sentence. Out on appeal, Bowers was now risking a capital sentence by going on this mission. Indeed, he was risking potential exposure not only of himself, but also his secret operative, Tarrants.[22]

It now seems likely that this was precisely Bowers's goal. His caution in avoiding police surveillance was exceeded only by his paranoia about informants. At one time or another, Bowers suspected almost every member of his group, including even his most loyal sycophants, like Burris Dunn, whom FBI documents describe as worshipping Bowers. This was not without justification. Several men, including senior White Knight operatives such as Delmar Dennis and one-time Grand Giant Robert Earl Wilson, had recently testified against Bowers in federal trials. Indeed, the FBI, especially in Mississippi, went to great lengths to plant and turn informants inside the KKK through a program simply known as Counterintelligence Program (COINTELPRO). These informants not only provided evidence in trials, but they also created a climate of suspicion that helped destroy targeted groups from within, parasitic behavior amplified by dirty tricks and provocations crafted by the FBI. No one was spooked by this more than Bowers himself.

It seems unlikely that Bowers would welcome a complete stranger like Tarrants into his midst without an excessive amount of caution. Tarrants himself described Bowers's unease at their first meetings. They met, again, after extensive countersurveillance measures, exchanging notes on paper rather than in conversation, burning the "correspondence" as they went.

While Tarrants successfully bombed a number of targets in Mississippi for Bowers, such behavior was not unknown among FBI informants. In Alabama, for instance, Gary Rowe participated in various acts of racial violence while informing for the FBI, something exposed to the world—and interested parties like Bowers—in 1965.[23] What may have bothered Bowers was that no one died in any of the numerous bombings. Yes, many civil rights–era church bombings often aimed to scare and terrorize would-be protestors and activists without killing anyone—but the wave of bombings Bowers ordered in 1967 were directed at Jews and had little to do with deterring activism.

One way to make sure that Tarrants was up to snuff would be to see if he would kill someone for the White Knights. The trip to Collins, Mississippi, likely would have resulted in just such a test, with the drive-by shooting of McLaurin's residence. Bowers never got the chance to implement this test, however, as Collins policemen, suspicious of the out-of-state Alabama license plates, approached the men when they pulled into a gas station. The car proved to be stolen, and the men were arrested.

Bowers then made another interesting move. According to the police report, Bowers told officers he was cold, and asked them to fetch his sweater from the car, the stolen vehicle. Upon removing the sweater, they found an illegal firearm. Between the interstate transportation of a stolen car and national firearms laws, Tarrants should have faced serious federal charges. Now Bowers had another kind of test: would the federal government bring charges against Tarrants?

If this was Bowers's intention, the answer likely intensified any suspicion he had of Tarrants. The government charged Bowers with illegal firearm possession, but he was quickly acquitted. Tarrants was not arraigned on those charges nearly as quickly. It appears as if the system simply went slower for Tarrants, who faced indictment that coming March in Mobile. But the source of the delay is less important than what it meant for Bowers's perception of Tarrants as a potential informant. Bowers needed far less than this to become suspicious of people he had known for years. The entire episode cries out for an explanation, as it dumbfounded even those who knew Bowers best. If this was a test, the implications are not without relevance for the King murder. For it appears likely that Tarrants was set up as the original patsy for the King murder, and may have been marked for death later to tie up loose ends.

9

IN WAITING

Tommy Tarrants found himself in law enforcement's cross-hairs for the first time since 1965. No one knew of his terrorist bombings and shootings in Mississippi, but his arrest with Sam Bowers meant that for the second time he was now facing charges of carrying an illegal firearm. On his attorney's advice, Tarrants returned to his family in Mobile and registered for classes at a community college, ostensibly to clean up his image in anticipation of a court date. But records show that Tarrants was not much of a student.[1] His mind was still dedicated to fighting the Jewish-Communist conspiracy against white America. According to his autobiography, the recent federal charges only amplified his antagonism toward the government and minority groups.[2] Bowers escaped conviction for the firearms charges in mid-January. While the Justice Department convicted other White Knights for their roles in the 1966 Dahmer murder, Bowers was acquitted on a mistrial. But in January of 1968, Bowers's luck with the law had nonetheless already run out. He was free but on appeal bond for his conviction for the MIBURN murders. Arrangements were already being made to transfer power as Grand Wizard to L. E. Matthews once Bowers finally went to prison, since his appeal was expected to fail.[3]

By early 1968, almost every major player in the White Knights faced or would face criminal charges. Many, including Bowers, temporarily kept a low profile. Increasingly, they worked through their front organization, the Americans for the Preservation of the White Race, to raise money for legal costs. Through that same group, senior Mississippi White Knights continued to actively promote J. B. Stoner's National States Rights Party and its outreach in Meridian and Jackson, mailing out his radical newspaper, *The Thunderbolt*.[4] Such low-level activity was simply window dressing. Behind the scenes, Bowers continued to plot more violence, with tactics in a wider strategy. Since 1964, a key component of his grand vision of a race war involved pushing law enforcement into a showdown in Mississippi. The strategy also included targeting key civil rights leaders for assassination, using strike teams.[5] In Bowers's scenario, leftist, black radicals would then retaliate, encouraging further retaliation not just from the "rednecks" Bowers manipulated, but "everyday" whites in Mississippi. Bowers never clarified how he hoped this would spread throughout the country, but he told Delmar Dennis that the White Knights were simply part of an even larger strategy to stoke a race war.

The lull in Mississippi Klan violence came to end on February 20, 1968, when the White Knights burned down the grocery store belonging to Wallace Miller, a one-time member who became an FBI informant and testified in the MIBURN prosecution. Two weeks later, the White Knights bombed the Blackwell Realty Company in Jackson for selling homes to blacks in white neighborhoods.

Having endured months of bombings, local and federal law enforcement fought back in unprecedented ways. Unable to secure convictions in local cases, Meridian police formed a special squad under Sergeant Lester Joyner. According to historian Michael Netwon, "Joyner's guerrillas," as they were known, "fired into Klansmen's homes and detonated explosives on their lawns."[6] The Jackson field office of the FBI was already experienced with fighting dirty against the local Klan. Research done by federal judge Chet Dillard strongly suggests that the FBI brought in an out-of-state mobster to beat and

intimidate a Klansman into providing information in the Mississippi
Burning murders.[7]

It is easy to question the legality of this law enforcement response,
but it is important to remember that the White Knights were unique
in their willingness to directly oppose policemen and special agents.
Recall that, following the September 1967 bombing of Perry Nussbaum's home, a group of Klansmen, including Danny Joe Hawkins,
stopped a group of FBI agents who were tailing them in a car, pulled
weapons on the men, and struck one of the agents. Law enforcement
found a hit list the Klan prepared with the names of FBI and local
police officials.[8] The record now shows that in March of 1968, Bowers
was asking members to assassinate legendary Mississippi FBI chief
Roy Moore.[9] Bowers's underground hit squad's recent attacks on Jewish targets only put more pressure on law enforcement to unleash a
serious counterattack on the White Knights. White Mississippians
who turned the other way when the Klan destroyed black targets were
upset by the attacks on Jewish targets. But the investigation was not
generating any leads. As Newton noted, Jim Ingram, who was a senior
FBI agent in Jackson at the time, referred to the Klan as "animals,"
and told his men to "just go out and pound them until you get some
results."[10]

For Bowers, all the violence was simply a grand diversion for both
local and federal law enforcement. The Neshoba investigation brought
a large federal intervention by the FBI into the state, with polls favoring military intervention if the situation worsened. Four years later,
by 1968, with membership rolls depleted, the White Knights were
alienating outside supporters. Yet Bowers might have been banking
on Southern history to overcome those disadvantages. Few things
could inflame an apathetic, white Southerner more than the outside
interference of the federal government. Cultural animosity to federal
intrusion informed Bowers's thinking in 1964, when he spoke of a
race war on the heels of the Neshoba murders. By 1968, Bowers could
also point to another development that might make his strategy even
more effective: the growing number of black militants willing to use
violence to retaliate against racism.

Stokely Carmichael famously claimed that "every courthouse in Mississippi ought to be burned down tomorrow, to get rid of the dirt and the mess."[11] This too was part of Bowers's original strategy—the racial polarization Tommy Tarrants described that would foment their dreamed-of race war. Only now, in the tense racial climate of 1968, it must have appeared as if the right spark could nationalize such a conflict.

IN 1967, DR. King, maintaining his stance of totally nonviolent protest, was losing influence with both the young blacks and middle-class whites who once formed the backbone of his civil rights coalition. In continuing to insist that nonviolence was not simply a tactic but a moral philosophy, he lost his youth appeal to groups like the Black Panthers, who brandished shotguns to oppose police brutality, often for show, but sometimes on the street. Increasingly, firebrands like Stokely Carmichael and H. Rap Brown attacked not only the political establishment, but also the strategy of nonviolence itself and Dr. King by implication. As Carmichael wrote, the idea "that a black minority could bow its head and get whipped into a meaningful position of power [was] absurd."[12] King's popularity with important political figures had also suffered, first for his speaking out against the Vietnam War and then for his focus on the issue of poverty, one that Washington—involved in a full-scale war in Southeast Asia—was not at all prepared to address.

His reliance on nonviolence, his opposition to Vietnam, and his new focus on poverty were all obstacles to King as he shifted his focus to his next major project: the Poor People's Campaign. The SCLC wanted thousands of Americans to march to and camp out in the National Mall in Washington, D.C., to call for what scholar Gerald McKnight described as a "fundamental reorganization of the American economy."[13] Dr. King hoped to align and unite, arguably for the first time in American history, the economic interests of poor blacks and poor whites. But King found it increasingly difficult to mobilize yet another peaceful march when so many young activists were drawn to Black Nationalism. Nor did the campaign, with its economic message, appeal to mainstream, middle-class whites. By arguing that the conflict in Vietnam was diverting resources from LBJ's other war, "the war on poverty," King did nothing to regain support from the White House. And J. Edgar Hoover, already paranoid about King's supposed communist affinities, resorted to an unprecedented rumor campaign against King through surrogates in the media.

With this context in mind, King delivered his famous "Drum Major" sermon on February 5, 1968. It is often remembered for King calling himself "a drum major for justice." But for most of the sermon, the term *drum major* represented something else. Perhaps with his outspoken Black Nationalist counterparts in mind, King spoke against the "drum majors" who led movements for their own ambition, without careful consideration of their tactics and the implications for their followers. These people drew "joiners" who followed a movement without understanding the actual cause. King contrasted this with another "rabble rouser," a supposed "agitator" who led by example by ministering to the poor in a small region in Palestine. Former friends turned against Jesus too, King reminded the audience, but he still became the most influential person in history. He did so, King asserted, by emphasizing love over hate. In the tradition of prophets bringing the flock back to their better impulses, King was reminding the audience of the power of nonviolence, not simply as a tactic but as a principle.[14]

In doing so, King was also validating himself as an ideal target for the sort of violence Sam Bowers had in mind. Killing Dr. King would reveal the ultimate truth—there could be no nonviolent solution. The only answer would be full-scale black-on-white warfare.

JAMES EARL RAY returned from New Orleans to Los Angeles in late December 1967 and waited. No one would have contracted Ray, with his history of nonviolent crimes, as a murderer for hire—not when professional killers were available. In any plot, Ray would be a peripheral figure, someone who could be used if circumstances required.

After returning from New Orleans with Charlie Stein and his two little nieces, Ray didn't get any of the legitimate jobs he was seeking, but his spending continued, suggesting that he may have obtained some narcotics to sell for profit while in the Big Easy. In fact, January 1968 was extremely busy for Ray. He continued his dance lessons and his locksmithing correspondence course. He also started a series of lessons at the International Bartending School. And Ray seems to have restarted his quest for female film subjects. He joined a swingers club and ran an advertisement in the *Los Angeles Free Press,* seeking "female for mutual enjoyment and/or female for swing session," getting the addresses of several interested parties and sending photos of himself. In support of these efforts, he ordered more sex manuals from Futura Press and a set of chrome handcuffs from a police equipment company in Los Angeles.

Ray also subscribed to a mail-forwarding service, only for the month of February 1968, and used that address for the responses to both his *Free Press* advertisement and swingers letters. Ray explained that he didn't want such letters coming to his apartment, but of course the use of an alternate address could also have been useful for other types of confidential correspondence as well. Such mail forwarding would have protected Ray's true location if any letters to or from him intercepted. And that would have been a very logical precaution if Ray had started any communication with people he might have suspected as being under FBI surveillance or mail monitoring.

And Ray wrote to the Orange County, California, chapter of the Friends of Rhodesia, first with questions and then with a thank-you letter stating that he anticipated leaving for Rhodesia in November 1969. The letter requested a subscription to the *Rhodesian Commentary.* Ray's consistent and ongoing interest in the racist regimes of South Africa and Rhodesia seems to undermine Ray's own statements that he held no racist views. Yet these were also countries that were commonly described as ideal destinations for criminals wanting to avoid extradition. In any event, it seems clear that Ray still had an overriding interest in leaving the United States for good. He was still a fugitive from the law, and by January 1968, he had been on the run for the better part of a year. Given Ray's conservative nature, he must have begun to wonder how long he could continue eluding law enforcement.

An objective look at Ray's activities in January 1968 shows a continuation of the same sorts of undertakings that he was pursuing for most of 1967, going all the way back to his stay in Canada. He wanted to get out of the United States and preferably off the continent. "White" Africa was obviously a preferred destination. He wanted to learn portable skills (bartending, locksmithing), he was not averse to picking up money from the sale of drugs when the opportunity presented, and he certainly seems focused on pornographic films as a moneymaking option. There is no indication of any major change in his behavior, no sign he was tied into a King conspiracy or practicing any more than his routine security precautions. Sending his photo to a number of women argues against his being involved in anything new or particularly risky. But that was all in January.

Things appear to have changed mightily for Ray in February 1968. With no obvious way to pay for it, James Earl Ray suddenly scheduled plastic surgery that would not begin until March 5. He stopped his scheduled dance lessons, forfeiting some of his deposit—anathema to the money-conscious Ray. He declined a bartending job offered to him after his class graduation, though it was exactly the sort of job he had been seeking for the previous two months. At his bartending school graduation, he was heard to remark that he would soon be leaving for Birmingham, Alabama, to visit his brother. He traded his console television to Marie Martin for her portable set, telling her he was returning to the South. And on March 17, he completed a change-of-address form forwarding all his mail to general delivery, Atlanta, Georgia. Notably, he indicated that address would only be good through April 25.

After his capture, Ray stated that the planned plastic surgery was because he feared that he might show up on the FBI's Ten Most Wanted Fugitives list and he needed to change his appearance.[15] Of course he eventually did make that list, but that would require a much more dramatic crime than any found in Ray's decades-long history of robbery, theft, and fraud. To explain himself, he claimed that he thought his appearance on the FBI's Ten Most Wanted Fugitives list would have resulted from his prison escape in 1967—but surely no career criminal would ever really imagine that a minor prison escape could earn that level of attention from the FBI.

Various authors have written about these "Top Ten" remarks with amusement, picturing Ray as out of touch with reality and possibly not all that bright.[16] Of course that view fails to acknowledge that Ray was absolutely correct; he would indeed be on the Ten Most Wanted Fugitives list within a matter of months. Authors, like William Bradford Huie, in search of a motive—but not conspiracy—use Ray's statement to define a point at which his ego overcame his caution and he decided to make himself world famous. Others, like Gerald Frank in his book *An American Death*, point to this as a sign of Ray's buried racial extremism, "coming out of the very atmosphere in which Ray grew up and lived." Frank argues that Ray's willingness to pursue King despite an expectation that he might become the most wanted man in America shows that he was not only willing to act on his racial animus, but that he did not expect to be caught, much less convicted, for the murder. A most-wanted listing would ensure that somewhere in the country someone or some group would take good care of Ray if he rid the world of the black civil rights leader.

With the information now available, we propose that views on Ray's motive such as the Ten-Most-Wanted-Fugitives-list motive Huie describes and I'll-kill-King-and-become-a-Southern-hero motive Frank suggests are simply incorrect. They do not accurately reflect either Ray's caution, his actions, his desire for money, or, for that matter, the sophistication and reach of those who had been trying to eliminate Dr. King since before 1964. Rather, our view is that Ray's change in behavior in February demonstrates that he was responding to what he thought was finally a truly concrete bounty offer on Dr. King's life.

•

ON MARCH 2, 1968, the man known to his classmates as Eric Galt graduated from bartending school in Los Angeles. In the graduation photo, James Earl Ray deliberately closed his eyes to make future identification more difficult. On March 3, 7, and 11, Ray spent a sizable amount of his remaining money on plastic surgery to alter his appearance. Again, Ray said this was to make a future identification more difficult.[17]

Ray's recruitment into a King conspiracy is further suggested by the manager of the St. Francis Hotel, where Ray had been staying since late January. Allan O. Thompson told investigators he remembered his switchboard operator reporting a series of phone calls to Eric Galt, sometime in March, possibly as early as March 1. The calls came from either New Orleans or Atlanta or both, and the caller left the name J. C. Hardin. Sometime in the middle of the month, a stranger whom Thompson presumed was Hardin visited the St. Francis looking for Galt/Ray. Thompson reported that another man, a shady character who wanted to avoid law enforcement attention, recalled seeing Ray meeting with a stranger at the same time. They met at the Rabbit's Foot Club, a bar not far from the St. Francis, and one that Ray was known to frequent.

The authors have identified J. C. Hardin after reexamining the FBI's investigation into Allan O. Thompson's claims. Having mined their national files for men who used the alias J. C. Hardin, the FBI presented Thompson with a number of photos. A police artist constructed an "incremental" drawing of the man as Thompson reflected on various facial features. Thompson noted a striking overall similarity between the man who visited the hotel and a photograph the FBI showed him. Inexplicably, the FBI dismissed the match because the hair in the photo was different, ignoring the fact that the J. C. Hardin photo they were showing was taken more than a decade before the King murder! Newly released files (with the redactions removed) make clear that Thompson identified James Wilborn Ashmore from Texas as J. C. Hardin.[18]

Ashmore had a steady history of criminal offenses, mostly for theft and forgery, and he served more than one stint in prison. Nothing directly indicated that he was connected to a group like the Dixie Mafia, but such information rarely appeared in FBI files prior to the 1970s. Donald Sparks was undoubtedly Dixie Mafia, as revealed in an extensive investigation by the Kansas state attorney's office, but no FBI file references him as such. A truck driver by trade, Ashmore was exactly the kind of man the Dixie Mafia would recruit for missions: someone who could routinely cross state lines without drawing the attention of law enforcement. More work needs to be done to develop Ashmore, who died in 1973 in California, as possible accessory in the King conspiracy. But it seems probable that he was another go-between in the Dixie Mafia/White Knights bounty plot, and the one who finally integrated James Earl Ray into the scheme. Newly discovered information makes this even more probable. The FBI originally located the Hardin alias for Ashmore in files that connected him to the Ole Miss race riots against the admission of James Meredith. Those riots not only incited many future members of the White Knights, it drew radicals from around the nation, including several mentioned in this book, such as Gale and Crommelin. The file that details Ashmore's role in the riots may have been routinely destroyed.[19]

And as of March 17, 1968, James Earl Ray was leaving Los Angeles for good and heading to the Southeast. His destination: Martin Luther King Jr.'s hometown of Atlanta. Martin Luther King Jr. also left Los Angeles on March 17 en route to Memphis.

10

STALKING

As spring approached in 1968, King was frequently traveling in efforts to mobilize support for the upcoming Poor People's Campaign. A movement that had been growing in Memphis to improve the condition of the city's sanitation workers captured his attention and soon his energy. Protests erupted in Memphis in February, with the proximate cause being the deaths of two garbage men forced to work in terrible weather conditions. For Memphis sanitation workers, this was the final straw in a long history of poor treatment. The sanitation workers earned such petty wages that many were on welfare, and they were forced to work long hours even in harsh conditions. Issues of class intersected, as they often do, with issues of race. The Memphis sanitation workers were also overwhelmingly African American. The strike quickly drew the support of local church leaders and civil rights activists, soon garnering national media attention, with images of hundreds of strikers wearing placards asserting I AM A MAN. That King found solidarity in such a struggle is not surprising.

Dr. King arrived in Memphis on March 18 and spoke to a tremendous crowd of both civil rights activists and laborers. He told the audience: "You are demonstrating that we can stick together. You are demonstrating that we are all tied in a single garment of destiny, and that if one black person suffers, if one black person is down, we are all down." King left shortly after, but members of the SCLC remained active to help maintain the Memphis Sanitation Workers Strike. For King, the strike represented an opportunity to broadcast the socio-economic themes of the Poor People's Campaign, and to once again demonstrate the efficacy of nonviolent protest.[1] He was not done with Memphis, but he was next heading to a speaking engagement in Selma, Alabama, the site of one of his greatest triumphs.

AT APPROXIMATELY THE same time James Earl Ray was making arrangements to move to Atlanta, Tommy Tarrants took a pilgrimage to the home of his hero, Rev. Wesley Swift, in Lancaster, California. According to Tarrants's autobiography, he made contact with Swift some months earlier, impressing Swift enough to be invited to become his understudy.

Swift gave one sermon during Tarrants's stay in Lancaster, on March 17, entitled "The Children of the Spirit." Echoing many familiar themes—blaming Jews for manipulating the money supply, for a communist conspiracy, and so on—he also made the following comment:

> But we the people of the kingdom realize that we are to destroy the powers of darkness. We are going to haul down the hammer and sickle because we believe God. HE declares that the powers of Gog and Magog, and the powers of darkness, are to be destroyed by the children of the kingdom. Their government is to be thrown down and their evil Priests are going to be removed from their places of authority.[2]

We do not know if Tarrants heard his idol deliver this sermon, but his other interactions with Rev. Swift have enormous implications for the King assassination. In his excellent book on anti-Jewish and racial violence in Mississippi, *Terror in the Night*, published in 1993, Pulitzer-winning reporter Jack Nelson used Tarrants as a major source. Tarrants is quoted as saying that he bought a rifle from Swift to shoot Martin Luther King Jr. "That was my ambition," Nelson quoted Tarrants as saying, "to shoot Dr. King. I hated Dr. King."[3]

In a 2007 interview with Jerry Mitchell of Mississippi's *Clarion-Ledger*, Tarrants seemingly backed off from such comments. By this time, Tarrants had been a mainstream Christian minister since the 1970s, having moved away from Christian Identity theology in prison, a life change so profound that it convinced the FBI and even his would-be victims to press for his early release (his sentence was commuted in 1976). Tarrants, while acknowledging to Mitchell that he bought the rifle from Swift in March of 1968, insisted he did so to "get acquainted with Swift. I thought a lot of him and listened to his recordings, was under that influence."[4]

Regarding the hatred and ambition to kill Dr. King that Nelson quoted Tarrants as expressing, Tarrants acknowledged "having those views," but said "a lot of people in the South hated Martin Luther King."[5] Because Nelson did not footnote or explicitly cite his sources and because Tarrants's quotes are separated from each other in the text, it's difficult to confirm whether they were recorded at the same time.

New information uncovered by the authors brings this matter more sharply into focus. In materials donated by Nelson's wife, Barbara Matuszow, to Emory University, the authors found the original tape recording (and transcripts) of Nelson's interviews with Tarrants. One of the recordings, from 1991, captures the relevant exchange. Nelson first asks Tarrants if the House Un-American Activities Committee (HUAC) interviewed him. It is highly likely that Nelson confused HUAC—which did not exist after 1975, but which at one time investigated the KKK—with the House Select Committee on Assassinations (HSCA). The HSCA, as noted earlier, ran a concurrent re-investigation of the JFK and MLK murders from 1976 to 1979. Indeed, Tarrants told Mitchell in 2007 that HSCA investigators did interview him in the late 1970s. Nelson, for reasons that are still unclear, then turned directly to the issue of the rifle purchase.

> NELSON: Did you testify before the House Un-American Activities Committee?

> TARRANTS: They sent . . .

> NELSON: Late '70s?

> TARRANTS: . . . two investigators down to see me at Ole Miss.

> NELSON: They must have quoted your testimony at some point in a report or something. *Did you say anything about buying a rifle to assassinate King?*

> TARRANTS: *Yeah, yeah, I told them. I told them that.*

> NELSON: When did you do that?

> TARRANTS: I bought, I think, I bought that from Wesley Swift as a matter of fact.

> NELSON: Is he still around?

> TARRANTS: Oh, no. He died of cancer, years and years ago.

> NELSON: He was in what city? In, ah, . . .

> TARRANTS: Lancaster, California.

> NELSON: Lancaster, California.

TARRANTS: Um, yea, yea. *That was my ambition* . . .

NELSON: Right.

TARRANTS: . . . to shoot Martin Luther King.

NELSON: So you bought . . .

MATUSZOW (NELSON'*s wife*): Oh, really?

TARRANTS: Yea. I hated him worse than any of the Blacks.[6]

The readers may judge for themselves if the explanation Tarrants provided to Jerry Mitchell, in 2007, captures the spirit of what Tarrants told Nelson on tape. Tarrants's responses to Mitchell leaves open to interpretation whether he misled Mitchell. It would benefit the historical record if he cleared up this matter. The authors have unsuccessfully reached out to Tarrants on more than one occasion.

The immediate temptation is to see the quotation and the timing of the rifle purchase as evidence that Tarrants was involved in King's murder. But the authors believe that Tarrants's other claim to Mitchell is likely true: that he had no role in King's murder. Upon closer inspection, what appears to be a suggestive circumstantial case against Tarrants for some kind of involvement in King's murder looks more like the result of a carefully orchestrated effort to frame him for the crime. The idea of a frame-up is well-worn in theories on the King assassination. For decades, the only man convicted in the crime, James Earl Ray, insisted he was a patsy in the murder. But Ray's actions from the end of March through the beginning of April substantively contradict this assertion. Instead they strongly suggest that he played a conscious role in the crime.

·

JAMES EARL RAY agreed to drop off a package in New Orleans for Marie Martin on his way to Atlanta. After that brief stop sometime between March 19 to 21, James Earl Ray ventured to Atlanta, but not before making a highly suspicious detour along the way, one that took him directly to the vicinity of Dr. King. Almost three years after marchers stood their ground against club-carrying Alabama policemen on horses, Martin Luther King Jr. returned to Selma, Alabama. Dr. King was there to give a speech on March 22, one that newspapers had publicized in advance. James Earl Ray, who according to any logical, direct route to Atlanta would have traveled through Birmingham, somehow found his way to Selma at the same time, and stayed at the Flamingo Hotel. Confronted with this coincidence, Ray claimed that he made a wrong turn. But Selma is completely out of the way of Birmingham, and available maps from the time show the "wrong turn" described by Ray wasn't even possible given the available exits.[7] Even some researchers sympathetic to Ray, notably Harold Weisberg, his chief investigator, acknowledge that someone or something related to King's murder lured him to the city.

King returned to his hometown of Atlanta on March 23, and Ray followed, traveling through Montgomery and Birmingham. Ray had never spent any time in Atlanta before in his life. On March 23, he rented a room at a cheap rooming house known to lodge drunks and vagrants on Peachtree Street. Once again, he used the alias Eric Galt.[8]

Other than the constantly inebriated rooming house owner and the owner of a Laundromat, both of whom had short and limited interactions with Ray, there is no one who can describe Ray's movements in Atlanta. Ray of course says he was in Atlanta waiting for his next directives from Raul. Until Raul told Ray to meet him in Birmingham at the end of March, Ray did nothing but hang out in his room—or so Ray says. There is evidence that suggests he made contact with someone in Atlanta, someone whom Ray never identified. Investigators found a receipt for a dinner for two at Mammy's Shanty, a local dive that, according to author Lamar Waldron (an Atlanta native), was frequented by racists.[9] When confronted about this by one

of his earliest chroniclers, author William Bradford Huie, Ray was
unable to explain it. Ray also could not adequately explain why he had
a second key made for his room, or why after the assassination police
found clothing among his possessions that would not have fit Ray.

Also suspiciously, Ray obtained a commercial map of Atlanta,
and as was often his custom, marked areas that were relevant to him.
On this map, Ray circled his rooming house on Peachtree, but also
Martin Luther King Jr.'s home (twice!). Ray also marked several
other locations. Ray never offered an adequate explanation for why
these areas were marked on the map.[10] But new evidence makes it
clear that the FBI also misrepresented the location of the markings
of the map. The FBI claimed that they walked to the other locations
that Ray circled on the map and that Ray also circled the headquarters for the Southern Christian Leadership Conference and Martin
Luther King Jr.'s church.

A new analysis by researcher Jerry Shinley suggests a reason why
both Ray and the FBI would want to cover up the markings on this
map and their implications. One of Ray's markings appears very close
to a restaurant that served as a front operation for Cliff Fuller, a Dixie
Mafia criminal who later turned into a federal informant. Another
mark appears very close to a nightclub frequented by Fuller's partner
in crime Harold Pruett. Fuller enjoyed relationships with criminals
in Mississippi, among other places. Ray may have been hiding his
contacts with the criminal underworld—something, again, that even
Harold Weisberg believed to be the case. The FBI, in turn, may have
been protecting their informant, Fuller, and the embarrassment it
may have caused to have such an informant caught up in something
like the King assassination. As will become clear and as has been
hinted at elsewhere, the FBI may have had more than one informant
in a position to have known about, and potentially stopped, the King
murder. But the FBI, throughout its history, has had a difficult time
balancing the need to protect informants while waiting to maximize
said informant's ability to implicate other outlaws, and the need to
preemptively stop a crime.

It is clear Ray stalked King in Selma and on through Atlanta. As such, it is important to recall the offer extended by Leroy McManaman to Donald Nissen. McManaman told Nissen that he could have a stake in the bounty in one of two ways. He could participate in the actual killing, or he could case King's movements and report them to the would-be killers. Specifically, McManaman mentioned casing King's movements in Atlanta—Nissen's destination following his immediate release.[11]

It makes sense that any conspiracy involving Ray would more likely use him in the "stalker" role, since he had no background as a professional killer or sniper. One could safely assume that as this secondary role was far less risky, it promised much less of the bounty. Whether that would sit well with Ray as he proceeded through the "mission" is another matter.

IN HIS AUTOBIOGRAPHY, Tarrants says he decided to leave Swift and visit his uncle in San Diego, after which his cousin joined him when he returned to Mobile. There, Tarrants says, he spotted FBI agents in round-the-clock surveillance of his residence. In going to California, Tarrants jumped bond for his upcoming trial for the firearms charge. Already upset with the government, Tarrants decided to pursue an even more serious form of resistance against the enemies of white Christians.

Inspired by the example of Robert DePugh, the leader of the Minutemen, who had evaded the FBI for months to avoid firearms and bank robbery charges, Tarrants decided that he, too, could become a lone-wolf terrorist while dodging capture. On March 28, one week before King's murder, he wrote a note that police discovered months later:

Gentlemen:
    I have committed myself totally to defeating the Communist-Jew conspiracy which threatens our coun-

try—any means necessary shall be used. Please be
advised that since 23, March, 1968, I, Thomas Albert
Tarrants III, have been underground and operating
guerrilla warfare. I have always believed in military action against the communist enemy.[12]

The connection to DePugh is significant for another reason. Files
on the Minutemen reveal multiple accounts from informants referencing assassination plots. The radical antigovernment group, heavily
influenced by Swift and Christian Identity zealots, articulated a secret
plan to be activated if DePugh and his colleagues were captured by
federal authorities. Hardcore members were to assassinate key political figures in retaliation, among them Martin Luther King Jr. Although DePugh and his main aide, Wally Payson, continued to elude
the FBI and remain in hiding from the time they were charged in
January 1968 until 1969, the seven other Minutemen arrested in connection with the same charges began their trials in March of 1968.[13]

At least one person who developed a relationship with Tarrants
insists that the young terrorist most identified with the Minutemen
as of 1968—more so than even the White Knights. Records show that
Tarrants met with a senior Minuteman leader, Dennis Mower, on his
trip to see Swift in the middle of March. This makes sense, as Mower
served as a key aide to Swift. Mower also enjoyed a close relationship
with Sam Bowers. But most relevant to our discussion, Keith Gilbert,
a one-time close ally of Mower, insists that Mower was behind the
1965 plot to blow up the Palladium theater when King visited. Notably, Gilbert claims that he was to be a fall guy for Mower—that
Mower manipulated him into a position where he would either die
in the attack or die from the death penalty if he survived the attack
and was captured. Gilbert says he tipped off the police about the 1965
plot for this very reason, and he did, in fact, shoulder all the blame for
stealing the dynamite. Based on this and his direct experiences with
Mower, Gilbert is convinced that Mower had something to do with
the King murder on April 4.

Tarrants's story in March parallels another radical's, whose account only recently became available in new files. Eugene "Sunset" Mansfield at one time was a Grand Dragon in a Texas KKK. But for several years, his racist activity was dormant. At least in the FBI files, his only recorded offense was an assault charge from 1966. Suddenly, on March 13, 1968, Mansfield left his job on an oil rig, forwarded his last check to L. E. Matthews's residence in Mississippi, and subsequently went to stay with him. Documents show that Matthews wanted to use Mansfield in a hit or a job. Indeed, documents indicate that in the last two weeks of March, Matthews was in and out of his usual residence, planning a "project" out of state. Matthews and Mansfield argued over the payment for this proposed hit or job. Unable to account for his whereabouts in the immediate wake of King's assassination, Mansfield became one of the earliest persons of interest in the crime.[14]

Tarrants also spent part of his time living underground with L. E. Matthews, but he never specified the dates to Nelson. The record indicates that Matthews encouraged Tarrants to visit a remote location in North Carolina known to be a national gathering place for white supremacists looking to perfect their paramilitary skills. According to Tarrants, he stayed with Swift followers in this area for an unspecified period.[15] The FBI did not yet know about Tarrants's months-long bombing campaign in Mississippi, much less his promise to become a one-man guerrilla army waging war against the American government. They *apparently* did not know about his visit to Wesley Swift, or the rifle purchase to "shoot King." In short, at the end of March 1968, Tarrants would have raised none of the alarms that Mansfield raised in discussing "hits" with the soon-to-be Grand Wizard of the most dangerous racist organization in the country. Yet as we will see, somehow Tarrants attracted just as much immediate interest from law enforcement in connection with the King murder. It seems entirely possible that as the calendar moved closer to April 4, someone was informing on Tommy Tarrants to law enforcement.

•

AS TARRANTS WROTE his antigovernment screed, Martin Luther King Jr. returned to Memphis. Originally intended for the week before, scheduling problems forced King to return to Memphis on March 28, having promised local leaders that he would lead a nonviolent protest on behalf of the striking sanitation workers. Disappointed with fund-raising and mobilization efforts for the Poor People's Campaign, King saw the Memphis Sanitation Workers Strike, with its national profile, as an opportunity to raise public awareness on issues of economic justice while demonstrating the viability of large-scale nonviolent protest.

But, if anything, Dr. King's experience leading the protest march undermined his future plans. A group of rowdy marchers at the rear of the procession began to break store windows, triggering a police response, and ultimately a riot. In the tumult, more than sixty people were injured and one demonstrator was killed. King himself had to be taken to the Holiday Inn Rivermont for protection, and he left Memphis unceremoniously early on March 29. Given the chaos of the prior two summers, and the shift toward militancy in parts of black America, King knew that outsiders would question the very possibility that the upcoming Poor People's Campaign could remain nonviolent. If potential sponsors and marchers believed that the Washington, D.C., effort, scheduled to begin in April, could turn violent, if they doubted King's ability to maintain discipline, it could seriously damage the credibility of this next project. King vowed to return to Memphis to demonstrate the efficacy of his entire philosophy.[16] Activities by his enemies in the Southeast and Mississippi suggested that they were just as resolute as King.

ON MARCH 27, James Earl Ray drove his white Mustang from Atlanta to Birmingham and visited the Gun Rack, looking for a hunting rifle. He spent considerable time looking at potential weapons, but ultimately left without making a purchase.

Two days later, on March 29, 1968, James Earl Ray visited the Aeoromarine Supply Company, a sporting-goods retailer that also sold rifles. Dressed in a shirt and tie, Ray looked out of place to a young hunting enthusiast, John DeShazo. The questions Ray asked confirmed DeShazo's impressions: Ray knew nothing about rifles. But Ray purchased a .243-caliber rifle and ammunition using the alias Harvey Lowmeyer.

On March 30, 1968, Ray reappeared at Aeromarine Supply to exchange his weapon. FBI experts later concluded that a preservative in the rifle's breech prevented its proper loading. But Ray made no reference to this, even though it would have provided him with a perfectly innocent reason to exchange the weapon. Instead, Ray said his "brother" or "brother-in-law" examined the .243 and concluded that they needed a better weapon if they were going to go "hunting in Wisconsin." His adviser told him to get a Remington Model 760 Gamemaster rifle. One of the more highly regarded hunting weapons ever produced, it was also more expensive than the .243, meaning the normally frugal Ray was stepping out of character.[17]

That Ray had some guidance in choosing a weapon seems likely, not simply because he gratuitously referenced another person, but because he demonstrated little or no understanding of rifles. Ray, of course, blamed it on Raul, claiming he was told to return to the store and purchase the Gamemaster. Under that scenario, Ray referred to Raul as his "brother" to protect his benefactor's identity. Others who share the authors' doubts about Raul's existence suggest that it was one of Ray's actual brothers who helped him with the rifle purchase. This cannot be discounted, but evidence is lacking.[18]

Our examination of out-of-state phone calls made from Sam Bowers's Sambo Amusement Company in Laurel, Mississippi, produced another possibility. On March 29, 1968, the day of the original rifle purchase, someone at Sambo called a number in Birmingham. It was the only phone call to Birmingham from the fall of 1967 through the summer of 1968. Bowers and his partner, Robert Larson, operated the company with no other employees. The timing is certainly curious, but the phone record does not identify who was called. Only recently, thanks to research by Charles Faulkner, the number was traced to the Birmingham Army Reserve, specifically to the senior army advisor for the Army Reserve Advisor Group. Extensive research, including by military historians, has not yet been able to generate a name, but both the timing and a call by Bowers or Larson to an army officer are suggestive.[19]

Following the purchase of the gun, Ray returned to Atlanta. Ray always denied this, and insisted instead that he was told by Raul to go straight to Memphis. The evidence to the contrary is overwhelming, however; that Ray returned and left his laundry at a dry cleaner in Atlanta was established not only by the recollection of the manager of the Piedmont Laundry, but by a dated receipt in her files. This is one of Ray's most important and revealing lies. Ray himself acknowledged that establishing a return trip to Atlanta would be highly incriminating. This is not simply because King also returned to Atlanta at approximately the same time. Rather, it would be Ray's subsequent trip, from Atlanta to Memphis, that would seriously damage his contention that he was an oblivious dupe for Raul. Martin Luther King Jr. did not specify his return date to Memphis until April 1, and for Ray to return to Atlanta on March 30, and then follow King to Memphis *with a gun*, was too much for even Ray to pass off on the public. Subsequently, Ray steadfastly insisted that he never took that route. Combined with the "accidental" stay in Selma during King's visit, and the Atlanta map with marks that "coincidentally" overlap King's home and church, a rational observer could not escape the conclusion that Ray was stalking King.[20]

Ray claims to have stopped and stayed at the DeSoto Motel in Corinth, Mississippi, on April 2. Weisberg did find motel help, albeit many months after the assassination, who claimed Ray stayed at the motel. The motel is right near a Mississippi drug store where beer cans, later discovered among a collection of Ray's belongings at the Memphis crime scene on April 4, were found to have been purchased. Weisberg did not get access to motel records that could positively confirm or deny this. Assuming Ray did make the stop, the trip raises more questions than it answers. It does not, as some researchers have implied, create any kind of timing problem or in any way preclude Ray's trip from Atlanta to Memphis. The fastest route from Atlanta to Corinth to Memphis traces the same path as the fastest route from Birmingham to Corinth to Memphis and would add less than two hours to what was, in all accounts, a multiday trip. But Weisberg, Ray's investigator, could not reconcile two issues with this Mississippi motel stay. For one thing, a trip to Corinth takes one off the straightest path to Memphis regardless of whether someone is coming from Atlanta or Birmingham. Secondly, Weisberg discovered the motel was a "hot-sheet joint," essentially doubling (discreetly) as a pseudo-brothel. Such places, as Weisberg noted, are convenient for all kinds of illicit activities, including meeting people to plan such activities. Weisberg became convinced that Ray met someone connected with the King assassination at the DeSoto.

But Weisberg could never get Ray to admit this, and therein lies a problem for anyone sympathetic to Ray's claims of innocence. Ray would not even claim to have met the ubiquitous "Raul" at the DeSoto. He denied even purchasing the beer. Weisberg, quite possibly correctly, believed that Ray was covering up for whomever it was he met at the DeSoto. Privately, he even confronted Ray with this fact (years later), only to have Ray snap back that Weisberg should not do the FBI's work for them. Weisberg, as he often did when Ray frustrated the investigator's ability to try to exculpate the accused assassin, chalked this up to some informal "code of omerta" among criminals.[21] Ray knew who the real conspirators were, under this thinking, but chose to protect people that Weisberg, in letters to Ray, insisted had completely framed him. The authors think it is far more likely that Ray was covering up for individuals who could implicate him in the King assassination, not for individuals who, by his and Weisberg's account, completely betrayed him. "Hot-sheet joints" are exactly the kind of place where the type of Dixie Mafia gangsters the White Knights approached with a King assassination bounty would meet to plan their various criminal activities.

Yet it remains unclear exactly what Ray envisioned as his role. To earn the full bounty, Ray would have to directly participate in King's killing. Simply handing a rifle to someone else would not be enough. Analyses of King's murder typically treat Ray as either an unwitting dupe or the driving force. A better approach might be to view Ray as someone with his own agenda, but one who was forced to work within the framework of a larger conspiracy in which he was, at least initially, a peripheral player. Recent evidence, discovered by researcher Charles Faulkner, indicates that at the time of the rifle purchase, Ray was acting in his own interests, possibly with an eye toward scoring a larger payment.

Faulkner found FBI documents detailing the investigation of the Lowmeyer alias, specifically the address Ray provided for Lowmeyer when he purchased the rifle in Birmingham: 1907 South 11th Street in Birmingham. This address belonged to a widow whose husband had died years before, and whose son had moved out not long after. In 1968, the son, William Arthur Jenkins Jr., worked as an attorney, but for years prior he was an Alabama state circuit judge. As a judge, Jenkins issued an injunction against King's protest marches in Birmingham in 1963, which King promptly violated, leading to his imprisonment. It was then that King wrote his famous "Letter from Birmingham City Jail," defending civil disobedience as a moral response to violations of higher law.[22]

Nothing indicates that Jenkins had anything to do with Martin Luther King Jr.'s assassination, but by associating himself with Jenkins, Ray was once again building a legend, suggesting his potential knowledge of figures involved in Southern anti-integration activities. We can only speculate that such "markers" were not intended for law enforcement. Nor does it make sense that the White Knights would want Ray to leave evidence that pointed in the direction of an obscure judge with no obvious radical connections. The use of that address, like the visit to American Independent Party headquarters, appears to have been a unilateral action on the part of Ray, one with an obscure future purpose.

The answer may be, as it always was with Ray, about money. Ray appeared to be performing the role of a stalker, one that presumably carried a lower payday. If Ray wanted "a bigger piece of the action," it's possible he had to create a racist "résumé" that would allow him to directly engage the plot's sponsors. Such a record would have to be sufficiently controversial to earn the respect of the sponsors without looking outwardly radical to law enforcement investigators. But if Ray wanted to expand his role in hopes of making more money, he was running out of time. The purchase of the rifle would be a sure sign to Ray that whatever plan was in motion, King would be killed sooner rather than later.

ON MARCH 31, 1968, Martin Luther King Jr. delivered a speech in Washington, D.C. The biblical theme was the Book of Revelation, and the promise of a new world, as he re-emphasized the transformative power of the upcoming Poor People's Campaign set for the next month. Entitled "Remaining Awake Through a Great Revolution," King told the crowd:

> We are going to bring the tired, the poor, the huddled masses. We are going to bring those who have known long years of hurt and neglect. We are going to bring those who have come to feel that life is a long and desolate corridor with no exit signs . . . We are not coming to tear up Washington. We are coming to demand that the government address itself to the problem of poverty . . . We do it this way because . . . the nation doesn't move around questions of genuine equality for the poor and for black people until it is confronted massively, dramatically in terms of direct action.[23]

Recognizing the price he paid for openly arguing against the Vietnam War (alienating him from his one-time ally, President Lyndon Johnson) and challenging the economic status quo in America, King said: "There comes a time when one must take the position that is neither safe nor politic nor popular, but he must do it because conscience tells him it is right."[24] Within a few days King would return to Memphis.

ON THAT SAME day in California, Rev. Wesley Swift delivered his final sermon of the spring, one that also featured the Book of Revelation. He told the audience:

> The word of God is for you the sons and daughters to use. This word of God is for your protection in the hour of emergency. The word of God shall see America through . . . This does not eliminate you from defending your home and battling the enemy. But it gives you the capacity to know that those of your household with you will come through this battle. For God did not stop the enemy from battling Israel, but he gave them the victory. He brought forth victory by the hands of his household for this is the very word of God . . . And the children—you and I—shall participate. And we shall have absolute victory.[25]

This Swift sermon is notable for two reasons. First, according to extensive research by Dennis Dunn, among officially transcribed Swift sermons, it is the only sermon that was not fully transcribed from the audio. An entire section on "current events" is not available to analyze and Dunn has been unable to obtain the tape. Just as noteworthy: Swift would not deliver another sermon for three months. This is one of the two longest gaps in Swift's career. Swift does not address his followers again until June 8, the day James Earl Ray is arrested. He called it "Ye That Have Killed for Gold." He then goes on his second, and only other notable hiatus from public preaching.

•

ON APRIL 1, 1968, King publicly announced his return to Memphis, as James Earl Ray was leaving dry cleaning at the Piedmont Laundry in Atlanta under the name Eric Galt.

The following day, as James Earl Ray drove his Mustang from Atlanta to Memphis, something strange happened at John's Café in Laurel, Mississippi. Senior Klan leaders frequently met at the restaurant, owned by one of Sam Bowers's closest aides in the White Knights, Deavours Nix. According to a report filed by Myrtis Ruth Hendricks, a black waitress at the bar, Deavours Nix received an odd phone call that evening. "I got a call on the King," she recalled him saying when FBI agents interviewed her on April 22; but she was unable to hear the rest of the conversation.

Hendricks recalled additional suspicious activity on April 3, 1968. According to her report, "two men, neatly dressed, with short stocky builds, came to Nix's place where she started to work at three p.m., and worked nights. While going to the bathroom, she observed a rifle with a telescopic sight, in a case in Nix's office. Later, the two men took the rifle and a long box, which took three men to carry out, and put them in a sixty four maroon Dodge with a fake 'continental kit' on the back."[26]

DESPITE A BOMB threat delaying his flight, Martin Luther King Jr. returned to Memphis, Tennessee, on April 3. With the march to Washington, D.C., less than three weeks away, King returned with the goal of proving that nonviolent protest could still work. The bad blood that developed between civil rights activists and the local police department boiled over as King's entourage, mindful of police informants infiltrating the ranks of sanitation protestors, refused the security detail usually provided.

King settled at the Lorraine Motel but not, at first, in his usual room, 306, where he often roomed and met with his close friend, Rev. Ralph Abernathy. As the two leading members of the SCLC, King and Abernathy traveled the nation together, forming a one-two punch, with King delivering eloquent sermons that appealed to middle-class and educated audiences, and Abernathy offering the same message in a "country" style. Someone, however, was temporarily staying in Room 306, and they waited until they got a call to reclaim their "suite" on the second floor.

King attended a meeting at the Centenary Methodist Church that day at noon, where he announced a plan for a mass march on April 8. But upon his return to the Lorraine that afternoon, federal marshals served Dr. King and his aides with a district court injunction, temporarily preventing them from engaging in future marches.[27]

On the evening of April 3, Martin Luther King Jr. delivered his last sermon at the famous Mason Temple church. Referencing both the particulars of the Memphis Sanitation Workers Strike and the general condition of the civil rights movement on the eve of the Poor People's Campaign, King struck an optimistic note, in what history now refers to as his "I've Been to the Mountaintop" speech. King described the wide arc of history from the Exodus of Egypt to the Emancipation Proclamation, marked by the common theme of mankind saying "we want to be free." Referring to the challenges to nonviolence, he reminded the crowd of the successes it brought in places like Birmingham.

He was equally optimistic about practical facts on the ground. Referencing the restraining order against a future march in Memphis, Rev. King was confident that his team of lawyers would defeat the "unconstitutional injunction." Of course, King was no stranger to violating injunctions, as he reminded the crowd of their past successes in Alabama. "We aren't going to let dogs or water hoses turn us around," he asserted. "We aren't going to let any injunction turn us around. We are going on."

King ended by extending the theme of the Exodus to its final denouement, when the liberator Moses, having led the Hebrews to the outskirts of the Israel, climbed to the peak of Mount Nebo and stood in awe of the promised land that he himself would never visit. King reminded the audience of the bomb threat that delayed his flight to Memphis. Prophetically, he ended his speech with the following words:

> And then I got into Memphis. And some began to say the threats, or talk about the threats that were out. What would happen to me from some of our sick white brothers? Well, I don't know what will happen now. We've got some difficult days ahead. But it really doesn't matter with me now, because I've been to the mountaintop. And I don't mind.
>
> Like anybody, I would like to live a long life. Longevity has its place. But I'm not concerned about that now. I just want to do God's will. And He's allowed me to go up to the mountain. And I've looked over. And I've seen the Promised Land. I may not get there with you. But I want you to know tonight, that we, as a people, will get to the promised land!
>
> And so I'm happy, tonight.
>
> I'm not worried about anything.
>
> I'm not fearing any man!
>
> Mine eyes have seen the glory of the coming of the Lord!![28]

11

ZERO HOUR

On April 3, several hours before Martin Luther King gave his final sermon at Mason Temple, James Earl Ray arrived in Memphis in his white Mustang. He checked into the New Rebel Motor Hotel using the Galt alias. He brought the newly purchased rifle, his prison radio, and other gear. In the years that followed, Ray, again, attributed a number of his actions to the elusive Raul, but could not keep his stories straight or even sensible. It is possible he was in Memphis to meet someone, perhaps to provide the newly purchased rifle to would-be conspirators. More than likely, he was debating his own next move. Would he continue to work within a prearranged bounty plot against King's life? Or would he try for a greater share of the bounty himself?

Anyone wanting to observe Dr. King's movements in Memphis did not have to work very hard—his stay there was widely covered on television and in local newspapers. Ray, who voraciously followed the news while in prison, claims he was all but oblivious to anything having to do with Martin Luther King Jr. while in Memphis. But fingerprints on a newspaper covering King's stay, including his lodgings at the Lorraine Motel fifteen minutes away from the New Rebel Motor, suggest otherwise.[1]

The following day, at 3 p.m., James Earl Ray inquired about rooms at Bessie Brewer's rooming house across the street from the Lorraine. Initially shown Room 8, Ray turned it down, claiming it provided too much in the way of amenities—cooking facilities, among other things. But Room 8 also happened to face South Main Street, without any view of the Lorraine. Ray elected to rent another room, 5B on the second floor, facing Mulberry Street, which provided a view of Martin Luther King Jr.'s room, 306, at the Lorraine. The vantage point from the window of Room 5B, at the rear of Bessie Brewer's, was awkward, certainly for anyone looking to try to shoot the civil rights leader across the street.[2] But the rooming house bathroom provided a clear view of the Lorraine and Room 306. As the evening approached, William Anschutz, another border at Bessie Brewer's, became frustrated: someone was occupying that bathroom for an unusually long period of time.[3]

POLICE SURVEILLANCE TEAMS monitored Martin Luther King's every move after he arrived in the River City on April 3, 1968. Memphis mayor Henry Loeb feared another riot. Cognizant that they lacked the manpower to respond to further civil unrest, local law enforcement formed special response teams, known as police tactical units (TAC), that, according to historian Michael Honey, "consisted of three cars, each of which held four men. A commanding officer could order a unit to a location, where they would quickly form a flying wedge and charge down the street."[4] Law enforcement also used African American officers to spy on gatherings of the Memphis Sanitation Workers Strike. Officer Ed Reddit and his partner Willie Richmond formed one of the surveillance teams, assigned to observe King from Fire Station 2, across the street from the Lorraine Motel, where King was staying. Labor leaders had uncovered Reddit as a mole, hence his reassignment to surveillance duty. The mutual distrust between the labor strike proponents and their adversaries in the law enforcement community carried an important implication for

April 4: King's entourage had refused police protection when King arrived in Memphis the day before.[5]

Fire department officials also worried about a riot and assigned their own men to watch King. But the two fire department officials tasked with watching the Lorraine were active in supporting the sanitation workers strike, and they clashed with Reddit, whom they saw as a turncoat. Reddit arranged for both firemen to be removed from duty on April 4, since both firefighters knew about Reddit's role as a spy within the civil rights movement and Reddit sensed their hostility toward him. Then strange events forced Reddit himself from his post.[6]

The Memphis police received death threats against Reddit, relayed from Philip Manuel, an aide to Arkansas senator John L. McClellan. According to an informant, radical Black Nationalists in Mississippi promised to kill Reddit. Reddit's superior, Lieutenant Eli Arkin, removed Reddit from duty on April 4 as a precaution. The story of the threat, it turned out later, was completely false, leading some to think that the entire affair was part of a wider conspiracy to kill King, to facilitate his murder by stripping the minister of local security. But Reddit did not serve any security function on April 4, and his partner continued to maintain surveillance on King.[7] A more likely explanation is that Sen. McClellan, an ardent segregationist, simply planted a false story as a dirty trick to undermine King, reinforcing an effort by Mayor Loeb to stop King's upcoming April 5 demonstration by way of a federal judge's injunction. A threat on a police officer could become the pretext to overcome First Amendment challenges to the injunction filed by King's friend Andrew Young. Sen. McClellan had pursued similar dirty tricks to undermine the Poor People's Campaign in the preceding months.[8]

Surveillance logs of the Lorraine Motel reveal little in the way of activity on the part of King or his entourage on April 4. King spent most of his time inside his motel room that he shared with his close friend and fellow activist, Rev. Ralph Abernathy, waiting in Room 306 to hear the outcome of Young's legal efforts. The night before, Abernathy sensed his approach was not working with the congregation at Mason Temple and coaxed Rev. King (exhausted from his travels) to the church to deliver his "I've Been to the Mountaintop" speech. The next day, the mood was lighter in the King-Abernathy suite. When Young returned with news that the injunction had been overturned, King, Abernathy, and others surprised the young attorney. If those surveilling King could see through walls, they would have witnessed King, Abernathy, and Young engaged in a playful pillow fight.[9]

The men spent the rest of the April 4 afternoon in meetings and answering phone calls, delaying them from visiting the home of local minister, Rev. Billy Kyles, for dinner. In the early evening, with Kyles trying to rush King along, and with other civil rights leaders waiting in the parking lot, King exited Room 306 and approached the railing of the second floor of the Lorraine. At 6:01 p.m. a bullet "fractured Dr. King's jaw, exited the lower part of the face and reentered the body in the neck area . . . It then severed numerous vital arteries and fractured the spine in several places, causing severe damage to the spinal column and coming to rest on the left side of the back."[10]

Several witnesses, including Reverends Jesse Jackson and Ralph Abernathy, pointed in the general direction of Bessie Brewer's rooming house as the source of the shots. Witnesses at Bessie Brewer's rooming house described a man rushing out of the building after shots were heard. He appeared to be carrying a long bundle in what looked like a blanket. The name in the registry used by the tenant who showed up at 3 p.m. was John Willard, yet another alias eventually traced to James Earl Ray. Guy Canipe, owner of Canipe Amusement Company immediately adjacent to Bessie Brewer's front entrance, reported someone dropping a package in front of his doorway; then shortly after, a white car sped by his store.[11]

Rushed to Saint Joseph's Hospital, King was pronounced dead at 7:05 p.m.

•

IF CHRISTIAN IDENTITY radicals arranged the murder of Martin Luther King Jr. with the goal of igniting a racial holy war, they never came closer to their vision than in the weeks that followed April 4, 1968.

The first signs of the violence that would plague America's cities in the wake of Martin Luther King Jr.'s assassination began in the place where King delivered his famous "I Have A Dream" speech about the promise of racial harmony five years before: Washington, D.C. On April 4, upon hearing of the assassination "in stunned silence and utter disbelief," a group of young black men, soon joined by Stokely Carmichael, patrolled the 14th and U Street sections of the nation's capital, first asking and then demanding that the local businesses close in honor of Dr. King's memory. Carmichael's presence drew a larger crowd, one that grew increasingly angry as the reality of the news settled in. Soon anger turned to violence, but local police pacified the crowd. Yet, this was the calm before the storm in the nation's capital, and in the nation as a whole.[12]

The civil disorder that followed has not been matched, in intensity or scope, since. By 8 p.m. riots broke out that in the course of two weeks would spread to more than one hundred American cities, the most widespread outbreak of civil disorder in the United States since the Civil War. *Time* magazine described it as a "shock wave of looting and arson" that would, over the next week, lead to thousands of arrests, millions of dollars' worth of damages, and the largest intervention of federal troops on domestic soil since Reconstruction. On April 5, Carmichael called the unrest the "beginning of revolution" and for a while it seemed that way. Even nonviolent stalwarts like former SNCC leader Julian Bond asserted, "Non-violence was murdered in Memphis."[13]

In front of an audience of 1,500 people in Cincinnati, an officer for the Congress for Racial Equality (CORE) "blamed white Americans for King's death and urged blacks to retaliate." In two days, Cincinnati experienced an estimated $3 million in damages. Similar chaos affected approximately 128 cities in twenty-eight different states. A survey of the violence by Dr. Carol E. Dietrich, in her entry in the encyclopedia *Race and Racism in the United States*, described the devastation in startling numbers:

> In Chicago, federal troops and national guardsmen were called to the city to quell the disorders, in which more than 500 persons sustained injuries and approximately 3,000 persons were arrested. At least 162 buildings were reported entirely destroyed by fire, and total property damage was estimated at $9 million.
>
> In Baltimore, the National Guard and federal troops were called to curb the violence. More than 700 persons were reported injured from April 6 to 9, more than 5,000 arrests were made, and more than 1,000 fires were reported. Gov. Spiro T. Agnew declared a state of emergency and crisis on April 6, calling in 6,000 national guardsmen and the state police to aid the city's 1,100-man police force.[14]

The hardest-hit city was Washington, D.C., where the rioting began. "The District of Columbia government reported on May 1, 1968, that the April rioting had resulted in 9 deaths, 1,202 injuries, and 6,306 arrests," Dr. Dietrich noted. Swift and Stoner could not have been more pleased that the heart of the "Jew-controlled" government lay smoldering alongside so much of America.

The jubilant reaction by far-right white supremacists was widespread.

Stoner, in fact, famously danced in the streets of Meridian, Mississippi at the news of King's murder—with members of the White Knights of the Ku Klux Klan of Mississippi! According to the FBI, Stoner predicted "the death of Martin Luther King would bring more Negro demonstrations and violence than anything since the Civil War." Stoner added that, "the Black Power niggers will say that nonviolence has failed and that violence is the only answer." The Swift follower "welcomed the riots which are expected to follow" and asserted that the NSRP was "glad to see others encouraging Negroes to protest."[15]

Sam Bowers and his colleagues celebrated the onslaught of rioting in America at John's Café in Laurel, Mississippi. A low-level White Knight—unidentified in tape recordings—told Jack Nelson in 1969 that Bowers and others expected a race war.[16]

Tommy Tarrants told Nelson, years later, that he celebrated the news of King's murder while hiding out at a paramilitary training compound run by Swift followers in North Carolina, waiting to launch his guerrilla campaign against the United States.[17]

In Pennsylvania, Rev. Roy Frankenhouser, of the Minutemen, defied a city ordinance and marched with white supremacists through the heart of his town. Stoner promised his own marches in May.

Wesley Swift, while on an unexplained sabbatical from his routine sermons, nonetheless led a Bible study on April 24, the first one since King's murder. He commented:

> The *U.S. News & World Report* had pictures of these Negroes looting the stores and coming out laughing. This article said there is no end to the rioting because Negroes are having a ball. They like this . . . these people shoot one another for excitement. They burn their own houses down just to see the fire. They loot everything. So how can you call them equal to the white man? . . . For the Negro has taken the place of the Indian as your enemy. The African Negroes are coming in, so the white man is going back to carrying a gun again . . . I think everyone should be armed today. The more of this rioting I see, I think you need . . . weapons.[18]

But a closer analysis of the events in Memphis, and the reaction of white supremacists in the wake of the assassination suggests that not everything went according to plan or expectation on April 4.

Without question, there was evidence that white supremacists were preparing to kill King in Memphis. Myrtis Hendricks, the wait-ress at John's Café, overheard Deavours Nix, Bowers's friend, "receive a telephone call on his phone which is close to the kitchen. After this call, Nix said, 'Martin Luther King Jr. is dead.' *This was before the news came over the radio about the murder.*"[19] [Emphasis added.] Congress found additional information suggesting that Sam Bowers, in par-ticular, shared insider information about a plot in Memphis while at John's Café, a frequent hangout for the White Knights.[20]

Additionally, J. B. Stoner's very presence in Meridian, Missis-sippi, raises suspicions of foreknowledge. FBI agents who had the rad-ical white supremacist under constant surveillance witnessed Stoner's celebratory dance. Law enforcement fully expected Stoner to follow his modus operandi—to go to Memphis in a counter-rally against King—and they placed him under watch fearing such rabble-rousing in Memphis. But on April 4, for reasons unknown, Stoner broke type. In fact, the Memphis Sanitation Workers Strike was notable for its ut-ter lack of counterprotests by racist groups. Unfortunately, rather than consider Stoner's pattern of establishing an out-of-town alibi in his previous racial crimes, the FBI's investigation into the assassination of Dr. Martin Luther King Jr. immediately eliminated Stoner as their number one suspect in a King plot because he was in Meridian.[21] In a practice condemned by a later congressional inquiry, the FBI assumed that anyone who wasn't in Memphis could not have taken part in a conspiracy against King—the same logic allowed them to eliminate everyone from Sam Bowers to Sidney Barnes from consideration as conspirators.

The Jackson field office spent a considerable amount of time try-ing to verify the whereabouts of KKK members on April 4, looking to see if their cars were in driveways or if the light in their homes were on. One member made it rather easy for the FBI to establish his alibi: on the evening of April 4, 1968, Meridian police ticketed Danny Joe Hawkins, one of Bowers's 1968 covert hit squad, for speeding the wrong way down a one-way street.[22]

Yet if Hawkins was attempting to establish some kind of alibi for the murder, he clearly could have found better ways *if he expected the King murder to materialize as it did on April 4*. For all his jubilation over the riots that followed the King murder, and for all the suspicious activity suggesting that Sam Bowers knew about a Memphis plot in advance, other informant reports suggest that the Imperial Wizard did not, at first, like the timing of the death. Something may have been expected in Memphis, but was it the shooting at the Lorraine?[23]

Events in Memphis do not suggest a well-planned conspiracy, certainly not if Ray was the designated shooter. For one thing, with professional killers available, it seems unlikely anyone would call on Ray to murder their "ultimate prize," Martin Luther King Jr. Ray lacked any pedigree as a hit man. A rooming house, furthermore, represents a poor choice for a potential shooting location. No one can guarantee that one would find a room facing the Lorraine, or at least one with a good vantage point. In fact, the room Ray did rent offered a very poor view of Room 306 at the Lorraine, where King stayed. This likely is what forced Ray (or any other assassin) to camp out in the bathroom, per William Anschutz's testimony (the boarder at the rooming house who testified that the assassin shot from the bathroom window). But a rooming house bathroom is also a less-than-desirable shooting location. At any time, someone can knock on the door look-ing for access to the community toilet or bath—including at the mo-ment a shooter is aiming and ready to pull the trigger. And a different problem presents itself with the choice of rifle, if, as the evidence seems to suggest, someone told Ray to exchange his original purchase for the Gamemaster. If the goal was simply to shoot a relatively stationary target from a short distance, one did not need the more expensive and reputable Gamemaster. Bessie Brewer's rooming house was just across the street from the Lorraine. If someone told Ray to "trade up" for the better rifle, the likelihood was that the weapon was meant for a more difficult shot from a longer distance.

The rather haphazard way in which evidence was disposed of at the crime scene also points to a less-than-ideal plan, a last-minute plot formed out of desperation. As a member of the Minutemen confided to the FBI, a professional killer would have used a disassembled rifle, putting the weapon together at the shooting location, firing a shot, then breaking the gun down so it could be smuggled out, for instance, in a briefcase. Here, not only the rifle, but numerous other items, including binoculars and hygiene products, were bundled together in a green blanket that was left in the entryway to Canipe Amusement Company.

Many have pointed to the bundle as convenient—a too-obvious attempt by conspirators to frame James Earl Ray. But anyone shooting from the bathroom in Bessie Brewer's rooming house had few good options available to him if he wanted to escape Memphis that day, short of the breakdown scenario the Minuteman described. Leaving the material in the rooming house would immediately connect the rifle to any missing boarders inside the building, including any possible fingerprints or identifying information left behind (something even a cautious assassin could not risk). Carrying the bundle to a vehicle would risk discovery and immediate capture at any kind of roadblock dragnet. In many ways, leaving the bundle on the street was the least bad option. In fact, whether intended or not, the materials in the bundle confused law enforcement for up to three weeks. Items in the bundle were initially linked to what appeared to be three or four different people. The rifle was linked to a "Harvey Lowmeyer," who purchased the weapon in Birmingham; other items belonged to "Eric S. Galt"; and a prison radio, found in the green blanket, was eventually traced to an escaped fugitive from Missouri State Penitentiary: James Earl Ray. Coupled with the reports of a potential shooter fleeing Bessie Brewer's rooming house, who rented the room under the alias John Willard, it appeared to the FBI as if they were dealing with a conspiracy of at least three to four people. It took weeks before they connected all the aliases to Ray, in part because authorities had to unearth the serial number on the prison radio Ray left in the bundle (he had scratched out the numbers and letters to the best of his ability).

The best explanation for all the facts is a scenario whereby Ray preempts a legitimate plot against King by choosing to parlay his limited role as a scout into a more lucrative role as the actual shooter. He apparently would do this without consulting with the plotters, assuming he even knew who the major players were, and he would do this at the last minute, hence the haphazard execution. Several additional pieces of evidence point in this direction.

First, this explanation helps account for one of the most enduring and perplexing mysteries on April 4: the citizens band radio broadcast that diverted law enforcement away from Ray's escape route. As Ray fled Memphis in his white Ford Mustang to Atlanta, someone led police on a wild goose chase. Some thirty minutes after the King shooting, a citizens band radio operator named William Austein heard a transmission from a fellow CB operator broadcasting a car chase. Contrary to routine procedure, the broadcaster would not identify himself, but he reported that he was chasing a white Mustang driven by King's killer, fleeing east on Summer Avenue from Parkway Street. The unknown CB operator wanted to make direct contact with the Memphis police. Austein halted a Memphis police cruiser and relayed periodic reports from the other man's radio broadcasts to a police officer who then relayed them to Memphis police headquarters. Lasting for ten minutes, the transmissions reported the chase of the Mustang through multiple turns and through a red light; the individual in the white Mustang even fired shots at the heroic citizen. The final broadcast occurred at 6:48 p.m., with reports that the vehicle was heading toward a naval base.

But it turns out that the broadcast was a hoax. An investigation never established who perpetrated the fraud, but in reaching out to police, refusing to identify himself, and trying to direct police attention to the northern parts of Memphis, the unknown CB broadcaster was attempting to pull police resources away from the southern route Ray likely used to escape the city.[24]

Some claim that the timing of the broadcast, over thirty minutes after the shooting, speaks against this being a conspiratorial act. But the delay could also suggest that the conspirators themselves were caught off guard. If James Earl Ray short-circuited a more elaborate plot against King, perhaps to obtain a larger share of a bounty, it would have placed any conspirator in Memphis in the uncomfortable position of having to guess what happened. The delay between the crime and the broadcast may well represent the time it took for conspirators to surmise that someone within their plot had literally jumped the gun. Under this scenario, using the CB stunt to shift police attention away from the likely getaway direction might be a logical, if delayed, maneuver. Conspirators had good reason to fear what a fleeing shooter might tell law enforcement regarding a wider conspiracy, and if the conspirators realized the unexpected shooter was Ray, they may have surmised that he was heading back to Atlanta. The KKK commonly used CB radios to intercept police broadcasts and stymie police investigations, so much so that Congress cited the practice as widespread in a 1966 report.[25] At one point, in their investigation of the MIBURN murders, the FBI was forced to call in help from the Federal Communications Commission to establish a completely independent communications network—one that was immune to CB radio intercepts by the White Knights.

The possibility that Ray preempted a shooting by professional criminals contracted by the White Knights is further suggested by events that occurred not far from the crime scene. One of the earliest reports from Memphis related to suspicious activity at the William Len Hotel, located just a mile from the Lorraine Motel. As they later described to the FBI, hotel employees observed two men acting suspiciously at 12:05 a.m. on April 5. The two guests had arrived the previous afternoon and looked nervous while waiting to check out at that odd hour. The suspicious men had registered on the afternoon of April 4 as Vincent Walker and Lawrence Rand and stayed in two separate but nearby rooms. Both men checked out in a hurry following King's murder. The FBI was interested in the two men and traced their activities once they left the hotel. One man hailed a cab and asked to go to West Memphis, Arkansas, but some distance into the trip, he insisted that the cab driver turn around and take him to the Memphis airport. The passenger appeared to scout the airport, then told the cabbie to return to the William Len Hotel. Outside, the cabbie met the second man and drove them both to the airport. They boarded the flight under the names W. Davis and B. Chidlaw. Their flight departed at 1:50 a.m. on April 5 and arrived in Houston at 2:50 a.m., at which point they took a shuttle and disappeared. The FBI checked the names and addresses on the hotel register, only to find that they were both aliases. So too were the Davis and Chidlaw names provided at the airport. A fingerprint check revealed no suspects, so the FBI gave up, guessing that these were criminals in town for a separate operation who left because they expected an increased police presence following King's murder.[26] It is worth noting that Cliff Fuller and Harold Pruett—two Dixie Mafia gangsters who may be connected to marks on Ray's Atlanta map—were last arrested in connection with burglaries in Houston, the last point of departure for "W. Davis" and "B. Chidlaw." Were Fuller and Pruett—or two other Dixie mobsters—caught off guard by Ray's unilateral decision to kill King himself?

New evidence uncovered by the authors in the past year suggests that Ray may even have had limited contact with the Walker and Rand characters at the William Len. Among hundreds of items of evidence collected by the Shelby County district attorneys in their prosecution of Ray was a matchbook from the William Len.[27] Unfortunately and oddly, there is no explanation for how this piece of evidence came into possession of the authorities—nothing on who collected it, nothing on where it was collected. A careful review of several different inventories of evidence, lists of material the FBI or Memphis police collected at different locations, reveals references to matchbooks but none that specify the William Len matchbook (and several that, in fact, could not be the matchbook in question). The exception is a vague reference to matches found in the hotel room Ray stayed in prior to shifting locations to Bessie Brewer's rooming house. If one assumes that every item of evidence was carefully noted (and the lists are thorough), then process of elimination would make this matchbook the William Len matchbook, but frustratingly, the list does not actually take note of the wording on the matchbook. In any event, the matchbook suggests the possibility that Ray met the figures from the William Len, and that may help explain the CB radio incident. The men in question would have been caught off guard by the shooting of King, but they would have been familiar enough with Ray to realize that the fugitive was the likely culprit. This understanding would explain why the CB radio trickster diverted police away from the direction Ray would take as he escaped from Memphis. After some delay, they would have realized who the actual shooter was and guessed as to where he was heading: Atlanta.

Whether Ray pulled the trigger or knew who did, his decision to return to Atlanta makes little sense even if, as he claimed, he realized that authorities would be looking for him. Ray always admitted that he knew that the King murder would trigger a massive manhunt. If he fired the shot he certainly knew they would be looking for him; but even by his own "I was as shocked as anyone" claims in the years that followed, Ray admitted that he realized he was cooked. Ray claimed that he put two and two together immediately—that he knew after he heard about the King assassination on his car radio in Memphis (a dubious claim itself, as the radio appears to have been broken) that he had been framed. That is why he fled Tennessee so quickly. But Georgia lay in the opposite direction of both Canada and Mexico, the two places any seasoned criminal would go if he wanted to escape a massive manhunt. Atlanta *is* where the money for the King bounty originated. And if Ray literally and figuratively jumped the gun on his fellow conspirators, it is where he would need to go to be paid. The evidence suggests that is exactly what he did.

PART THREE

12

MANHUNT

By April 5, as America's cities continued to burn, the FBI launched the largest manhunt in its history. In reality, they were launching three manhunts, but only the hunt for the Memphis shooter was apparent to the public.

The first was for James Earl Ray, and while it was initially confounded by Ray's use of many aliases, it eventually succeeded, thanks to an impressive amount of lab work and shoe-leather investigation. Yet in narrowing its field of view on Ray over time, the initial manhunt also overlooked key leads discovered early in the case. A second manhunt started almost as soon as the first, for reasons still unclear. Indeed, this manhunt's very causes and its contours are obscured by incomplete records and deliberate obfuscation by the FBI. Its target was Tommy Tarrants. Had it been pursued properly, it likely would have exposed the intended patsy in the King assassination, and by implication, the real killers. But the third manhunt was even more disappointing than the second. This was the search for Donald James Nissen, who predicted King's murder in June 1967, but who now was missing from Atlanta. This manhunt forced a reinvestigation of that old lead, revealing new information that, taken together with the search for Ray and the search for Tarrants, should have exposed the full dimensions of the plot against King. Instead, the FBI missed another opportunity to do justice by Martin Luther King Jr., just as they had missed the chance Nissen provided to save King's life in the first place.

The first manhunt—for Ray—started as a search for three different people, all of them Ray's aliases and none of them Ray himself. A report from the New Rebel Motor Hotel allowed them to connect the reports of a fleeing white Mustang to Eric S. Galt; the guest registry at Bessie Brewer's rooming house suggested that John Willard, occupant of Room 5B, was the missing man who fled the building; and most importantly, the rifle, discovered in the bundle of items in the green blanket outside Canipe Amusement Company, pointed to Harvey Lowmeyer. They traced the rifle to the Aeromarine Supply Company, and from that, to the Lowmeyer name. The FBI was running the fingerprints collected from various items in the blanket bundle, including the rifle, but it would be weeks before they realized that all of them belonged to the same man: James Earl Ray, whose prison radio was also in the bundle.[1]

In that first month, while they were more open to conspiracy angles, the FBI considered a number of leads described in this book. This included the Barnes-Crommelin-Gale-Carden-Smith plot in Birmingham (after the 1963 bombing of the 16th Street Baptist Church), the bounty offer to Sparks, the attempt on King's life by Keith Gilbert, and others. But problems with compartmentalization of information often meant that they did not treat these leads as seriously as they should have.[2] For the Birmingham plot, for instance, the FBI did not check the files of Sidney Barnes housed in the Mississippi field office; that file contains a taped transcript between Barnes and his friend Willie Somersett (the same informant who taped Joseph Milteer predicting the murder of JFK in 1963), in which Barnes describes the plot as continuing on through 1964. Recall that Somersett provided Barnes with a marked rifle to help Miami police trace the plot.[3] The boast by White Knight Billy Buckles, about using a criminal for a major operation in 1964,[4] was never connected to the Sparks bounty reports, which the FBI didn't even believe was an actual plot.[5] Information revealed in 1999 showed that Bowers used the Ben Chester White murder as a trap to lure King into an ambush, but this was in files on that murder, and never even considered in the King assassination investigation.[6] Time and time again, information wasn't cross-referenced across file streams.

And yet, quite mysteriously, as the FBI initiated the second manhunt, they focused their interest on the chief terrorist for the White Knights of Mississippi, Tommy Tarrants, a man who knew Barnes, Bowers, and Swift. In early April when the government was still under the impression that King was killed by a conspiracy of Galt, Willard, and Lowmeyer, the potential range of suspects was far wider than even those three names. Absent a picture of any of the men, they considered the possibility that any one of them were aliases (just not for James Earl Ray) and hence almost everyone was a potential suspect, save those, like Stoner and Bowers, who were curiously eliminated from consideration because they were not in Memphis. But as wide-ranging as the first three weeks of investigation were, nothing yet explains why the FBI was interested so early in Tommy Tarrants. An FBI agent was at Tarrants's home in Mobile as early as the evening of April 4; decades later, the agent, Gerard Robinson, told the authors that this visit was odd for three reasons. First, the visit took him outside his normal zone of activity on the outskirts of Mobile. Second, the FBI sent him to the residence without his partner, a direct violation of fundamental procedures, put in place for reasons that would become obvious that day when Tarrants's father greeted him with a shotgun. Finally, he was not told specifically why Tarrants was of interest to the FBI in Mobile—and they never told him after. Robinson realized just how dangerous Tarrants was ten weeks later when Tarrants's capture for the 1967 and 1968 bombings in Mississippi became national news. But in April of 1968 the FBI had no idea who the southern Mississippi bomber even was— they simply labeled him "the Man." The extent of Tarrants's known crimes as of April were the gun charge he faced in Mississippi from the previous winter, and the fact that he jumped bond.[7] Federal law enforcement had no idea as to the extent of Tarrants's racist violence.

The importance and mysteriousness of the timing of the FBI's interest in Tarrants cannot be overstated. Just two days later, on April 6,

Tarrants's picture was shown at the Gun Rack in Alabama, the first place Ray had attempted to buy a gun. Keep in mind, again, that at this point, Tarrants's only offense was jumping bond on a firearms charge.[8] Yet his picture was shown at the same time as Eugene Mansfield, the one-time Grand Dragon from Texas who suddenly left his job in Alabama to live with White Knights Grand-Wizard-to-be L. E. Matthews and who talked to Matthews—*prior to the King assassination*—about "hits" and "doing a job." In addition, Mansfield did not have an alibi on April 4. The FBI's central headquarters knew all of this from the Jackson field office and urgently reported it to the Birmingham field office. Hence it makes complete sense that Mansfield's pictures were shown that day.[9] In fact, the authors can find the reasons why every one of the first wave of pictures in the FBI's documents were shown at the Gun Rack. Likewise, the authors can find justification for why the FBI showed subsequent sets of pictures at the store on later days—for instance, when they showed a picture of Jimmy George Robinson, an NSRP member who assaulted King in 1965; or when they showed a picture of Byron de la Beckwith, the man the FBI concluded had assassinated Medgar Evers with a rifle similar to the King weapon, in 1963. Just as oddly, every picture the Birmingham FBI agents displayed on April 6 came from readily available mugshots from local and state law enforcement agencies in Alabama. The exception was Tarrants—his picture was the only one sourced to an FBI file from Mobile.

The unique attention paid to Tarrants, who *at that time* had no profile as a dangerous extremist, raises serious questions that will be explored later. The interest continued through the middle of April, when the FBI showed Tarrants's picture to right-wing militants in Los Angeles, on suspicion he might be "Eric Galt."[10] When we took this information to former FBI agent Jim Ingram in 2009, who ran the Mississippi bombing investigation that eventually captured Tarrants, he was stunned that Tarrants had been an early suspect in the King murder. "He wasn't on our radar," Ingram insisted.[11]

•

ERIC GALT, JOHN Willard, and Harvey Lowmeyer definitely were on the FBI's radar. The FBI spared no cost, manpower, or hours, as evidence flowed from Memphis. They visited every possible location to find the source of left-behind underwear, or the location of a beer can purchase. They conducted thousands of interviews. Eventually, on April 11, they found Ray's abandoned white Mustang, registered to Eric Galt in Atlanta—not far from the Lakewood General Motors factory—and traced the registration to the September sale in Alabama. Most importantly, the FBI lab manually slaved through thousands of fingerprints until they matched every identifiable print that they could. Several sets of prints, as will be discussed later, were never matched to Ray or anyone else despite dogged efforts to compare them against potential innocent contributors, such as police officers and FBI agents. But on April 19, the Bureau reached the stunning conclusion that every item could traced to one man: James Earl Ray. The FBI then realized that Lowmeyer and Willard, whom they saw as two separate conspirators with Galt, were aliases for the escaped fugitive from Missouri State Penitentiary. Photographs of Ray soon ran nationwide.[12]

But then the FBI also grew weary of prospective conspiracy leads. This was unfortunate, because many developed after April 19, including Myrtis Hendricks's story to the Dallas field office about John's Café. She entered the field office with her boyfriend, who confirmed elements of the story, but who voiced great fear of retaliation by the Klan against relatives still living in Mississippi. In addition to the story about Deavours Nix receiving news about King's murder before the shooting, Hendricks offered background information that helps shed additional light on what may have transpired in Laurel, Mississippi. She described discreet and suspicious conversations she overhead between Nix, Bowers, and at least one man with whom she was not familiar, in days leading up to King's murder. In one notable exchange she recalled that the day before the King murder, Bowers and Nix "worked" the stranger, insisting, about a matter that Hendricks could not identify, that "only you"—the stranger—can "make this happen."[13] Reports from other informants, and Hendricks's description, make it likely that this individual was L. E. Matthews, the man who took over the White Knights when Bowers went to prison.[14] It is worth noting that a separate stream of informant reports, unconnected to Hendricks, shows that fellow White Knights could not reach Matthews because he was arranging for an "out-of-state project" for the Klan. Additionally, Matthews housed both Tommy Tarrants and Eugene "Sunset" Mansfield in his home in the weeks before the King murder.[15] Both men, as noted earlier, would become some of the first suspects in King's murder. Matthews's unique position in relation to several suspects in the King case is an important dynamic worth remembering as the story of the investigation of King's murder unfolds.

There were other, additional leads that, like the Hendricks lead, developed after April 19 and did not get the attention they deserved. This included the reports on the 1964 offer to Donald Sparks. The FBI did interview an uncooperative Sparks in jail about the 1964 rumors, but never dug deeply enough into the story to see the obvious connections to McManaman. From the end of April forward, conspiratorial leads were often held in abeyance or minimized if there wasn't an obvious connection to Ray or, even less logically, if the individuals in question could not be placed in Memphis on April 4. This is what allowed the FBI to eliminate J. B. Stoner as their top lead—he was, recall, literally dancing in celebration in Meridian upon the news of King's murder—within hours of the crime.[16] This, despite their own records showing that the lawyer rarely remained within the same zip code when he knew that a crime, such as a bombing, would take place on his initiative.

DESPITE A MASSIVE manhunt for people using his various aliases and ultimately for Ray himself, Ray managed to stay one step ahead of his pursuers for several months. Having made a mad dash back to Atlanta, he left and ultimately abandoned his white Mustang near the Capitol Homes housing project. Ray claimed he went back to Atlanta to recover certain belongings, but author Lamar Waldron points to several features of Ray's return to Atlanta that support the notion that Ray was continuing to reach out to potential assassination sponsors, like Hugh Spake. The Capitol Homes housing project is located near the General Motors Lakeland auto factory; this is, again, where Spake worked and where, according to Waldron's source, unidentified businessmen and white supremacist Joseph Milteer secretly syphoned off money from union dues to finance a bounty against Martin Luther King Jr. Witnesses described Ray leaving the Mustang and consulting what appeared to be a small black address book, something never found among Ray's possessions.[17] Most intriguingly, information indicates that Milteer himself was in Atlanta at the time, something significant enough to capture the attention of one of Milteer's closest friends. In an otherwise inconspicuous exchange, Milteer's friend says, "Looks as though you and the hunted suspect were in the Capitol area about the same time—they found a car there they say."[18] It is unclear if by "Capitol," the friend meant the state capital, Atlanta, in general, or the Capitol Homes project specifically. But, as investigative reporter Dan Christensen noted in his series of articles that featured Milteer, this was one of the only instances in which Milteer, or any of his correspondents, referenced King's assassination, even though they despised the civil rights leader.[19]

Ray certainly did not spend much time in Atlanta, suggesting, again, that he had little specific knowledge of which businessmen sponsored the plot or where to find them—that he, again, "jumped the gun" and, by shooting King, assumed a place in the conspiracy that was not intended for him and that he had not adequately planned for. As it had been the previous spring after escaping Missouri State Penitentiary, Ray's immediate goal became escaping North America. He once again returned to Canada, only this time with the knowledge he needed to make good on his objective.

Ray claims he made his way to Toronto by April 6 via train and bus. The owner of the rooming house at 102 Ossington Street where Ray rented a room, Feliksa Szpakowska, told investigators that Ray first registered on April 8. The discrepancy suggests Ray's stay in At-

lanta was longer, and that he lied, one might speculate, to hide his
efforts to find the bounty sponsors. Either way, Ray spent close to
a week in Toronto attempting to obtain a fake passport. Using the
Ossington Street address, Ray asked for a copy of a birth certificate
under the name Paul Bridgman, on April 10. Not long after, someone
claiming to be from the passport office contacted the real Paul Bridgman inquiring whether Bridgman already had passport. If the caller
was Ray or someone helping him obtain false identification, they got
bad news: yes, Bridgman told him, he already had a passport application on file. Not surprisingly, Ray never obtained Paul Bridgman's
birth certificate after Szpakowska received it on April 14. Instead, one
Ramon George Sneyd, another resident of Toronto, received a call
asking if he had a passport—Sneyd said no. Ray also soon rented a
second room at a flophouse, one located a mile away from Szpakowska's, at 962 Dundas Street and managed by Mrs. Sung Fung Loo (Ray
claimed he rotated back and forth between the two rooming houses
to further complicate efforts to find him). It is at Dundas where Ray
received the birth certificate for Sneyd.[20]

Questions remain as to whether Ray had help in creating these
documents. All the men Ray used as aliases, including Galt, were real
Canadians; some lived close to each other in Toronto. Some authors
make much of the fact that the men vaguely resemble Ray—but Ray
had circled their addresses on a map of Toronto, suggesting that he
may have scouted them to see if they looked anything like him. Ray
always insisted that he and he alone developed the fake identities.
This forced even his own lawyers and investigators to question Ray's
honesty. Historians like Philip Melanson, who also believed that Ray
used Raul as a composite of several accomplices to throw off authorities, imply that Ray was covering for people, presumably government
agents, who helped him with fake identities.

But if Ray was covering up for others, he certainly would not be
protecting government agents; he spent his entire life blaming the U.S.
government and government agents for framing him. It is possible, on
the other hand, that Ray was covering for those in the Canadian crim-

inal underworld who ran a pipeline for fake identification at the time. One of the most accomplished criminals in Missouri State Penitentiary, George Edmondson, referenced this enterprise to the FBI and insisted that Ray would have been aware of it. John Nicol, a Canadian reporter, tied Ray to a Canadian hoodlum, George Kapakos, someone with extensive underworld ties; Nicol argued that he was among those who helped Ray obtain his aliases. What cued Nicol to the address was an incident in which Ray was stopped for jaywalking by Toronto police; Ray provided the address of 6 Condor Avenue to the authorities and claimed, later, that this was a random place he had never visited but that belonged to a woman whom he had identified in a lonely hearts advertisement in a Canadian newspaper. This, Nicol asserted, was another lie Ray told to cover for criminal accomplices. The address was for a brothel run by Kapakos's wife and Ray had circled it on the map.[21]

On April 16, Ray visited a Toronto travel agency and arranged for a round-trip flight to England. Operating, once again, under the false assumption he might need a Canadian citizen to vouch for him, Ray initially arranged for a ticket three weeks in advance. But the travel agent corrected Ray's misperceptions this time, and Ray filled out the necessary paperwork to exit North America. While waiting for his passport to be delivered, Ray claimed he once again went to Montreal until May 1, looking for a ship to take him to an African country without an extradition treaty. But investigators believe that Ray, if he did visit Montreal at all, spent additional time in Canada—Ray's vaccination records show a Toronto doctor during this time, and Sung Fung Loo told investigators that Ray ended his stay at her flophouse on April 26. After almost a month in Canada, Ray flew to London on May 6, and then to Lisbon, Portugal, on May 7, where he spent ten days continuing to try to find some means to travel to an African country from whence he would not be extradited.[22]

Back in the United States, the FBI was receiving interesting reports from two informants close to Jerry Ray, James's brother, with whom he was in close contact. Over several decades, Jerry Ray offered public statements, sometimes to the media and other times to authors, either implying his brother's guilt or strongly defending his innocence and then sometimes recanting or claiming to have joked. But those were statements made with the expectation of public attention. In June 1968, Jerry Ray made *private* statements to his then-girlfriend and landlady in Newark, New Jersey, neither of whom he realized were FBI informants. The informants asked Jerry Ray if "he thought his brother shot King. Ray replied by pointing out if he were in his brother's position of having an 18 year sentence to serve once he was apprehended and someone offered him money to kill someone he did not like and thereafter be able to leave the country, he would do it . . ." Later he added that James was "paid either $100,000 or $500,000," but would not elaborate.[23]

It is unlikely that James Earl Ray had *yet* received the $100,000 or more, as he was running out of cash in London. Eventually, he ran out of money and robbed a bank in London on June 4. By this point, information on Ray was widely disseminated throughout Europe via Interpol. Detectives finally arrested Ray on June 8 on his way to Brussels at Heathrow Airport. He was soon extradited to American custody. Ray had hoped that in Brussels he could find former British mercenaries, veterans of combat in the Belgian Congo, who could help him find his way to an African country out of the reach of American authorities.[24] The same day of his arrest, June 8, 1968, the Reverend Wesley Swift finally returned to give his first sermon since the King assassination. He titled it "Ye That Have Killed for Gold."[25]

One popular view of Ray's escape is that, up until his being taken into custody in London, Ray had moved swiftly and smoothly out of the United States, through Canada, and multiple European countries. That view argues that he had been well funded by co-conspirators who maintained ongoing contact with him. But we find little evidence to support that view and much that contradicts it.

Ray was forced to make a last-minute effort to sanitize his car and his apartment before heading out for Canada. He did a poor job of that, leaving behind key evidence in both locations; there is no indication that he had made any preparations to cover his trail prior to the shooting in Memphis. The only precautions he appears to have taken during the entire period were to buy the rifle in a name other than Galt (he used the name Harvey Lowmeyer) and to register at the Memphis rooming house under yet another name (John Willard). Up until the evening before the Memphis shooting, he was still using the Galt name for motel registration. However, he had no counterfeit identification papers for either the Lowmeyer or Willard names, so he had to use the Galt name as he fled the country.

Rather than a well-planned and sophisticated escape, we see Ray leaving the United States by bus, building his own fake identity in Canada, buying the cheapest possible ticket overseas ($340 round-trip to London), and then making his way to Portugal, where he fruitlessly tried to contact companies who provided mercenaries for service in Africa, apparently hoping they would employ him and provide the transportation and paperwork to get him there. With only $840, Ray could have flown directly to Rhodesia and at least been safe from extradition, but apparently he didn't have that relatively modest amount. Even if he had made it back through London to Brussels, what would have become of him is unclear. Certainly he didn't have the money to play tourist forever. He was so desperate for money that he was forced into multiple robbery attempts in London, finally stealing $240 from a London bank. When he was taken into custody at the airport, Ray had a total of $143 on his person.[26] While there is ample evidence that Ray had help of some sort in the lead-up to the April 4 shooting, Ray's escape afterward follows the same pattern demonstrated throughout his criminal career—the execution of the crime was more successful than the execution of the getaway. And that further suggests that Ray never was able to contact the people he needed to reward him for King's murder; those people never planned for Ray to be the actual shooter.

If they had lost interest in conspiratorial activity when they identified Ray in April, the FBI became only more narrow-minded once he was captured. This extended even to suspicious activity by Ray

himself. Ray for instance, once wrote his other brother, John, a mysterious letter in which he directed his brother: "Don't discuss any
part of this case with anyone until I get back especially the libel part.
I think pity will have a good thing. If you see Fu Manchu or the
Tongue tell them am OK. Take it easy." John Ray never explained
this, especially who "Fu Manchu" and "the Tongue" were.[27] John
Ray did tell reporters that his brother would never "name names
under any any circumstances. That is not his way." He added, in that
same article, that James had told him that "I'm not the only one in
on this."[28]

ACCORDING TO TARRANTS, he received word of King's murder,
both to his surprise and to his glee, while hiding out at a paramilitary
camp run by Swift followers in the city of Franklin in the mountains
of North Carolina. The FBI, months later, was able to find witnesses
to Tarrants's presence at the camp, and to document his relationship with the family who owned the property, especially the son,
J. A. Hendrickson.[29] Tarrants told author Jack Nelson that he had no
insight into anything that happened to King, and there is no evidence,
to this day, that Tarrants knows about the FBI's mysterious and as-
yet-still-unexplained interest in him as a possible conspirator in King's
murder. Tarrants told Nelson he stayed in North Carolina until
April 18, when he went back to Mobile and then stayed in New Orleans for several days. Tarrants was short on details in describing this
stay, but records show he at least visited his old mentor, white supremacist Sidney Crockett Barnes, in Mobile. Tarrants says that for
the next several weeks, until June, he floated back and forth between
North Carolina and Mississippi, sometimes visiting White Knight
Danny Joe Hawkins, sometimes bringing Danny Joe with him to
North Carolina. Along the way, he committed a number of robberies,
including of a grocery store in Mississippi.[30]

    It was only at the end of May 1968 that anything developed that
could justify consider treating Tarrants as a suspect in the King mur-

der. The Jackson field office received a tip that Tarrants was "the Man," the "mad dog killer" who had terrorized Mississippi's Jewish and black population for the past several months.[31] By this point, all bets were off with Mississippi law enforcement groups when it came to Klan opposition. How they dealt with Tarrants and the underground hit squad is probably the most controversial manifestation of a war that had been raging for months. Having raised outside money from Jewish groups, mainly the Anti-Defamation League (ADL) to pay two White Knights, Raymond and Alton Wayne Roberts, to become informants, the Meridian Police Department and the Jackson field office gathered information confirming that Tarrants and Danny Joe Hawkins were part of Sam Bowers's secret terrorist group. But rather than arrest the men, law enforcement arranged for the Roberts brothers to lure the two men into a trap by encouraging them to bomb a synagogue in Meridian. The record makes it clear that law enforcement had no intention of taking these men alive in this sting.[32]

On June 28, 1968, an informant called law enforcement and told them that two men, Hawkins and Tarrants, were on their way to do the job. Law enforcement was waiting and opened fire on their car. The passenger was mortally wounded, but the driver, Tarrants, managed to exit the vehicle, seriously wounded, returning fire. Eventually law enforcement caught Tarrants, but a surprise awaited them. The passenger killed in the car was not Danny Joe Hawkins, as planned, but Kathy Ainsworth.[33] Hawkins had pulled out of the bombing at the last minute. Tarrants went to prison for the crime, while Kathy Ainsworth became a martyr to the white supremacist cause. During the several years he was in prison at Parchman, Tarrants converted to mainstream Christianity, and with the help of two FBI agents, obtained early release in 1976.[34]

There are circumstantial reasons to suspect that this shooting was set up as a deathtrap with the provocation of the White Knights themselves. Hawkins's last-minute decision to leave the bombing is one suspicious fact. More disconcerting is the role of the Roberts brothers. Despite betraying Sam Bowers's most trusted operatives, the Roberts brothers decided to stay in Mississippi before they went to prison for their role in the MIBURN killings and returned to Mississippi after they served prison time. But they faced no repercussions from a vengeful Bowers. It is noteworthy then, that weeks before the bombing, someone reported Bowers as saying that "the Jews will finance the White Knights."[35] One can take this statement metaphorically and interpret it as saying that Bowers thought his attacks on Jewish targets would rally support for his group. But one can also see it more literally, and wonder if the Roberts brothers transferred some of the money raised from the ADL to Bowers's organization, in effect acting as triple agents, overtly White Knights, covertly helping the FBI and Mississippi police, while *really* doing Bowers's bidding all along. Why would Bowers want Tarrants and Ainsworth killed? We've already discussed the possibility that Bowers thought Tarrants was an informant. But it's just as possible that Tarrants and Ainsworth represented loose ends related to the King assassination. Information developed in the next chapter certainly suggests that, whether Bowers set up a trap for Tarrants that June 28, those in the Swift network felt it necessary to sully Tarrants as a source by framing him for King's assassination.

WITH BOTH RAY and Tarrants in jail, one fugitive with an important connection to the King assassination remained on the loose: Donald Nissen. That manhunt began in early April, as soon as the FBI realized that Nissen had skipped Atlanta in violation of his parole. Reviewing his June 2, 1967, assertions about a White Knights bounty offer from Leroy McManaman at Leavenworth prison, the FBI gathered background information on Nissen's likely locales and associates, and began to look for him. But at the same time, perhaps more importantly, they retraced their steps in investigating the substance of Nissen's account.

This began with Jackson agents to Sybil Eure in May 1968. In

June 1967, Eure had acknowledged a working relationship with McManaman, but claimed ignorance about any connection whatsoever to a bounty on King's life. Now, almost a year later, her story changed. Eure now claimed that everything was just a major misunderstanding. In the spring of 1964, when McManaman was staying with her, Eure was experiencing financial difficulties. At the same time, she followed reports about the Mississippi Burning murders in the news. Those reports mentioned that Sheriff Lawrence Rainey in Neshoba was part of the KKK and helped orchestrate the murders. Having a dark sense of humor, Eure joked to McManaman that all they had to do to get $100,000 was visit Sheriff Rainey and promise to kill Martin Luther King Jr. McManaman simply misconstrued the joke, and passed it off to a fellow prisoner as a legitimate bounty offer.[36]

There are some serious problems with this new version of the story. First, it doesn't resolve how Eure came to know McManaman in the first place, and why he was in Mississippi in apparent violation of the appeal bond. Second, it doesn't explain why, having made numerous visits to McManaman at Leavenworth since 1964, and having exchanged several letters with the prisoner, the joke was never cleared up. In revealing Eure to Nissen as a cutout in a major criminal operation, McMamanan was, after all, exposing a woman he supposedly intended to marry to great risk. You'd think the matter would have deserved some discussion between the pair before he made the approach! Finally, and most importantly, there is an issue of timing: when McManaman stayed with Eure during the spring of 1964, the Mississippi Burning murders had not even happened yet. McManaman was gone before the end of April, and the Neshoba killings occurred on June 21, 1964.

It is remarkable that the Jackson office did not recognize the contradictions immediately, given that they were directly involved in the recent prosecution of the Neshoba murders. But they once again took Eure at her word, and continued their search for Nissen, who traveled around the country, on the run.

Nissen eventually called the FBI and agreed to turn himself in on condition that Special Agent Wayne Mack of the Phoenix field office was the arresting officer. Nissen knew Mack from his criminal days in Arizona, and though they were on opposite sides of the law, they enjoyed friendly relations. Mack was heading to St. Louis for an in-service training and agreed to pick him up. Nissen told the same story to Mack and his partner as he did to the Dallas FBI, but also detailed the threat issued against him near the Atlanta Federal Building in December 1967.[37]

But if Nissen did talk about Ayers to the FBI, they would have been well aware of the eccentric Georgian by August 1968. This is because Ayers engaged in a series of odd and public behaviors shortly after Dr. King's death. First, on April 11, 1968, Ayers infiltrated King's funeral, posing as an usher, even seating presidential candidate George Romney. Things became more sinister than strange not long after, when Ayers posed as a chauffeur and convinced the deceased minister's father, Martin Luther King Sr., to ride with him to the Atlanta Fulton County baseball stadium. A reporter recognized Ayers as an associate of James Venable, and managed to lure King Sr. away from Ayers, as the two were moving toward a dark and isolated part of the ballpark.[38]

Ayers was not the first person with inside knowledge of a King plot to reach out to King Sr. In one of his last acts before going into hiding in Florida post-assassination, Nissen arranged a secret meeting with King Sr. With a secretary recording the conversation, Nissen detailed his Leavenworth story to the grieving father. He excluded some details of his experience, including, ironically, his experience with Ayers, because he remained uncertain about his own safety and legal culpability. Efforts to obtain the tape have been unsuccessful largely because of delays, at the King Center, in fully inventorying their holdings. One wonders to what degree King Sr., aware of both stories after Ayers's attempted "kidnapping," was piecing together the story behind his son's murder.[39]

What came next is even more provocative. Ayers appeared outside the White House gates, carrying a folder, asking to speak to President

Johnson. The Secret Service arrested Ayers, letting him go soon after dismissing him as an apparent "kook."[40] This would affirm a speculative argument the authors made earlier in the book: that Venable chose Ayers in part because of the salesman's well-known eccentricity. Anything Ayers would say before or after the King murder could be dismissed as the musings of a mad man. But what the Secret Service did not know is that this eccentric was someone whom multiple sources independently suspected of involvement in the King murder. In fact, Ayers appears to be the first suspect volunteered by law enforcement in Georgia—on April 7, before James Earl Ray had even been connected to Atlanta by way of his Mustang.[41] This report predated two independent reports from associates of Ayers in Alabama, both voicing suspicions, based on his comments and odd behavior, that Ayers had something to do with the King murder.

One of these sources was a lawyer named Bubba Jones who told the FBI on April 14 that he had defended Ayers against DWI charges in February of 1968. At that time, two months before King's murder, Ayers, according to Jones, "talked of killing any SOB in the country with a high powered rifle and a scope. He also talked of how easy it was to kill some prominent person. He also seemed to be incensed with racial problems." Jones, having heard this talk, called KKK leader James Venable, "who said to tell Ayers to get in his car and get back to Atlanta." Jones then followed up with the FBI's Mobile office, reporting that Ayers boasted that he "had a high powered rifle behind the dresser in his hotel room."

One is left to speculate about what motivated Ayers and what was in that folder he brought to the White House. The early interest in him—before Ray was connected to Atlanta and before Ayers infiltrated King's funeral proceedings—also raises eyebrows. Ayers's brother told the authors that Ayers may have associated with Venable, he may have been influenced by Venable, but he was not a hardcore racist. One is left to wonder if Ayers was trying to speak about his role in the crime out of a sense of guilt. If so, no one took him seriously due to his flamboyance. Interviews with Ayers are not available in the current files. The Secret Service claims to have no files on Ayers despite the public references to their interactions with him, following his "visit" to the White House, in newspapers from the time.

But the FBI took one last, logical step in investigating Nissen's account: they finally interviewed Leroy McManaman. They had visited Leavenworth in June of 1967, where they found corroboration for Nissen's story from his cellmate, John May, who acknowledged, just as Nissen claimed, that Nissen described the bounty plot and told the machinist that McManaman was interested in a procuring a special gun for the assassination attempt. May did not take Nissen seriously at the time, but he made an interesting side comment: May himself had heard about $100,000 bounties in bars in North Carolina before he went to Leavenworth. The FBI then approached other inmates with connections to McManaman who, predictably, claimed no knowledge of the plot. But at that time, remarkably, they never interviewed Mc-Mamanan himself. Now, more than a year after first visiting the federal prison, the agents from the FBI's Kansas office first interviewed Leroy McManaman in September 1968.[42]

McManaman's claims were interesting. He acknowledged he did not like King but denied any connection to any kind of plot. Apparently forgetting Eure's "joke," he denied any knowledge of a bounty. He did however admit that he intended to marry Eure once he left prison. Finally, he denied ever knowing or associating with Nissen.[43] Taken together, these are highly problematic answers. If he was operating on Eure's joke when he approached Nissen, why couldn't he remember it? How could he not know Nissen when the two, according to prison records, worked so closely together in the prison shoe factory? If Nissen did not know him at all, how could he know the name of the woman McManaman wanted to marry, much less her address? And if the two had no contact, what reason would Nissen have to implicate McManaman in a crime, a gratuitous act that resulted in Nissen jumping parole—for fictitious reasons, if you believe Mc-Manaman—and going back to prison? The FBI asked none of these follow-up questions and let the matter rest.

Nissen insists that he told the FBI about his interactions with Ayers and his package delivery to Eure's Jackson home in 1967 when Mack interviewed him in August 1968. If that is the case, the material has been excised from the record. This could be to protect the FBI's reputation, as Nissen's story, and their failure to adequately follow up on it, puts the Bureau's competence into serious question. It could also be that Special Agent Wayne Mack, who enjoyed a friendly relationship with Nissen, may have kept that material out of Nissen's report to protect Nissen, either from harm from unknown conspirators or from potential criminal charges that really were not warranted. A more likely explanation is that Nissen withheld that information himself and that he is confusing his interrogation by the FBI with revelations he later made to prison authorities. Nissen went to prison in Indiana in 1969 for his parole violation and he continued to fear for his life. Nissen says he explained his predicament to the prison warden, who followed up and became sufficiently concerned to transfer Nissen to another prison in 1970. At the time of this transfer, Minnesota's Sandstone Prison, where the warden sent Donald, was one of only a handful of prisons just designated as Protective Custody Units under the new federal witness protection program.

Presumably, a warden would not transfer a prisoner merely on the word of an inmate, so the authors attempted to obtain the records of that transfer with no success to date. But the authors suspect that Nissen, he says he did, told the prison warden the stories about Ayers and Eure and the package, while he withheld that information from the FBI in St. Louis when he first turned himself in. We do not doubt his sincerity, but with more than forty years of time separating his account to investigators from his account to us, he may simply be confusing what he told the warden with what he told the FBI.

Although the Bureau of Prisons found Donald's story credible and serious enough to send him into protective custody, the FBI did not take him seriously enough to fully develop the leads Nissen had given them. As it had with his original report, the FBI took a superficial approach with Nissen's 1968 account. Had they integrated the information from all three manhunts, they may have been able to solve the case in 1968. The last hope for an official resolution did not come for almost another decade. But not before James Earl Ray, his brothers, and various white supremacists attempted to mislead those who questioned the official narrative of the King assassination.

13

MISDIRECTION

Following his arrest at Heathrow Airport on June 8, James
Earl Ray soon found himself on a plane to the United
States to stand trial for the murder of Martin Luther
King Jr. in a Tennessee court. Having then been placed in virtual solitary confinement in a jail in Shelby County, Tennessee, Ray pleaded
guilty on March 10, 1969, conceding the charges read by Judge Pres-
ton Battle in the Memphis courtroom. The surprisingly quick end to
the trial—before one even began—resulted in a ninety-nine-year sentence for Ray and spared him a death sentence. But even as he agreed
to several pages' worth of stipulations of fact, James Earl Ray started
to plant the seeds of confusion that would characterize the case in
the decades that followed. Aware that United States attorney general
Ramsey Clark had discounted the possibility that he had any confed-
erates (something Clark later admitted he said to calm a tense nation),
Ray publicly took exception on one issue. "I don't really accept the
theories of Mr. Clark," he told the court on March 10. "I mean on the
conspiracy thing," he clarified.[1] By March 13, Ray had fully recanted
his confession, blaming it on poor advice from his lawyer, Percy Foreman. Ray had already been working with journalist William Bradford
Huie for months on a series of long-form articles in which he would

develop the "Raul" story for public consumption. But Huie, like the numerous appellate courts that Ray presented his story to in the decades that followed, did not buy his tale of complete innocence, and for good reason.

If the authors are right, James Earl Ray faced a much more complicated challenge than a criminal proceeding. He wanted the bounty money, or a large share of it, and the evidence makes clear that he could not find a sponsor willing to give him his due. But he risked a conviction that could have easily elicited a death sentence. If Ray, on the other hand, conceded his guilt to obtain a lesser sentence, he still faced decades, even life in prison, where bounty money would do no good. If he chose to go further, and identify potential conspirators, he might be released much earlier—but he would forgo any chance of a bounty. Moreover, with any cooperation, he'd be exposing himself to grave harm. While in custody and facing trial in Tennessee, Ray would be kept in isolation, but once convicted, he'd be in a state prison with a giant target on his back. Dixie Mafia hoodlums or white supremacists could kill or maim him. Even if such people did not attempt to kill Ray, a lack of friends on the inside would make him a prime target for black prisoners who would have resented him for participating in a King plot. Ray's actions going forward are best explained by this core dilemma—having to thread the needle between staying alive and safe in prison while preserving his chances to get the money he felt was rightly due to him if he could find a path to freedom.

One can find Ray's attempted solution to this problem in his choice of—and use of—attorneys and investigators. Other than the attorneys who were assigned to defend Ray in his initial trial, he chose two basic groups of people to advance his cause. On the one hand, Ray surrounded himself for decades with lawyers with very strong connections to white supremacists. This likely served two purposes: signaling to the group of people Ray broadly understood as backing the plot that he intended to keep their involvement a secret, and attempting to reach out to lawyers who could serve as middlemen between Ray and the sponsors he never found, in the same way mob attorneys serve as conduits between lower-level mafioso and senior leaders. In the case of the former, Ray could obtain a measure of protection from those same Dixie Mafia and white supremacist inmates while in prison by assuring conspirators outside of prison that he was "playing ball"; in the case of the latter, he could secure money in the event he obtained an early release from prison. That is where the second group of attorneys came in: people whom Ray could convince of his innocence and who could work tirelessly to see him freed, even in the face of his negative public image.

Even before he was extradited to the United States, Ray's choice of attorneys reflected these two parallel tracks. The British courts asked Ray for Americans to represent him in his extradition hearings. Ray offered three choices: F. Lee Bailey, a nationally known defense attorney famous for winning a not-guilty verdict for Dr. Sam Sheppard in a 1966 retrial for his wife's murder; Melvin Belli, the California-based mob attorney who represented Jack Ruby for shooting Lee Harvey Oswald; and Arthur Hanes Sr., the former mayor of Birmingham, Alabama, who won acquittals for four men accused of murdering civil rights activist Viola Liuzzo.[2] Ray would have to wait to find a more reliable group of people to invest in his sincere innocence: Bailey and Belli turned him down. But in Hanes, Ray connected with an attorney who at least, in theory, could reach the kind of white supremacists who might free Ray.

Hanes would claim that he chose to take on Ray's case because he was convinced Ray was the patsy in a conspiracy against King. But an investigation strongly suggested that North Carolina–based KKK operatives offered Hanes $12,500 in another case as a proxy payment to convince Hanes to represent Ray.[3] That such a deal came from North Carolina is significant. Joseph Milteer, the Wesley Swift acolyte who the authors believe tapped into his network of rich racist friends to help raise the money for the King bounty, had, according to research from author Lamar Waldron, extensive connections to property and friends in North Carolina.[4] Tommy Tarrants stayed in a paramilitary camp run by Swift devotees in North Carolina when King was shot in Memphis. Margaret Capomacchia connected those camps to the Sullinger family out of Florida. Ferris Sullinger is noted in government documents as being one of the chief sponsors of Swift's church and other white supremacist groups.[5] On the other hand, Ray's choice of Hanes is not suspicious on its face, given Hanes's well-regarded reputation as lawyer.

It was that reputation that encouraged the courts in Tennessee to maintain Hanes as Ray's main lawyer. Eventually the chief duties for representing Ray in court fell to Percy Foreman, another court-designated attorney with a strong reputation as a litigator. Foreman is the attorney who convinced Ray to accept a guilty plea. Even then, Ray planted the seeds for his eventual defense. Having heard the judge detail the official narrative of the case, Ray acquiesced to every charge but took exception to one: the idea that there was no conspiracy. Eventually, as will be detailed shortly, Ray would blame Foreman for misleading him into accepting any guilt at all and highlighted the conspiracy as the core of his counternarrative. But this is an ad hoc defense. While there are many aspects of Foreman's counsel that deserve scrutiny and even criticism, Foreman knew what the long-time criminal Ray also knew: the evidence against him was damning, and a death penalty verdict by a jury was a distinct possibility. Yes, the ballistics markings tying the Gamemaster rifle Ray bought in Birmingham to the fatal bullet that killed King were inconclusive, and the witnesses from Bessie Brewer's rooming house were uncertain in their identifications of Ray as the shooter because many, on April 4, were inebriated. But there were also these facts: Ray's movements closely track King's from Los Angeles to Selma, to Atlanta to Memphis; he purchased a rifle in Birmingham found near the scene of the crime; only his fingerprints were found on that rifle; he purchased binoculars the day of the crime; he registered at Bessie Brewer's rooming house across from Lorraine from whence witnesses heard the shot; he fled Memphis immediately after the shooting and eventually escaped the continent in search of a country with no extradition orders.

To work his way around this incriminating set of facts, Ray arranged through Hanes to work with a famous writer, William Bradford Huie, to construct a counternarrative to the official version of events. In an exchange of letters—virtual essays in some cases—between Huie and Ray, Ray attempted to explain away everything, arguing that he was a complete and total patsy, one whom Foreman browbeat into what amounted to a guilty plea. As noted in various places in the book, Ray offered the mysterious figure of "Raul," a gun-running, drug-running man of mystery with hints (that would grow stronger as Ray's narrative evolved) of intelligence community connections. When Ray planned to escape from North America via Canada in 1967, Raul convinced Ray to instead remain in North America in gun- and drug-running operations. Raul promised, but failed to deliver, time and time again, the papers Ray would need to flee the country. Instead, as Ray claimed to realize only after King's murder, Raul was manipulating Ray into visiting places and engaging in activities that would, after the fact, make Ray look very guilty as a potential King assassin. Ray's movements only tracked King's in those last two weeks, Ray claimed, because Raul moved the escaped fugitive around like a pawn on a chessboard. Raul told Ray to buy a weapon. Raul told Ray to meet him in Memphis, and then to leave the weapon at Bessie Brewer's rooming house. Raul sent Ray away, and then (presumably) shot King, fleeing in the same style car, dropping the rifle with Ray's belongings outside Canipe Amusement Company, leaving Ray to be captured and suffer the blame for one of the most important crimes in American history.[6]

Huie leaned toward the possibility of a conspiracy for much the same reason the authors and others do: Ray did not strike him as a violent racist. Yet Huie suspected that violent racists likely sponsored King's murder. To Huie's credit, he did not fully trust Ray either. He set out to evaluate and confirm Ray's claims, assertion by assertion. Huie found some tantalizing evidence of a conspiracy—the dinner for two at Mammy's Shanty,[7] the fact that Ray returned the rifle for a better weapon and cited someone else (his brother or brother-in-law) as the reason. But Huie ultimately—and the authors believe mistakenly—dismissed Ray's claims because of holes in Ray's story and Ray's reluctance to go into detail on key matters. Huie came to realize what other historians, even those sympathetic to Ray, later observed: that Ray's ability to remember even minute details about his life after he escaped from Jefferson City became noticeably less acute when he began to describe potentially incriminating activities. This is noticeable, for instance, when Ray described his activities and whereabouts during his stay in New Orleans in December 1967.

One could argue—as we do—that these gaps in Ray's descriptions could represent opportunities for a guilty Ray to have engaged with conspirators, that Ray was hiding the involvement of others. But on Ray's key conspiratorial claim—his manipulation by Raul—Huie could find no one to confirm any interactions between Ray and the mysterious Raul figure. Ray also blatantly lied to Huie about important parts of his story. In his original account, Ray claimed that Raul fled with Ray; after presumably shooting MLK and fleeing Bessie Brewer's, Raul got into Ray's white Mustang, found Ray, and urgently ushered him into the vehicle. At that point, in Ray's original story, Raul insisted Ray hide himself under a white bed sheet as they fled Memphis.[8] Ray later admitted this story was false, telling Arthur Hanes that it was a joke meant to mock Huie's pursuit of a Klan angle in the case (white sheet, white hood). But Huie may have viewed that claim the way many others view it—an unlikely subject for a joke when the fake alibi is also being communicated through Hanes, the man responsible for saving Ray from the electric chair. Huie ultimately, and the authors believe wrongly, concluded that Ray solely murdered Martin Luther King Jr.

Ray openly branded Huie a traitor to the cause, someone desperate to monetize the simplest story, the official narrative. To an extent Ray was right—Huie made a small fortune from the book that resulted from his interactions with Ray. Percy Foreman, who helped negotiate the deal with Huie, also deserves criticism, as his dealings with Huie represented a potential conflict of interest. The claim there would be that once Huie decided to write a book invested in the official narrative, Foreman had a fiduciary interest in Ray accepting blame for the crime. But this ignores Huie's legitimate concerns about the Raul story, flaws, as we will detail later, that only get worse over time. One clear example: Ray told Huie that the decision to exchange the Browning rifle for the Gamemaster rifle in Birmingham at the end of March came from Raul. Raul, in this initial telling, opened the Browning rifle from its box, handled the rifle, and then returned it to Ray when he found it wanting. Ray did, as previously noted, cite someone else as motivating the rifle update when he returned it, and by all accounts, the escaped fugitive did not have the knowledge of weapons to know why a Gamemaster would be superior to the Browning. The problem is that Ray's fingerprints are the only ones found on the Gamemaster. When he was confronted with this, Ray changed his story: Raul no longer directly handled the rifle in Birmingham; in fact, he never took it out of the box. When he fired the fatal shot, Ray contended, Raul must have used gloves.[9]

Ray could not convince Huie of his innocence. He could not get Bailey or Belli to defend him. In the period before Percy Foreman became co-counsel, when Hanes was his only attorney, Ray reached out for additional help. One of his first choices in that search is among the most suspicious—so suspicious that the attorney himself likely turned Ray down for fear of how it may have appeared. Ray tasked his brother Jerry with obtaining the services of Percy Quinn as a lawyer. This decision defies any innocent explanation, as Quinn's main, and often only, clients were the White Knights of the Ku Klux Klan of Mississippi.[10] Quinn did not even have a listed phone number or legitimate office in southern Mississippi. He worked from within his own home.[11] When the authors asked Jerry Ray about this, he could not remember how he acquired or who provided him with contact information for Quinn. Jerry also said someone referred Quinn to James while he was awaiting trial in a Tennessee jail.[12] But, as noted earlier, from the start, Tennessee prison authorities kept Ray in isolation from other prisoners well into his trial. Quinn did represent Klan members (including, notably, Sam Bowers) in several widely publicized trials in the late 1960s, but Quinn also lost almost every one of those cases. That Ray reached out first to an attorney for a group that actively tried to kill King for years and that, as established in this book, offered a bounty to kill King in federal prisons across the country, is a strong sign that Ray knew, at least in general terms, who the driving force was behind King's murder. One can surmise that Quinn understood (or was made to understand) the risks involved in having Sam Bowers's chief attorney represent the accused King assassin. Quinn turned Ray down.

But bad optics did not discourage Ray from attempting to employ some of the most ardent and overt racists in the country as his attorneys, even if one forgives him Hanes because of his legal reputation. The list includes neo-Confederate Jack Kershaw, whom Ray kept as legal counsel for years, and who personally sculpted, in the 1990s, a twenty-five-foot monument to the KKK's first Grand Wizard General Nathan Bedford Forrest in Tennessee.[13] It also includes Raulston Schoolfield,[14] who once ran for governor in Tennessee on a segregationist platform. In the courtroom, Raulston's most famous effort came in defense of John Kasper,[15] who later ran for president of the United States on the ticket for the National States Rights Party.

Kasper's vice presidential running mate was none other than J. B. Stoner, whose involvement with Ray's defense is deeply suspicious. That Stoner sought Ray as a client is not dubious on its face, as Stoner loved the publicity that came with defending anyone accused of a racist crime. Ray's decision to welcome Stoner on his legal team, on the other hand, despite Hanes strongly advising against it, is highly suspicious.[16] Hanes knew that with a jury trial pending, Ray needed to avoid even the appearance that he murdered King out of racial animus. Stoner, nationally known as one of America's worst racists, wouldn't help Ray's cause. Stoner, oddly, then hired Ray's brother, Jerry Ray, as his security guard. Years later, when Congress reexamined the King murder, James Earl Ray waived attorney-client privilege for everyone who represented him in the past, except for J. B. Stoner. This was convenient for Stoner, whom Congress thought should be treated as a suspect; under the cloak of attorney client privilege, Stoner frustrated that inquiry.[17]

Stoner's involvement as Ray's attorney, and his decision to hire Jerry Ray as a security officer for years, suggests that Stoner was some kind of conduit between Ray and the conspirators. If so, the timing and substance of a note Ray wrote and placed in the garbage—recovered by prison guards—is highly suggestive. Author Pate McMichael, building on the work of investigative reporter Marc Perrusquia, suggested the note was written at approximately the same time that Ray began meeting with Stoner in prison custody. At the bottom of half of the note, Ray wrote: "I got a murder charge instead of 10,000 for listening to promises. No more fool pants."[18]

Stoner's association with Jerry Ray deserves more attention than most historians of the case assign to it. It is often treated as an afterthought even though Jerry Ray and Stoner maintained the relationship for years. One might be tempted to think that this is a marriage of convenience, with Jerry keeping an eye on his brother's attorney while Stoner used Jerry to improve his racist bona fides, but this ignores the degree to which Jerry Ray appears to have embraced Stoner's ideology. The HSCA, for instance, found a letter, sent to the NSRP member and signed by Jerry Ray, in which Jerry Ray openly condemns Jews and their satanic-communist conspiracy.[19] Jerry's very association with Stoner, like his brother's decision to hire the NSRP leader as an attorney in the first place, only reinforced the perception of James's guilt—the racial-animus theory—in the minds of investigators.

Many began to question if Jerry Ray himself was a co-conspirator in the crime. James Earl Ray consistently referenced his unnamed "brother" in explaining a host of his decisions, from leaving Los Angeles in March 1968, after which he proceeded to stalk King, to upgrading his rifle purchase from a .243 Browning to a .30-06 Gamemaster in Birmingham. The authors cannot dismiss the possibility of Jerry Ray's involvement but it seems unlikely that James Earl Ray would invoke his brother, even ambiguously, if it could expose Jerry Ray to consequences with the law. Similarly, it seems unlikely that Jerry Ray would implicate his brother if, in fact, Jerry shared criminal culpability.

And time and time again, Jerry Ray said things, in public and in private, that painted James Earl Ray in a guilty light. We have already discussed the private conversation he had with his FBI-informant love interest and her landlady, in which Jerry said James killed someone he already didn't like (King, in the context of the conversation) in hopes of getting anywhere from $100,000 to $500,000. But Jerry also gave public interviews where he implied the same guilty knowledge. In interviews with George McMillan, Jerry insisted that the Raul narrative was "just a story Jimmy made up" for William Bradford Huie and that his brother's account of a drug-smuggling operation from Canada was a "lie." But almost from the moment McMillan's book was released, Jerry claimed he was misquoted or pulling jokes on McMillan and reasserted his faith in the Raul story. Jerry also said in newspapers that James Earl Ray had provided him with phone numbers of conspiratorial contacts in New Orleans that Jerry was keeping in a safe deposit box.

Historians and others sympathetic to James Earl Ray have had to completely disavow Jerry at times; others selectively quote Jerry's statements that help James Earl Ray but ignore the statements that hurt him. The authors believe Jerry may have been part of the misdirection game himself, walking, in many ways, the same tightrope as his brother James between assuaging the actual conspirators (like Stoner) and working toward obtaining his brother's release.

No group of people were more frustrated by Jerry than the other team of legal experts Ray assembled to help his cause, a group of left-leaning attorneys and investigators who became convinced of James Earl Ray's counternarrative. Almost to a person, they included the earliest critics of the Warren Commission's report on the assassination of John F. Kennedy on November 22, 1963. This included Mark Lane, Bud Fensternwald, Jim Lesar, and Harold Weisberg among others including comedian and civil right activist Dick Gregory. The first three represented Ray in some capacity or another as attorneys; Weisberg, as noted earlier, was one of Ray's chief investigators. Weisberg, in particular, would write James Earl Ray with his frustrations about Jerry Ray and the inflammatory statements Jerry made to interviewers. But there was little Weisberg or anyone else could do.[20]

Weisberg would hear out Jerry and James's other brother, John Ray, when it came to conspiratorial leads. Most notably, Weisberg, at the two brothers' urging, became interested in the 1965 Ohio plot, in which Venable and likely Stoner offered $25,000 for a group of men to massacre King and his family when King spoke at Antioch College.[21] As noted earlier, Weisberg operated under the assumption that James Earl Ray was protecting the real conspirators, and this assumption appears to have extended, in some way, to Ray's brothers. But Weisberg also doggedly stuck to the notion that Ray was completely innocent of the crime. To be fair, a portion of his thinking was informed by his opinions of the physical evidence in Memphis. But it is also is clear that James Earl Ray took advantage of deeply rooted skepticism that Weisberg, and several of his other attorneys, held in respect to federal investigators and the government as a whole, doubts that lingered from the inquest into President Kennedy's murder. Some of Ray's legal advisors even suspected that agencies of the U.S. government participated in the president's murder and, just as importantly to Ray, that the agencies framed accused assassin Lee Harvey Oswald. That the U.S. government was once again claiming that a "lone nut" (James Earl Ray) assassinated another liberal icon (King) amplified preexisting biases in favor of Ray's story about Raul.

These critics deserve substantial credit for raising some of the biggest problems with the official investigation of King's murder. This included the issues with physical and eyewitness testimony in Memphis, Ray's gun purchases and movements, Ray's purported motivations, and other matters, many of which have been described in this book. They were dogged and determined enough in developing and publicizing these findings that they helped push Congress to reopen the case.

But the same passion for justice that these early critics brought to the Kennedy assassination investigation left them open to manipulation by James Earl Ray. These men wrote books detailing the flaws in the Warren Commission report, in support of the idea that Lee Harvey Oswald was a patsy, and here they had another purported lone assassin asserting the same thing. Both Ray and Oswald used fake names and aliases; both Ray and Oswald traveled to places like New Orleans and Mexico. Only now the accused assassin survived with sufficient knowledge of the grand conspiracy to point a finger at the mysterious figure known as Raul. To Ray's proponents, who shared leftist and antiwar sensibilities and who saw evidence of right-wing government manipulation in the life of Lee Harvey Oswald, the idea that some government contract agent would manipulate a patsy into murdering an antiwar liberal like King had enormous appeal.

But the differences between Oswald and Ray would also be obvious if these left-leaning experts brought the same critical faculties they used in defending Ray and attacking the Warren Commission to bear on Ray's story. Oswald's trip to Mexico City two months before the president's murder included provocative visits to the Cuban and Russian Consulates and left a trail of mysterious record keeping, on the part of the CIA, that led congressional investigators to speculate that someone impersonated Oswald during his visit. Ray's trip to Mexico, on the other hand—other than the unverifiable parts from Ray himself—clearly show someone interested in finding low-level narcotics and engaging in pornography. Ray's transparent lies about aspects of his Mexico trip, namely that Raul ordered him to purchase the cameras and other material that clearly were meant to help Ray film salacious acts—defy belief. Contract hit men for the government have no need for ceiling mirrors. The use of fake names is also common for criminals like Ray; it is not common for "everyday" individuals like Oswald.

In fact, it is not uncommon for a criminal to invent a fake person

altogether, like Raul, to deflect some or all of the blame for a crime.
Recall that Ray and his partner in crime, Walter Rife, invented a
fictional scapegoat early in Ray's criminal career when they invented
Walter McBride as a fall guy for their escapades. The most obvious
hint that Ray was following inquiries into the Kennedy assassination
and using that to curry favor with well-known critics like Lane came
during the height of New Orleans district attorney Jim Garrison's very
public investigation into the Kennedy assassination, when Garrison
tried businessman Clay Shaw for conspiracy to assassinate the president in 1968 and 1969. Garrison famously appeared on *The Tonight
Show* with Johnny Carson to advocate his case, and in so doing highlighted a picture of three men—purported tramps—in Dealey Plaza
(the site of the Kennedy murder) who each appeared to be dressed
abnormally well for hobos. Garrison pointed to one man in particular,
commonly referred to as "Frenchy," as a suspicious character. Not long
after, James Earl Ray identified Frenchy as looking remarkably similar to Raul.[22] Decades later, in the 1990s, JFK researchers identified
Frenchy as a legitimate tramp; not long after, James Earl Ray gave
a positive photo ID of another individual as being Raul—only this
individual looked absolutely nothing like Frenchy.[23]

His ever-shifting stories did give some on his legal team pause
about Ray, but they tended to keep their reservations private. Weisberg and Fensterwald exchanged letters lamenting Ray's mendacity.[24]
Weisberg, as noted earlier, came to believe that Ray was protecting
others, the real King conspirators, by lying to authorities and to his
own legal team. Weisberg passed this off as simple self-protection and,
because he maintained faith in Ray's total innocence, only worked privately, and gingerly at that, to press Ray for what he really knew. To
his credit, Weisberg recognized the implications of Ray's fabrications
and evasions for any claim of involvement by the U.S. government
in the King murder.[25] Logically, Ray would not be covering up for
U.S. government–sponsored killers while he simultaneously accused
the U.S. government, in television interviews, in books, and through
his attorneys, of arranging King's murder. In letters to other research-

ers, Weisberg ridiculed theories that, for instance, implicated J. Edgar
Hoover and the FBI in King's murder. Ray would not cover for them
(indeed he listed them among the conspirators). Weisberg, instead,
believed Ray was covering up for those in the criminal underworld.
The authors agree with Weisberg that Dixie Mafia–type hoodlums,
like James Ashmore (using the alias J. C. Hardin), linked Ray into
the conspiracy; unlike Weisberg, we would add that Ray likely also
knew, more generally, that certain white supremacist groups helped
mastermind the King assassination. That is why we, again, believe he
accepted the help of someone like Stoner, with connections to almost
every KKK group in the country, especially in the Southeast, to represent him. Outwardly and in practice, however, lawyers like Lane
behaved in the same way as Stoner, openly accusing the government
of involvement in the King death, even as they privately made excuses
for Ray's evasiveness to each other.

They sincerely believed Ray's essential narrative of the unwitting
dupe, looking past his ad hoc changes and adjustments. For thirty
years, for instance, no researcher was able to identify the place where
Ray allegedly was having an auto tune-up when MLK was murdered.
Mark Lane did unearth two people who claimed they worked on Ray's
car only to have both men exposed as liars in the late 1970s.[26] What is
never discussed is whether Lane received support for that claim from
Ray—to believe otherwise would mean that Lane, a skilled and experienced lawyer, offered alibi witnesses for Ray without ever bothering
to ask Ray about them. But if one believes the opposite, that Ray
privately endorsed these alibi witnesses before they were exposed as
hoaxers by the HSCA, it would represent the second time that Ray
offered a false alibi (recall the getaway, white-sheet story he told to
Hanes and Huie).

Of course, the alibi story has never made sense from the per-
spective of the kind of well-conceived conspiracy and frame-up Ray's
defenders posited. To believe Ray would mean that Raul, the man
who masterfully manipulated Ray and managed his movements in anticipation of Ray being framed as a patsy, made a huge mistake when

it mattered most. He let Ray wander about Memphis at the very moment the actual shooting was to take place. No amount of supposedly planted evidence would matter if Ray simply had a verifiable alibi. He could have any number of alibi witnesses for instance, or a receipt that confirmed where he was. If so, Raul and the whole conspiracy to frame Ray would have come crashing down. But Ray could never find anyone reliable to verify that he was getting his Mustang fixed. In fact, despite four decades' worth of investigative attention, no one has even found the supposed location where the repair occurred. Lane tried and failed.

Perhaps owing to this, Ray once again found another lead counsel to replace Lane: British attorney William Pepper. Pepper is more responsible than virtually anyone else for convincing the country—and King's closest family members—that Ray is innocent and that a high-level U.S. government conspiracy is behind MLK's death. Ray's influence on Pepper may well be similar to his influence on his other lawyers. In Pepper, Ray identified a former ally of King's from the civil rights movement who, like many of King's aides, saw the 1968 King as a major threat to the establishment regarding Vietnam and other issues. We will explore the flaws in this thinking in the Appendix, but suffice it to say a belief in a power elite theory of King's murder has allowed Pepper to march forward even as his critics, time and time again, shoot down his claims.

Pepper has offered no fewer than three different people as the actual shooters in King's murder. As each accusation is proved wrong, he simply flips to the next possible suspect. In his latest offering, he paid the person for the interview in which the known criminal claims responsibility. Pepper used clearly fraudulent documents and dubious witnesses to accuse a U.S. Special Forces member, Billy Ray Eidson, of leading the team of shooters in MLK's death. Pepper claimed that Eidson was then taken out of the country and killed for his sinister knowledge. Pepper had to pay Eidson millions of dollars after he showed up, alive and well, in 1997 on ABC's *Turning Point*, and directly confronted Pepper about his scurrilous accusations.[27]

This did not stop Pepper from using the same sketchy documents and sources to launch a famous civil case in 1998, one in which the King family sued one of Pepper's chief suspects, Memphis restaurant owner Loyd Jowers, for wrongful death. Pepper claims that Jowers provided the murder weapon to the actual King assassin, as part of a bounty a local mob figure offered at the behest of New Orleans mob kingpin Carlos Marcello. Jowers, after twenty-five years of saying something completely different, volunteered this to Pepper. Pepper could not rest there, claiming that Marcello, in turn, operated on behalf of and in conjunction with U.S. military and intelligence assets to kill King,[28] a claim based largely on the same materials and witnesses who falsely implicated the U.S. Special Forces captain. Yet Pepper's civil trial resulted in a guilty verdict against Jowers, a verdict that advocates for Ray's innocence often cite in social media as the final word in an MLK conspiracy. But the verdict was all but rigged in advance, for reasons that James Earl Ray's advocates frequently ignore.

The fact that Pepper could use sources that he knew, from a previous civil trial, were bogus, is because the opposition party in the civil suit—Loyd Jowers—had no interest in winning the case. Quite the opposite. As Pepper notes in his own book, Jowers *wanted* to parlay his admission into a book and movie deal that would earn him hundreds of thousands of dollars. Jowers, in fact, by Pepper's own admission, falsely accused one of the early "shooters" Pepper proposed. But this obvious lie did not deter Pepper. Nor did his numerous witnesses' lies and changing stories convince Pepper that he may be representing a guilty man (Ray). If Jowers's attorney, Lewis Garrison (no relation to the New Orleans district attorney), had wanted, he could have used Pepper's own book on the case, *Orders to Kill*, to impeach the credibility of virtually every one of the witnesses Pepper presented at the 1998 civil trial. But Garrison did not and Peppers did not because both sides were working toward the same result. The civil suit filed by the King family was for only $1! Memphis and Tennessee law enforcement openly and publicly dismissed Jowers's story. Jowers knew he could avoid prosecution and any serious civil fees while having a jury "officially" confirm his guilt—an official verdict that, by Pepper's own admission, Jowers hoped would garner hundreds of thousands of dollars from a movie deal.

The mutual arrangement, whether by design or by implication, is obvious from transcripts, and even quantifiable. There was only one procedural objection offered by Jowers's attorney, Lewis Garrison, over a multiday trial. These are the most basic objections, like "no foundation" and "calls for speculation."[29] Garrison did not even object to a husband offering direct testimony in place of his wife (who was ill)—perhaps the most obvious example of hearsay in trial history. In contrast, one can find dozens of these sorts of objections on any day in the O. J. Simpson civil trial for the murder of Ron Goldman and Nicole Brown Simpson.[30] The difference is obvious: Simpson stood to lose millions if he lost his case (and he did), and Jowers stood to lose a single dollar and possibly *gain* a lucrative movie deal if he lost. As Mark Lane noted to pro-Ray researcher Martin Hay: "It was not a real trial . . . both sides offered the same position and I have reason to doubt that the position they offered was sound. The jury, having seen no evidence to the contrary, had no choice. In my view, the court system should not be utilized in that fashion."[31]

Ray's earliest supporters, like Lesar and Weisberg, do not deserve to be grouped with Pepper. They sincerely hoped to expose the kind of government conspiracy they saw at work in the JFK assassination. They identified many of the problems with the official version of the case that the authors cite in this book. But they fell into the fallacy of the excluded middle: they failed to see that in between the theory that Ray was the total dupe of a massive conspiracy and the theory that Ray was the lone shooter was the possibility that Ray was complicit, in some fashion, with a conspiracy. They needed only to look at the other group of attorneys, and question Ray's motives in working with them, to see where that conspiracy led.

James Earl Ray apparently lacked his lawyers' faith that they could secure his release, even as nearly decades' worth of advocacy helped propel Congress to reexamine King's murder. At the same time the HSCA began its new investigation in 1977, on the eve of their first interview with the convicted assassin, James Earl Ray escaped from Bushy Mountain maximum security prison with six other inmates. The escape was, by all accounts, "imaginative and risky" and involved "widespread cooperation by other inmates." Most importantly it involved what appeared to either be a stroke of good luck or a measure of careful design: the prisoners escaped past the one watchtower, out of six, that was unmanned that night. Representative Louis Stokes, one of the senior members of the HSCA, found the timing and circumstances—the prison warden also happened to be on vacation—to be coincidental at best. It raised the possibility of outside help at a time when Ray ran the risk of exposing conspirators to investigators. "If there was outside participation, the reasons for it are obvious, and the escape would have been perpetrated for one of two reasons; either that once Ray got out he would never be heard from again or that he could have been lured out for the purpose of killing him."[32]

If Ray had help, he did not disclose it, just as he never disclosed his accomplices in the King murder. He did manage to win over one other convert to his cause. The court stenographer at Ray's trial for his escape, Anna Sandhu, not only bought Ray's claim of innocence in the King murder, she developed a relationship with and eventually married Ray in 1978. For years, she publicly proclaimed his innocence and worked for his release from prison. But relations with Ray became strained over time. In 1993, Ray called Sandhu, angry that she had not visited him. Sandhu asked Ray for $800 to help fix her car. Ray offered to give her the sum under one condition: if she did not pay it back, he would send someone to shoot at her house. Sandhu did not sense Ray was joking. "You're starting to sound like a somebody who would kill Martin Luther King," she recalled telling him, years later. "Yeah, I did it," he replied, "So what? I never got a trial." The two divorced shortly after. Asked what would motivate Ray to kill King, Anna Sandhu Ray speculated that he did it for money. "He didn't do anything for free," she told reporter Jerry Mitchell in 2013. "He was the kind of person whose whole world revolves around money."[33]

IF RAY HOPED to mislead his lawyers and the public at large in search of his elusive payday, the white supremacists who bore ultimate responsibility for King's death also began their own effort to foil the investigation. The conspirators who raised the money for the King bounty and who advanced the plot to Memphis began playing games with investigators. Notably, Tommy Tarrants's arrest in the Meridian sting on June 28, 1968, triggered a new wave of reports connecting him to possible involvement in the King murder. Both sets of reports emanated from a trip law enforcement informant Willie Somersett took. The Miami Police Department, which sponsored the trip, thought so highly of Somersett that they asked him to travel the United States and investigate the King murder, using his contacts in white supremacist circles.

In July, Willie Somersett visited his old friend Sidney Barnes in Tommy Tarrants's hometown of Mobile, Alabama. Barnes, as detailed previously, was part of an assassination plot against King in 1963, and while Somersett secretly taped him, Barnes confessed that this plot continued through 1964. Barnes also mentored Tommy Tarrants and Kathy Ainsworth in the ideology of Christian Identity and enjoyed close relationships with members of the White Knights in Jackson, Mississippi, where Barnes and his zealously racist wife, Pauline, in 1969. In July of 1968, Barnes invited Somersett to come to Mobile, where he told his friend an explosive story. A CB radio in Tommy Tarrants's car was used to jam police radio broadcasts in Memphis the day of King's assassination. This would not be out of character for Tarrants; he had described using police radios to monitor police frequencies when he engaged in petty racist activities as a teenager in Mobile. The story closely echoes the CB radio diversion that in fact happened that day. Barnes continued, saying that Tarrants hid out with him for some time in Mobile not long after the King murder. A receipt found in Tarrants's belongings at the Meridian bombing crime scene, recently discovered in Mississippi FBI files, conclusively establishes that Tarrants spent time in April with Barnes. The report from Somersett, however, on Barnes's July 1968 revelations, never appears to have reached the FBI.

One set of reports from Somersett did make it to the FBI, however, and it corroborates much of what Barnes said. Somersett also visited Margaret Capomacchia, Kathy Ainsworth's mother, mourning her daughter's shooting death. Capomacchia also revealed important information on the King assassination, apparently provided to her by her daughter. Capomacchia independently affirmed everything Barnes had to say about Tarrants: the CB radio jam in Memphis and his stay with Barnes. But she directly accused "him" of involvement in the King murder. She also accused several other members of the White Knights of participating in the King conspiracy. Somersett reported concerns about her mental stability and returned for a second round of conversations.[34] There, Capomacchia focused her attention more on Tarrants, explaining that he had fled to North Carolina and stayed with someone Somersett reported as "Henderson," who threw Tarrants out when he became "too hot." At that point, Tarrants went to stay with Barnes.[35] The FBI investigated Capomacchia's story and found it inconclusive; given her mental instability, she must be making it all up. While Capomacchia identified several key figures in the Mississippi White Knights, all of them had alibis, and one of them had already been exposed as an FBI informant.[36] Moreover, while the Miami PD valued Somersett as an informant, the FBI discontinued using him several years earlier, after a number of the stories he relayed about white supremacists, including other assassination plots, turned out to be false.

The FBI may have been right to doubt the report, but not for the reasons discussed. It appears Barnes and Capomacchia were likely using Somersett as an unwitting conduit of disinformation. This is not surprising. It turns out that certain members of the white supremacist community, notably J. B. Stoner, suspected Somersett as a snitch as early as 1962.[37] When Somersett taped Barnes in 1964, the FBI returned to the Mobile racist and more or less exposed Somersett as an informant. Barnes implied as much in future informant reports.[38] It is not a surprise that Somersett started to report more and more unreliable information to the FBI—white supremacists were likely deliberately feeding him misinformation. Most importantly, by 1967, reports of Somersett secretly taping Milteer—in which Milteer, in early November 1963, predicted JFK's assassination and spoke about other plans to assassinate Martin Luther King Jr.—had already reached American newspapers. They did not name Somersett as a source, but how could Milteer, with his extensive contacts in the white supremacist movement, not know and not tell others? Somersett was compromised by 1967, and the fact that Barnes and Capomacchia—who were friends—were both willing to tell the same story to him is significant. They clearly were using Somersett to pass dubious information to the FBI.

But this is not the end of the story. In placing Tarrants inside their purported King plot, the two racists also linked him to individuals who, again, had clear alibis for the King murder. Once the FBI dismissed these people as suspects, they didn't care about the rest of the story related to Tarrants, and he was dismissed as an accomplice in the King murder. They may well have been right: Tarrants maintains that he was in North Carolina at the time of the assassination. But, paradoxically, Tarrants was also likely a key to exposing a Christian Identity plot, not because he participated in the murder, but because he was set up as an early patsy in the crime. Going back to the very early, inexplicable interest in Tarrants as a suspect in the King murder makes it seem likely that someone was reporting incriminating information about him to the FBI, such as the fact that Tarrants obtained a rifle from Swift in March for the express purpose of killing King. But things went awry in Memphis, and this early effort to frame Tarrants failed. It would have been obvious to the FBI that only one group was positioned to implicate him that early: the network of racists he worked with. They were the only ones who knew in March and April that Tarrants was a radical terrorist. Thus, a possible explanation for Barnes's and Capomacchia's is that they were using Somersett in a "modified limited hangout." In the world of spies, a modified limited hangout involves providing a story that is a mix of truth and false-hoods; when the false part of the story is exposed, the hope is that the receiving party throws the baby out with the bathwater and discredits even the true parts of the story. In providing the disinformation on Tarrants, Barnes and Capommachia may have hoped to poison any interest the FBI had in Tarrants as a patsy in the King murder. They would effectively be reversing their original goal of framing Tarrants because Ray short-circuited the real plot. Or perhaps the effort was simply aimed at poisoning Tarrants as a source for law enforcement on other criminal activity. The record shows that Barnes was very concerned that Tarrants would ultimately expose white supremacists to law enforcement.

It would take several years, but federal investigators eventually became interested in Barnes, Stoner, and several other names mentioned in this book. Owing to the work of all Ray's attorneys and investigators, but most notably to the Warren critics, Congress opened a new investigation into the King and Kennedy assassinations in 1976. Congress established the House Select Committee on Assassinations to investigate lingering questions about both murders, in an atmosphere of increasing public skepticism over the federal government in the wake of the Watergate scandal and revelations about government surveillance and black bag operations, including those FBI director Hoover directed at Dr. King. The HSCA would ultimately conclude that a conspiracy was in fact behind the murder of the civil rights leader, and that James Earl Ray murdered King in hope of collecting a bounty. But they failed to identify the correct sponsor or the motivations for the conspiracy.

14

AFTERMATH

For five decades, the Department of Justice and the FBI, Congress, and scholars have failed to deliver justice in the King assassination. The pieces were there, even before the murder, but the relevant players never put them together. Understanding why may point a way forward to finally resolving the case.

In 1968, the FBI was actively supporting what was a local prosecution of James Earl Ray. The Memphis district attorney was gearing up to present a case to a Tennessee judge and a Tennessee jury. Any conspiracy by itself complicates a criminal prosecution, but a conspiracy to murder across state lines makes matters even more difficult when the victim is not a federal officer. It would have complicated issues of jurisdiction and extradition and would have made coordination between prosecutors and investigators more difficult. But in 1968, developments in the application of federal law made this concern moot.

Federal prosecutors in the Civil Rights Division of the Justice Department were becoming increasingly adept at using Title 18 Section 241 of the United States Code to convict groups of conspiracy. This component of federal law states the following:

> If two or more persons conspire to injure, oppress,
> threaten, or intimidate any person in any State, Ter-
> ritory, Commonwealth, Possession, or District in the
> free exercise or enjoyment of any right or privilege se-
> cured to him by the Constitution or laws of the United
> States . . . They shall be fined under this title or impris-
> oned not more than ten years, or both; and if death re-
> sults from the acts committed in violation of this section
> or if such acts include . . . an attempt to kill, they shall
> be fined under this title or imprisoned for any term of
> years or for life, or both, or may be sentenced to death.[1]

Indeed, attorneys at the Department of Justice had, in October 1967, successfully prosecuted several Klansmen, including Sam Bowers, for conspiring to kill the three civil rights workers in the Mississippi Burning case.

Attorneys in the Civil Rights Division were increasingly applying creative and broad interpretations of what qualified as a constitution-ally protected activity—the "right or privilege" part of the criminal code—to mount federal conspiracy prosecutions against the Klan. They did so in the Mississippi Burning case; they did so earlier with the murder of civil rights worker Violet Liuzzo in Alabama in 1965; and they did so with the murder of black World War II veteran Lem-uel Penn, in 1964, in Georgia.

The Justice Department had gained a tremendous amount of ex-perience in navigating and collating the FBI's investigative records, handling FBI informants, and seeing through the smoke screens the Klan set up to prevent successful prosecutions, such as the use of false alibis and other obstructionist tactics. And the Justice Department was becoming more and more adept at developing the narrative of conspiracy, tracing though mazes of coincidences and circumstantial inferences to weave together prosecutions that could successfully con-vict even those individuals, like Sam Bowers, who were smart enough to keep a safe distance from their crimes.

It is prosecutors—not investigators—who are focused on establishing issues of motive and, in the case of a conspiracy, aligning the behavior of the perpetrators with suspicious activity on the part of other potential plotters. In the case of Ray, more than one witness told investigators that Ray was motivated by money and that bounty offers on King were circulating in Missouri State Penitentiary before Ray's escape in April 1967. These other purported conspirators are often connected to broadly defined groups like the KKK or unnamed Southern businessmen. Donald Nissen's story, albeit in a separate federal prison, linked a bounty to the Mississippi White Knights, a specific group with a documented history of trying to kill King. Starting in 1967, this group was increasingly interacting with the National States Rights Party through J. B. Stoner, another individual who had tried to kill King; and when Ray failed to escape North America in 1967 through Canada, he traveled to Birmingham, the most publicized haven of violent NSRP activity in the United States, and lived just blocks from the NSRP's headquarters.

Based on the timeline Nissen provided, Ray arrived within weeks of the bounty money being transferred from Atlanta, Georgia, to Jackson, Mississippi. The evidence is fuzzy as to how and when Ray was recruited into a specific plot against King, but after his sojourn in Mexico and move to Los Angeles at the end of 1967, the apolitical fugitive suddenly started making contacts at the California headquarters of racist third-party presidential candidate George Wallace. It is known that at least one radical extremist with connections to Milteer, Stoner, and Swift—James Paul Thornton—had once worked at that campaign office. Whether Ray was seeking out Thornton (who had moved to Atlanta) or found others to reach, it is impossible to tell. Ray never adequately explained it, and investigators for the FBI, much less for the Justice Department, never asked. New evidence in this book suggests that Ray's fellow prisoner and friend, Louis Dowda, may have visited California to bring Ray information about a potential bounty. The authors have also identified James W. Ashmore as "J. C. Hardin," the man who called Ray and visited him in Los Angeles in February and

March 1967. All this information is in the FBI's own files; it stands to reason that Justice Department lawyers could have subjected all these people to additional interviews, but they did not even notice the coincidences in many cases.

In any event, starting March 17, 1968, Ray abandoned other potential vocations (pornography, bartending) and avocations (dancing) right at the time that he was running out of money; he began to follow King's movements throughout the Southeast. In stalking King, especially in following him to Atlanta, Ray was fulfilling one role Leroy McManaman proposed in his bounty offer to Nissen. It was also in Atlanta where Ray appears to have eaten with another person at Mammy's Shanty, a restaurant that researcher and Atlanta native Lamar Waldron says was a hangout for racist types.[2] The FBI never pieced this together, but perhaps a Justice Department investigation could have.

Certainly, an open-minded Justice Department investigation could have seen what Ray did at the end of March 1968 in Birmingham as representing not only one of the most telling signs of a conspiracy but also one of the most intriguing potential links to Sam Bowers. Showing an obvious lack of knowledge of guns, Ray purchased one rifle on March 28. The gun store staff said Ray seemed so lost that he was "out of place."[3] Yet the frugal Ray returned on March 29 and exchanged the weapon for a highly regarded but more expensive rifle, the .30-06 Gamemaster, whose bullets shared the same basic characteristics as the fatal round, removed from Dr. King. Ray told the staff that his "brother-in-law" told him to make the trade; but Ray did not have a brother-in-law, and his actual brothers cannot be definitively placed in Birmingham. If someone with knowledge of guns did insist on the weapons exchange, it is worth noting that March 29, 1968, was the only time, over the course of many months, that someone at Sam Bowers's company, Sambo Amusement, called Birmingham, Alabama. While it is uncertain who made the call and to where, the records show that it was to the Birmingham Army Reserve.[4] The FBI should have investigated to establish this more clearly and followed up with interviews of Bowers and Robert Larson; but the records of the Birmingham call come from separate Jackson files on Bowers and never made it into the MURKIN FBI headquarters file. Perhaps a prosecutor at the Civil Rights Division could have made the connection—and forced a follow-up investigation—where the FBI did not.

Any prosecutor would, and the Memphis prosecutors did, focus on Ray's actions immediately after the gun purchase—the quick return trip to Atlanta and his travels to Memphis—as key to any conviction of Ray. Even Ray admitted that this coincidence was devastating and denied it—in the face of clear contrary evidence—to the day he died. As noted earlier in the chapter, at the same time Ray was making these trips, in the days immediately leading up to King's murder, witnesses described Sam Bowers and one of his top aides acting very suspiciously at John's Café. To the FBI, Sam Bowers's presence at John's Café on April 5 was a reason to exclude him as a suspect. Who knows how the Justice Department, whose experience with Klan conspiracy trials made them leery of alibis on many levels, would have done with something like the Hendricks story?

Even if one adopts one of the scenarios we present—that Ray, contrary to his assigned role as a "caser," shot King to collect a larger share of a bounty, surprising other conspirators and forcing all parties, including Ray himself, to scramble—it would not absolve Bowers and company of guilt in a federal conspiracy case. Such a charge only requires that parties to a murder actively plan and intend to kill King, regardless of how such a plan played out. Because the murder was planned outside of Memphis, federal lawyers could have prosecuted someone like Bowers under federal laws.

But if the law permitted the Justice Department to pursue such a case, if the Civil Rights Division had already demonstrated the ability to develop a conspiracy argument especially against racists in civil rights crimes, why didn't they do so? After all, the FBI was and is the chief investigative unit for the Department of Justice and their attorneys. Part of the problem was that Attorney General Ramsey Clark, having seen the riots that were destroying dozens of America's cities, assured the press on April 5, 1968, that only one man had killed Martin Luther King Jr.; Clark would later admit this was premature and done to pacify the public. But his statements would obviously circumscribe the behavior of any of his subordinates, who, if they did pursue a conspiracy case, would effectively be publicly embarrassing their boss if it came to fruition with a prosecution.

But it is questionable whether the Justice Department could have uncovered a conspiracy, even on their best day, even if they had an interest in doing so, for J. Edgar Hoover was making sure that was all but impossible.

Hoover hated Attorney General Clark. It was Clark who had terminated Hoover's ongoing wiretapping program against Martin Luther King Jr. According to Hoover biographer Curt Gentry, Hoover considered Clark to be a "jellyfish" or a "softie" when it came to crime.[5] To Hoover, Clark was the worst attorney general he had ever worked with. Congress reviewed Hoover's interaction with Clark's Justice Department as part of the HSCA's reexamination of the King murder in 1978. In their "Staff Report on the Performance of the Department of Justice and the FBI," the HSCA found that Director Hoover had personally ordered that certain instructions from the attorney general be ignored so that the "course and direction of the investigation remained exclusively in the hands of the FBI."[6] The staff report concluded that the FBI investigation reflected "arrogance and independence of various personnel" and "poor and counterproductive relationships between the Bureau and lawyers at the Justice Department." It also noted that Director Hoover's lack of respect for Attorney General Clark had become an attitude "more or less" universally held within the Bureau.

According to the HSCA staff report, Hoover himself directed that details of the FBI investigation be filtered from the reports sent to the Justice Department and that only high-level summary information on the status of the investigation be provided. The hope for a serious, separate investigation of Barnes, Stoner, and Bowers did not emerge until almost a decade after the murder, with the establishment of the HSCA in 1976.

The Watergate scandal had raised serious doubts about the motives and machinations of the government, and the steady efforts of independent researchers to raise questions about the Martin Luther King and John F. Kennedy assassinations had forced a critical mass in public opinion, leading to the formation of this select committee. But while it represented a clear improvement over the original, deficient FBI investigation, the HSCA was also flawed, for reasons both within and beyond their control.

PICKING UP THE PIECES

In many ways, Congress's investigation showed the potential that existed in 1968 for uncovering the truth, had the Justice Department been a clearinghouse for all the relevant information in the FBI's records. In 1978, the HSCA reviewed all four of the major file threads the FBI produced, cross-referencing the central and local MURKIN records, the distinct files dedicated to dangerous individuals and groups, and the security file on Martin Luther King Jr. at FBI headquarters. After collating that information, they conducted follow-up investigations and interviews, much like the Justice Department would have done in 1968 and 1969.

Hence, when it came to J. B. Stoner, Congress took the possibility of his involvement far more seriously than did the FBI, dedicating an entire subsection of their final report to the militant extremist. They did not accept the idea that Stoner must have been innocent because he was not present in Memphis on April 4, 1968. They found the fact that Stoner came to represent James Earl Ray and that he also employed Ray's brother far more suspicious than did the FBI. The HSCA conducted secret executive interviews with Stoner and apparently confronted him with contradictions in his public statements. Notably, they found it troubling that Stoner openly boasted that he had information related to a conspiracy in the King murder but that he would not disclose this relevant data to their committee.[7]

Congress also reexamined the possibility that the White Knights were involved in the King assassination and gave that research angle far more credence than the original FBI investigators had. They specifically cited the FBI's failure to investigate the White Knights as a group that "demonstrated both a propensity for violence and a clear antagonism toward Dr. King."[8] It was Congress that was first able to show how the separate Jackson field office reports on Bowers's and Nix's activities in John's Café provided corroboration for the Hendricks story. They re-interviewed Hendricks, who denied the substance of her testimony, but only after expressing fear of a reprisal from her former boyfriend, Thomas McGee; it was McGee who told the FBI in 1968 that he was afraid of retaliation from the Klan if Hendricks's story became public. When Congress approached the other informants who corroborated aspects of Hendricks's story in 1968, they also refused to cooperate in 1977.[9]

Sidney Barnes refused to cooperate, too. The HSCA gave renewed attention to Barnes's involvement in the September 1963 plot against King involving Carden, Gale, and Crommelin. It was one of the few plots detailed in their final report. But when it came time to interview Barnes about these matters, he steadfastly refused to be interviewed.[10]

This illustrates a clear weakness in the HSCA investigation of the King murder. Congress has some subpoena power, but resisting such efforts or lying to Congress does not carry the same kind of consequences as one would face in confronting the Department of Justice and a possible grand jury investigation. Even if one does cooperate or comply with a congressional subpoena, it is incredibly rare for charges of perjury to result from false testimony to such a committee. One can simply wait out a select committee, which is formed by Congress for only a specified amount of time and with a limited budget.

As a shrewd attorney, Stoner would have been more aware of this advantage than anyone, but his status as a one-time attorney for Ray gave Stoner even more cover, for he was protected by the cloak of attorney-client privilege. As detailed, James Earl Ray waived this protection for all his other attorneys. *But Ray refused to do so for Stoner*, meaning that the extremist could not testify about his personal exchanges with Ray, even before a secret, executive session of Congress.

This was suspicious enough for Congress to call attention to Ray's exceptional treatment of Stoner in their final report.[11]

The limits of their budget and subpoena power meant that the HSCA continued to suffer from the flaws of the original FBI investigation in 1968, even as they criticized the FBI for those flaws. Budget and time constraints, for instance, prevented the HSCA from interviewing Deavours Nix or Sam Bowers. Yes, the HSCA castigated the FBI for the silly notion that someone would have to be in Memphis to participate in a conspiracy. But the reality was that unless they could conduct serious interviews with the likes of J. B. Stoner, the HSCA was still left with an FBI investigation that cleared the racist lawyer based on his whereabouts. The same was true for Barnes and Bowers; if the original FBI investigation was limited, so too was any effort to build on that investigation, especially if follow-up interviews were hampered by uncooperative witnesses.

The willingness to widen the scope of the investigation by cross-referencing the various streams of files the FBI produced could take the HSCA only so far. Without the sophisticated data-mining capabilities that exist today, the likelihood of missing information was significant. If the HSCA even learned about the Nissen story, much less took the account seriously, it does not show up in their final report, and the HSCA never approached Nissen. There is no mention of the Dixie Mafia or individuals like Donald Sparks or LeRoy McManaman in the HSCA report. The HSCA investigated information from Willie Somersett, but their report focused on a different angle: the claim by Somersett's benefactor in the Miami Police Department, Lieutenant Charles Sapp, that Somersett provided information about King's murder in the days immediately prior to the crime in Memphis.[12] The final HSCA report makes no mention of Somersett's informant reports on Capomacchia or Barnes, which implicated the White Knights in King's homicide. Although the Barnes material was not provided to the FBI in 1968, journalist Dan Christensen quoted from Somersett's reports to the Miami Police Department in a series of articles at the same time.[13] Christensen leaves out Barnes's name but identifies Tarrants as the person whose car was used in a radio diversion in Memphis.[14]

Administrative records show the HSCA was interested in Tommy Tarrants, likely spurred by Christensen's articles, but do not disclose why; in any event, it appears as if the FBI destroyed their Mobile field office file on Tarrants just before Congress became interested in the one-time terrorist.[15] It was that file that contained the picture of Tarrants that the FBI showed the employees of the gun store in Birmingham; that his picture was included at all, and before the FBI showed photos of other known racist killers, is a mystery the HSCA also failed to explore. Tarrants says the HSCA interviewed him,[16] but his name does not appear in HSCA's final report. It appears, by process of elimination, that Tarrants was one of two identity-protected sources the HSCA referenced in their analysis of potential white supremacist conspirators in the King murder. As someone who was on the verge of being released from prison after turning from Christian Identity theology to mainstream Christianity, Tarrants would have been an invaluable source on right-wing Christian extremists. He had personal connections and interactions with Barnes, Bowers, Carden, Crommelin, and key members of the Minutemen and the National States Rights Party, all of whom the HSCA investigated in connection with the King murder. Of course, disclosing Tarrants by name— someone who had just turned against what these violent men stood for—would have been dangerous to the new convert. Most of these men were still alive and could pose a threat to him. Lacking the cooperation of many of these extremists but limited by the FBI's premature decision to clear them of a conspiracy based on their alibis, the HSCA dug deeply into the separate sets of files compiled on these men and their groups; this material was independent of the King crime and connected to investigations into other violent acts and conspiracies.

The HSCA deserves credit for thoroughly examining this material. But the files on these individuals and groups were housed in dozens of field offices across the country. If any of these extremists moved or did business in a different state, if any of the groups had affiliates in a different region of the country, FBI field office investigations were opened and files were created. It is not clear that the HSCA had access to, for instance, the Jackson field office file on Sidney Barnes or the Birmingham field office file on the White Knights of the Ku Klux Klan. In the case of Barnes, the Jackson file not only details his extensive connections to the White Knights—something the HSCA left for a footnote in their final report—but also shows that the Jackson office thought he was a bomb maker for Klan groups.[17] Most relevantly, Barnes's Jackson file also included the Mobile field office reports showing that Barnes possessed and intended to deliver a rifle to Noah Carden as part of the plot on King's life in 1964, a plot that was not even mentioned in the HSCA report. Perhaps most intriguingly, the Jackson field office file on Barnes includes an exchange between Barnes and one of L. E. Matthews's associates, Elaine Smith, in 1969, in which Barnes is reported to have said that he was "friends with James Earl Ray."[18] If the HSCA learned of any of this, they left it out of their report.

Instead, the HSCA relied on new interviews with unnamed sources to all but clear Barnes, Bowers, and others. One source, who claimed to have had personal relationships in 1968 with Barnes, Carden, and Crommelin, insisted that he did not know of any plot against King's life. This same source said that Barnes was all bark and no bite and that he would talk about violence but never participated in any actual crimes. If the HSCA lacked the Jackson field office report on Barnes, it may have been difficult for HSCA investigators to challenge their source.[19] Separately, the report notes an anonymous source who was once involved with White Knights terrorist activities in the 1960s. This source argued that the White Knights were a local group who did not operate outside Mississippi. In other words, the source maintained the White Knights could be discounted because they would not have been involved in any attack on King across state lines in Tennessee.[20]

That Tarrants is one of the two sources is, from his own account, as noted previously, obvious. This also makes sense in light of the interview cited in earlier chapters, in which Tarrants admitted getting a rifle to kill King from Wesley Swift, two weeks prior to the assassi-

nation. What is unclear is if Tarrants gave his information to the FBI
or to the HSCA directly, and this is important. Because if the HSCA
received the information directly, they did not disclose it to the public
in their report. It certainly undermines the credibility of at least one
of their sources. If, instead, the FBI interviewed Tarrants on behalf
of Congress, it may be they were trying to protect something else—
something that could have blown the case wide open but would have
exposed the FBI to an unprecedented level of embarrassment.

This raises serious questions about the identity of the second,
undisclosed source, whose description closely matches that of L. E.
Matthews. In fact, it is hard to imagine any investigation into white
supremacists, especially the White Knights, ignoring Matthews. He
knew all the key players and assumed leadership of the group after
Bowers went to prison. Notably, he is identified as being in John's
Café at the relevant times when Myrtis Hendricks reported suspicious activity. But Matthews's name is conspicuously absent from the
HSCA report, making him a very strong candidate to be the anonymous source.

But if he was the second source, one who cleared the White Knights
and others from suspicion, Matthews himself should have been a suspect. Not only was he at John's Café at the relevant times, documents
indicate he was, in the two weeks prior to the King murder, engaged
in some vague but important "out-of-state project."[21] By itself, this undermines the source who claimed the White Knights would never work
out of state. But one must also remember that Matthews housed both
Tarrants and suspect Eugene "Sunset" Mansfield in the weeks leading
to King's murder. It is important to note, again, that there is an informant report saying that Matthews and Mansfield discussed a "hit" for
money, something that caused the FBI to investigate Mansfield. There
is no evidence that the HSCA considered any of this.

That may be because Matthews was a source for the government
long before he gave anonymous information to the HSCA. Even as
he was poised to assume leadership of the White Knights, Matthews
may have been what the FBI calls a Top Echelon informant, the most
valued and most carefully protected of assets. Four key pieces of in-

formation point in this direction. The first is the fact the FBI and the DOJ never sent—or really even attempted to send—L. E. Matthews to prison for his crimes after 1968. They tried repeatedly for almost every other senior White Knight, but not Matthews, whom their files nonetheless identify as one of the White Knights' chief bomb makers. The most conspicuous example of this "negligence" involves Byron de la Beckwith's attempt to provide explosives to individuals wanting to blow up the offices of Jewish lawyer A. I. Botnick in New Orleans. Authorities in New Orleans intercepted de la Beckwith on his way to the bombing, itself a clear sign that an informant was involved. When it came time to try de la Beckwith, the most damning evidence against him were the reports by FBI agents who claimed to have witnessed de la Beckwith receive the bomb, which de la Beckwith then placed in his vehicle; they were found when he was arrested in New Orleans. But the man who gave de la Beckwith the materials—Matthews— was never charged, much less convicted for his role in the crime, even though he was the leader of the White Knights at the time! This represents the second piece of evidence pointing to Matthews's role as an informant. The next piece is more circumstantial but suggestive— KKK activity petered out to a mere drizzle once Matthews assumed his role as the Grand Wizard.

Finally, there is the fact that the FBI will not provide to the authors more than five pages of material (two of which are duplicates!) on Matthews from his headquarters file. This is unheard of for anyone of any influence in the KKK—their files often run into thousands of pages. In fact, the FBI did not release any material on Matthews from before 1983! Experts on the government's handling of Freedom of Information Act requests say this suggests that Matthews was some kind of informant. In normal cases, when there is sensitive information, the FBI will withhold material or redact large portions of material. But if the person is a top-flight informant, the FBI may release some material on the individual and simply pretend as if other material does not exist (they have to say how much material they withheld otherwise).

If Matthews was a Top Echelon informant for the FBI, it would help explain one of the key mysteries of the King case, described in

this book: the early and significant interest in Tommy Tarrants as
a suspect in the crime. As noted earlier, it makes no sense that an
agent visited Tarrants's home on April 4, after King's murder, or that
agents displayed Tarrants's picture in Birmingham and Los Angeles
on April 6 and April 16, before he had been connected to any serious
acts of racial violence in Mississippi. But that assumes the FBI did not
know about the substance of Tarrants's visit to California to get a rifle
from Wesley Swift with the intent to kill King. If someone informed
the FBI of that, it makes perfect sense that the FBI paid close attention to Tarrants in connection with King's murder. It also explains
why, per Tarrants, his Mobile home was subject to around-the-clock
surveillance from law enforcement the week *before* the King murder.
If Matthews, who knew Tarrants and housed him before his trip to
California, was the source who tipped off the FBI on Tarrants's visit
to Swift in March 1968, everything becomes clearer.

But it also means that a top FBI informant knew about the King
assassination and may have participated in the planning of the murder, and the FBI failed to prevent the killing. In this scenario, the
FBI may not have had a sense of urgency about Matthews's reports or
they may have been waiting to catch someone like Bowers in the act.
In either case, they miscalculated, and then they were left deciding
whether to follow through on the information and risk exposing a valued informant, or let the informant continue to do his job. This kind
of catch-22 is not unknown in FBI history. It happened in the case
of Gary Rowe, an FBI-paid KKK infiltrator who was in a car when
Klansmen murdered civil rights activist Viola Liuzzo. It happened
when Boston mobster Whitey Bulger murdered rivals while working
for the FBI. In both cases, the FBI avoided taking action against their
assets until it was absolutely necessary, often when they had no choice
because of public revelations. But as embarrassing as those cases were,
they would have paled in comparison to the scandal that would have
been caused had the FBI revealed that one of their assets was involved
with and/or failed to prevent the King assassination.

This might also explain why the FBI chose to destroy the Mobile
file on Tarrants in 1977, in violation of standard FBI procedure, and

why they apparently at least considered destroying the entire Miami MURKIN file at some point. In the case of the Miami file, the FBI told the authors that they had destroyed it, when, in fact, they had provided a copy to the National Archives. Internal records show that the Miami file, alone among MURKIN files, was one the FBI wanted to avoid providing to Weisberg in FOIA requests. No one has yet to see it, but it is the file that likely contains all the information from Capomacchia (and possibly Barnes) related to Tarrants. Any hardcore investigation of Tarrants by Congress or anyone else, as the authors noted earlier, would lead to an investigation of the White Knights, and possibly alarming questions about L. E. Matthews.

The net effect of these HSCA interviews with unnamed sources was the same as when the FBI cleared Stoner, Barnes, and Bowers for having alibis outside of Memphis on April 4, 1968. Their operating principle—that the Klan was parochial—was just as misleading. It was generally true that most Klans operated within their own states or local jurisdictions, but we have developed extensive information that, especially when it came to murdering Dr. King, the White Knights and members of the Swift network were more than willing to work across state lines. J. B. Stoner had offered to bring his "boys from Atlanta" to kill King and Rev. Fred Shuttlesworth in Alabama in 1958. William Potter Gale traveled from California to Alabama to join a plot against King in 1963. A very close associate of White Knight Burris Dunn's, who overheard conversations between Dunn and Bowers about King over several years, was confident that, however parochial the White Knights were, they would have made a special exception in working across state lines if King was the intended victim. Informant Delmar Dennis told investigative journalist Jerry Mitchell that the White Knights were national in their reach.[22]

Part of the problem for the HSCA was their preconceived notion—one shared by many—that the Klan was a bunch of local hillbillies, fractured by internal rivalries, limited in their tactics, and with no particular strategy. With such prejudices, the Klan appears very much like a modern-day inner-city gang. They have their turf that they control, but they do not broaden their activities outside their immediate region. For the most part, this is true, as author Patsy Sims amply details in her excellent work on the Klan (appropriately titled *The Klan*).

But what the HSCA missed was the power of Wesley Swift's Christian Identity End Times vision to unify key leaders at the top of organizations such as the National States Rights Party and the White Knights of the Ku Klux Klan of Mississippi. Especially from 1967 to 1969, these men increasingly came together to join forces; Stoner, whose closest associate, Connie Lynch, was a Swift minister, became very active with members of the White Knights in Mississippi starting in 1967. Bowers used Barnes's protégés Tarrants and Ainsworth—members of the Swift Underground—for his bombing campaign in Mississippi in 1967 and 1968. After Ainsworth's death, Barnes moved to Jackson where he and his wife, Pauline, preached Swift's theology to anyone who would listen. At Barnes's invitation, Gale visited Mississippi on multiple occasions to minister and deliver Swift's message. Imperial Wizard James Venable accepted and embraced a California affiliate of his National Knights of the Ku Klux Klan that was run by one of Swift's closest aides. Joseph Milteer, an associate of Venable and Stoner, traveled the country, meeting with and attending functions organized by Swift's followers. Swift's message had captured the imagination of people like Bowers and Stoner, to the extent that his taped sermons were played at parties across the South. Just as modern terrorist leaders do now, Wesley Swift motivated a group of diffuse adherents in states across America to pursue an End Times race war. And killing King was a fundamental plank in the strategy to induce that race war.

WHAT THE ACADEMICS HAVE MISSED: RELIGIOUS TERRORISM

If the HSCA missed the religious component of a King plot, modern scholars, with their post-9/11 focus on religious terrorism, could help investigators understand the dynamic that may have led to King's murder. Reanalyzing elements of the white supremacist movement in the 1960s in the context of religious terrorism would represent a significant shift for some in the field of terrorism studies, but it might provide valuable insights—not only into the violence surrounding the civil rights movement but also possibly into the modern evolution of current religious terrorist organizations such as Al-Qaeda. Decades later, Osama bin Laden, through the power of his religious vision, managed to inspire individuals and groups from America to travel and train in Afghanistan and then wage jihad in Somalia.

Such a change would not require any kind of revisionist history but a reapplication and reconsideration of what is already known about the origins of certain domestic terrorist groups, what is known about religious terrorism as a concept, and what is already documented concerning the acts of violence in the 1960s. Recent scholarship, for instance, has already called attention to the underlying religious motivations of domestic terrorist groups such as the Order and the Aryan Nations who terrorized America in the 1980s and 1990s. They may be seen as extreme outgrowths of the Christian Identity message,[23] but their religious denominations were formed by devotees of Wesley Swift and were modeled on Swift's Church of Jesus Christ Christian, which was created in 1946.

In making such comparisons, one must be careful, as the Swift network in the 1960s was layered on top of, and their goals hidden from, the rank-and-file members of organizations such as the White Knights. But given this limitation, one can still see these groups loosely following the kind of template described by terrorism scholar Dr. Bruce Hoffman in his analysis of religious extremists for the RAND Corporation.[24]

According to Hoffman, religious terrorists are more willing to resort to "indiscriminate violence" than are secular terrorists, for such acts are not only sanctioned in their religious worldview but also necessary "for the attainment of their goals." The White Knights and National States Rights Party were so violent that even other Klan groups, notably the United Klans of America, sought to distinguish themselves from Bowers's and Stoner's organizations.[25]

Hoffman adds that religious terrorists are less concerned in obtaining the sympathy of outsiders as they are with satisfying the religious imperatives of their current membership. On this front, the evidence is mixed. Stoner, from the start, attacked Jewish synagogues when this was generally frowned upon by everyday Southern reactionaries. Bowers had repeatedly attempted to push the White Knights in an anti-Semitic direction in 1964 and 1965 but with no success. It was not until law enforcement pressure drained the White Knights of most of its rank-and-file membership that Bowers was able to use his inner-circle operatives, some of whom shared the same enthusiasm for Swift's theology, to focus their violent attention on Jews more than on blacks. It is important to note that for a member of the Christian Identity denomination, all Christian Anglo-Saxon whites are, in essence, their followers. The everyday white is still a "true" Israelite but with a false consciousness; once the race war comes, all these people will "wise up" and battle the forces of Satan.

Thus Bowers and his ilk, while more extreme than any other group at the time, could not, as Hoffman articulates about other religious terrorists, resort to "almost limitless violence against a virtually open-ended category of targets—that is, anyone who is not a member of the terrorists' religion or religious sect."[26] If he killed white Christians, Bowers would not only limit his power and influence over his remaining flock but also literally eliminate potential soldiers in the End Times race war to come.

Finally, and most relevant to a discussion of the King assassination, Hoffman notes that, in contrast to secular terrorists who "regard violence as a way of instigating the correction of a flaw in a system that is basically good or as a means to foment the creation of a new system," religious terrorists instead "seek vast changes in the existing order." We discussed earlier how this connects to a strategy of propaganda of the deed. A thorough analysis shows that the violent activities Bowers sponsored—as well as those Stoner and his followers committed—do not make sense as mere acts of reactionary racism or vigilante terrorism. It doesn't require much prescience to predict that killing four young girls in a church in Birmingham or killing a conservative civil rights figure like Medgar Evers in front of his family would foment strong reactions like a race riot. Such riots would represent the best hope of drawing federal troops into the state and escalating the violence. But federal intervention in state affairs ran counter to the very currents of southern culture. Only diabolical men such as Bowers would want intervention, because it could provoke a race war, the one Wesley Swift prophesied.

THE ARC OF THE UNIVERSE

To a follower of Swift at the beginning of 1968, such a prophecy must have seemed almost at hand. The racial tensions spotlighted during the nonviolent period of the civil rights movement from 1954 to 1965 did not disappear with the passage of the Voting Rights Act. As global economic forces began to take working-class jobs overseas and out of America's ghettos and inner cities, blacks were left with new political rights but even fewer economic opportunities. Frustrations began to fester, and even as Dr. King shifted his focus from political justice to socioeconomic justice, more and more blacks began to gravitate from his larger message of nonviolence to the more militant message of someone like Stokely Carmichael, who famously coined the term *Black Power*. It was Carmichael who once said, "Every courthouse in Mississippi ought to be burned down tomorrow to get rid of the dirt and the mess."[27] To Sam Bowers, who hoped that provocations in Mississippi would erupt in federal intervention, and then reprisals from black militants, Carmichael's words must have been music to his ears. And while blacks did not burn down the courthouses of Mississippi, by 1968 violence was becoming the outlet of choice for many victims of de facto racism.

In 1965 the race riots in the Watts neighborhood of Los Angeles, California, started a trend that would plague America throughout the decade. The next few years saw riots in Chicago, Illinois; Newark, New Jersey; Detroit, Michigan; and dozens of other cities across the country. Some estimates say that in the "long, hot summer" of

1967 alone, there were more than 150 race riots across the country. The civil disorder had changed the entire national security posture of the United States, involving the United States military in domestic intelligence gathering in unprecedented fashion. No longer was the national security infrastructure concerned about communists in Martin Luther King Jr.'s organization; they were focused on identifying black militants.

By 1968 America was a racial powder keg ready to explode, and the fuse of King's assassination pushed the country closer to Swift's dark dream than anything else in the nation's history. It created the waves of violence and rioting that the national security establishment so feared and Sam Bowers and J. B. Stoner so desired. The military and National Guard were deployed in America's cities in ways not seen since the Civil War. As much as structural flaws and philosophical limitations impeded law enforcement's investigation of the King assassination, it must be remembered that the tension in the nation also circumscribed their efforts.

But in the end, just as Senator Bobby Kennedy pacified a crowd on the evening of April 4 in Indianapolis, Indiana, by appealing to King's vision of mutual understanding and racial harmony, it was Martin Luther King Jr. who triumphed, even in death. The riots calmed. Sam Bowers and his ilk largely faded into the background, and the Klan has never approached its level of influence and violence since King's death, although recent events, like the white supremacist gathering in Charlottesville, Virginia, seem ominous and remind us that King's admirers must stay vigilant.

King, whose shift to socioeconomic issues had cost him popularity with white America before his death, has become an icon of righteous citizenship and racial harmony. Few historical figures are as respected across America's increasingly polarized, ideological spectrum. His ideas have been adopted by President Barack Obama, who kept King's picture in the Oval Office, and by Glenn Beck, who held a major event in King's honor. This reverence has even made some of King's contemporaries uneasy, as some commentators have sought to remind Americans that King died on his way to the Poor People's Campaign, after marching in solidarity with union workers.

But if King's ideas about racial justice are celebrated, if his views on economic justice are debated, one of his core goals, legal justice, has until recently largely been ignored. Time and time again, King marched in memory of or eulogized those whose murders shocked the nation into guilt over its larger inequities. King demanded justice for the victims, even as racists plotted to kill the minister on such visits. The names of those victims join King's on the civil rights memorial outside the Southern Poverty Law Center in Alabama in honor of those who lost their lives in the civil rights struggle, but also as a sad reminder that so many of their homicides have gone unsolved.

Starting in the 1990s, cultural and structural changes in the South allowed some of these crimes to be prosecuted. Notably, Sam Bowers went to prison in 1998 for the murder of Vernon Dahmer, the killing he ordered in 1966, and Bowers died behind bars forty years after Dahmer. Emboldened by such successful prosecutions, the Justice Department formed a Cold Case Initiative to investigate civil rights violence. To date, it has had very little success. But the Justice Department's renewed efforts lack legitimacy for another reason: they do not include an investigation into the murder of Martin Luther King Jr.

In response to the claims of James Earl Ray's attorney, William Pepper, whose theories had gained favor with some of King's family members, the Justice Department did briefly reanalyze the King assassination in 2000. Having once again dismissed Ray's improbable Raul stories, and having found that Pepper's chief witness to a conspiracy, Loyd Jowers, was someone who was clearly motivated by money and not honesty, the Justice Department correctly dismissed Pepper's arguments. Narrowly focused, this effort in 2000 did not examine many of the key outstanding issues in the case.

A renewed effort by the Cold Case Initiative should not simply focus on the material developed in this book but also on crime-scene evidence that has never been subjected to the latest forensic analysis. The authors have located the fingerprint evidence in the King murder and have taken high-resolution digital copies of prints that were never tied to James Earl Ray. The FBI made exhaustive efforts to tie several of these prints to potentially innocent contributors, such as FBI agents and police officers, with no success. The Justice Department attempted to run these prints through the FBI's fingerprint database system, the Integrated Automated Fingerprints Identification System (IAFIS) in 2000 with no success, but technology was new and the database was not as robust.

The authors can now report a major development in this area. Thanks to the efforts of Dr. Cliff Spiegelman, a statistics expert who specializes in (among other things) the application of probability theory to forensic science, the authors were able to reach out to various crime labs in the United States. Michele Triplett, forensic operation manager for the King County crime lab in Seattle, was gracious enough to offer her services; one of her best fingerprint analysts at the lab, Cynthia Zeller, has reviewed several prints and sent them through Next Generation Identification (NGI), a newer and more robust update of the IAFIS system that allows for palm print checks as well as fingerprint comparisons. Balancing her time with ongoing cases, Zeller has uploaded more than a dozen prints from various King assassination crime scenes into the system. As of yet, there have been no matches generated by the database—that is to say, nothing in the FBI's central database triggered a match. But similar concerns remain from the from the original Department of Justice IAFIS analysis of King assassination prints in 2000: it is not clear if the database includes prints that go back before 1968; it is not clear if the FBI ever obtained the fingerprints from a number of KKK members; and the Seattle crime lab lacks the authority to request that other, independent state and city crime labs run searches through their local databases. When time permits, some of these issues may be resolvable, and the authors continue to collect fingerprints in hopes that Ms. Zeller and Ms. Triplett can find potential suspects.

Such a delayed response to the murder would not have surprised Martin Luther King Jr., who liked to tell audiences frustrated with the pace of social reform that "the arc of the universe is long, but it bends toward justice."[28] Decades have passed since his murder, but the time has come for a serious pursuit of justice. Digging into the King murder mystery may force us to revisit parts of our history that are uncomfortable or painful to remember. It may disclose oversights or connections to informants that are embarrassing or shocking. It may disclose additional, private information about Dr. King himself, details that remind us of his human flaws but that also remind us of his courage in fighting for justice even in the face of scurrilous rumors aimed at besmirching his character and dignity. But these efforts could not be more uncomfortable and painful, more embarrassing and shocking, than King's murder itself, which deprived the country of a leader who challenged America and Americans, however burdensome it was, to be a better country, to be better human beings. Perhaps it is only through such sacrifice and suffering, as Bobby Kennedy reminded that crowd in Indianapolis, that we truly achieve understanding. "Even in our sleep," Kennedy told the audience, quoting the Greek poet Aeschylus, "pain that does not forget falls drop by drop upon the heart until, in our despair, against our will, comes wisdom, through the awful grace of God."

ACKNOWLEDGMENTS

This book would not have been be possible without the generous contribution of time, insights, and critiques by a number of individuals. The authors would especially like to thank Jerry Mitchell, Rev. Ed King, Charles Faulkner, Dr. Gerry McKnight, Dan Christensen, David Boylan, Keith Beauchamp, and Dan Dunn for their contributions and support of our efforts. We also offer our special thanks for support and encouragement to our family members Lawrence Wexler and Kathy Hancock, and to our good friends Debra Conway and the late Sherry Feister.

We are also grateful to others who were very helpful in our research into the King murder and the network of white supremacists and associated individuals surrounding the case. We especially appreciate the comments and contributions of Joy Washburn, Rev. Ken Dean, Ernie Lazar, Jason Kull, Roanna Elliott, Pat Speer, William Kelley, Dr. Chester L. Quarles, Carmine Savastano, Dr. John Drabble, Rex Bradford, Mark Zaid, Kel McClanahan, Lamar Waldron, Donald Tomasello, Scott Kercher, and Alan Kent.

Dr. Cliff Spiegelman, Michele Triplett, and Cynthia Zeller deserve enormous credit for risking their professional reputations to analyze the fingerprints in a case as controversial as the MLK assassination. I hope together we can find that break that changes the course of history.

In addition, a number of individuals provided important information to the authors via interviews. That list includes Janet Upshaw, retired Detective Fred Sanders, and several others who, due the sensitive nature of their comments, we will not identify. Special thanks go to Donald Nissen, who, for fear for his life, stayed quiet for many years, but who—in the face of those same fears—finally confirmed his own experiences with a White Knight bounty offer on the life of Martin Luther King Jr.

We would also like to express our appreciation to several former FBI agents who were interviewed for this book. Whatever flaws plagued the original FBI investigation into Martin Luther King Jr.'s murder, those problems should be attributed to the bureau's institutional impediments, and to the man who put those structures in place, Director J. Edgar Hoover. Individual field agents commonly worked the case to the best of their ability, producing key investigative reports and data. We feel that their individual work was severely limited by organizational and reporting procedures as well as Director Hoover's own personal biases—including his extreme dislike of Dr. King. The former agents we'd most like to thank for their dialog with us are Stanley Orenstein and Gerard Robinson. The late Jim Ingram was also especially helpful in providing early insights to the authors, and he continued to encourage our research until he passed away.

Likewise, staff members at several institutions were most helpful to our work. We would like to thank the staff of the Civil Rights Museum in Memphis; of the National Archives and Records Administration at College Park, Maryland; of the Record Information and Dissemination Section of the FBI; and of the library research staff at the University of Michigan—especially Julie Herrada, for her relentless pursuit of material from the "Dixon Line."

The support we received from our publisher has made what could have been a stressful experience one that was, instead, enjoyable and meaningful. Jack Shoemaker, Jennifer Alton, Megan Fishmann, Jennifer Kovitz, and Wah-Ming Chang helped us add a new level of quality to our work. And this project would not have been possible without Charlie Winton, who has been our advocate, mentor, editor, and friend all in one package.

APPENDIX

PHOTOGRAPHS

REVEREND WESLEY ALBERT SWIFT: Once an active leader in a KKK group, Swift, a Californian, formed the Church of Jesus Christ Christian in 1946. Under his interpretation of the Christian scripture, Armageddon would come from a race war that would "cleanse" the world of Jews and other minorities. Tapes of Swift's sermons were sent across North America through a mailing list and his message was amplified through a network of traveling ministers. (*Source: FBI field office.*)

SAMUEL HOLLOWAY BOWERS JR.: The Imperial Wizard of the White Knights of the Ku Klux Klan of Mississippi, Bowers was heavily influenced by the racist message of Wesley Swift. Under Bowers's leadership, the White Knights were the most violent Klan group in America in the 1960s according to the FBI. (*Source: The Mississippi department of Archives and History*)

SIDNEY CROCKETT BARNES: An extremist who left Florida for Alabama in the 1960s, Barnes was one of Wesley Swift's most devoted followers. He helped spread the Christian Identity message and the vision of an End Times race war to a number of individuals in the Southeast, including a young Tommy Tarrants, who become a terrorist for Sam Bowers. Files show that Barnes plotted to kill Martin Luther King in 1963 and 1964. (*Source: Jackson field office*)

J. B. STONER: A leader and cofounder for the racist National States Rights Party, Stoner would run on the NSRP ticket as their vice presidential candidate in 1964. Alongside Connie Lynch, a minister for Wesley Swift, Stoner inflamed audiences across the country with his message of white supremacy. He was one of James Earl Ray's attorneys.

THOMAS ALBERT TARRANTS III: This mug shot of Tommy Tarrants was taken after his arrest, in 1967, for possession of an illegal firearm. Tarrants was arrested with Sam Bowers after their vehicle was pulled over for reckless driving in Mississippi. Responsible for several acts of violence in Mississippi, Tarrants was not connected to these crimes until May of 1968. Yet he was inexplicably investigated in connection with the King murder within days of the act. Tarrants rejected the Swift message in favor of traditional Christianity in the 1970s and is now an evangelical minister. (*Source: Jackson field office*)

DONALD EUGENE SPARKS

DONALD SPARKS: Sparks was a home burglar and a contract killer in a criminal network that would later be popularly known as the Dixie Mafia. FBI records indicate that the White Knights of the Ku Klux Klan of Mississippi approached Sparks with a bounty contract on Martin Luther King Jr.'s life in 1964. A member of Sparks's criminal gang would later be connected with a bounty offer, from the same group, in 1967. (*Donald Sparks's 1967 FBI Most Wanted Photo. Source: FBI*)

Bessie Brewer's rooming house the day after King's murder. It shows extensive brush still present, contradicting the claims by some that the area was cleared immediately after King's murder. Some argue that an assassin may have fired from within the brush rather than from the building itself; others assert that the brush was too thick and thus not an ideal shooting location. (*Source: Shelby County Registry of Deeds*)

This photo shows the rear side of Bessie Brewer's rooming house Canipe Amusement Company. The accused assassin, James Earl Ray, allegedly dropped a bundle of incriminating items, including the murder weapon, in the alcove outside Canipe. Some argue he was afraid he would confront police officers with the material in hand. (*Source: Shelby County Registry of Deeds*)

The rear of Bessie Brewer's rooming house, the side facing the Lorraine Motel, where Martin Luther King Jr. was staying. Accused assassin James Earl Ray allegedly fired the shot that killed King from the second floor. (*Source: Shelby County Registry of Deeds*)

The bathroom on the second floor of Bessie Brewer's rooming house. This is where law enforcement and prosecutors believe accused assassin James Earl Ray fired the shot that killed King. (*Source: Shelby County Registry of Deeds*)

The view of the Lorraine Motel from the opening in the second-floor bathroom window at the rear of Bessie Brewer's rooming house. A shooter would have had a clear view of King from this vantage point. The markings indicate the location of King's body (C) and his room (B). (*Source: Shelby County Registry of Deeds*)

View of the rear of Bessie Brewer's rooming house from the second floor of the Lorraine Motel across the street. (*Source: Shelby County Registry of Deeds*)

The green blanket that contained several key pieces of allegedly incriminating evidence, including a rifle and binoculars, found in the alcove in front of Canipe Amusement Company. The material in this bundle would, over time, lead the FBI to James Earl Ray. Ray would claim that someone else planted the material to frame him. (*Source: Shelby County Registry of Deeds*)

A laundry receipt from the Piedmont Laundry in Atlanta, Georgia, for Eric Galt, James Earl Ray's alias, dated April 1, 1968. This receipt, as well as the confirmation from the laundry's owner, presented a dilemma for James Earl Ray and his attorneys. Hoping to avoid the incrimination charge that Ray was stalking King prior to the Memphis murder, Ray asserted that he went to Memphis before King even decided on a return date to lead another sanitation workers' strike. This receipt was strong evidence that Ray first went to Atlanta, King's hometown, and went to Memphis only after King announced his plans. (*Source: House Select Committee*)

The contents, sans rifle, found wrapped in a green bundle outside of Canipe Amusement Company. Through diligent work, the FBI was able to trace several of these items to accused assassin James Earl Ray. (*Source: National Archives*)

The Remington Gamemaster .30-06 rifle found in the bundle outside Canipe Amusement Company. Authorities claim this was the murder weapon, but ballistics tests were inconclusive. The rifle was traced to a gun shop in Birmingham, Alabama, and eventually to James Earl Ray. Ray bought a different weapon the day before but returned that gun for the Gamemaster. The store owner remembered Ray as claiming that he exchanged weapons on the advice of his brother-in-law. Ray claims this was a false reference to Raul. (*Source: National Archives*)

James Earl Ray's Wanted photo, issued by the FBI in their massive manhunt for the alleged King assassin. It was only by the third week of April 1968 that the FBI finally connected Ray to the numerous aliases he used in Memphis and elsewhere. (*Source: Shelby County of Deeds*)

Both of these pictures were separately identified by James Earl Ray as being (or strongly resembling) the mysterious figure Raul, the man who Ray claims manipulated his movements and eventually helped frame him for killing King. The photo on the left is of an individual photographed in Dealey Plaza after President John F. Kennedy's assassination; Ray said this person bore a "striking resemblance" to Raul. The photo on the right is a passport picture of an individual identified by Ray's last attorney, William Pepper, as being Raul; Ray positively identified this person as Raul. The Justice Department, in their 2000 investigation, checked this individual's whereabouts on the day of the King murder and determined he had a firm alibi. In either event, the readers may judge for themselves if Ray's two pictures could possibly be of the same person. (*Source: Justice Department*)

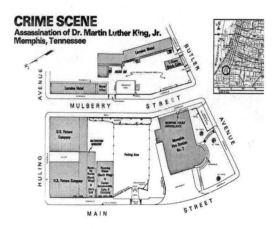

A schematic layout of the crime scene. (*Source: National Archives*)

PEOPLE

DR. WESLEY SWIFT: A militant extremist and Klan organizer who
formed the Church of Jesus Christ Christian in 1946 in Lancaster,
California, where he lived, Swift advocated a variation on Christianity that held that Jews were really the offspring of Satan, and that they
manipulated other, non-white minorities, into a conspiracy against
white Christians. Swift believed the world would be purified of Jews
and minorities through a race war. His sermons on these matters,
distributed through a network of newsletters and tape recordings, inspired militant white supremacists across the country, including Sam
Bowers, J. B. Stoner, Sidney Barnes, Colonel William Potter Gale,
and others.

SAMUEL HOLLOWAY BOWERS: Bowers was the Imperial Wizard,
or leader, of the White Knights of the Ku Klux Klan of Mississippi
in the 1960s. Under Bowers's leadership, the White Knights became,
according to the FBI, the most violent Klan group in America. A
devoted follower of Wesley Swift, Bowers was personally responsible
for plotting the murders of the three civil rights workers in the Mississippi Burning case and for ordering the firebombing of the home
of voting rights activist Vernon Dahmer in 1966, which resulted in
Dahmer's death. Bowers also plotted the murder of farmer Ben Chester White in hopes of luring Martin Luther King Jr. into an ambush if
King came to protest the White killing. Congress investigated Bowers as a potential suspect in King's murder, but investigators never
interviewed him. Bowers was convicted for his role in the Mississippi
Burning murders in 1967 and sentenced to ten years in prison; he was
not convicted for the Dahmer murder until 1998, when he was sentenced to life in prison. He died in prison in 2006.

JESSE BENJAMIN "J. B." STONER: A Nazi aficionado, J. B. Stoner
was one of the most active and outspoken white supremacists in America from the 1950s on through the 1970s. Stoner was the legal counsel

for the supremacist group the National States Rights Party and one of its leading voices, running for office, including, in 1964, vice president, under its banner on a number of occasions. With his close associate Conrad "Connie" Lynch, a minister in Wesley Swift's church, Stoner led counter-rallies against King's marches and other similar protests. He was suspected of plotting numerous bombings across the Southeast against black and Jewish targets. He offered a contract on Martin Luther King Jr.'s life in 1958 and was investigated by Congress in the 1970s as a possible suspect in King's murder. He was protected by attorney-client privilege, however, as he was one of convicted assassin James Earl Ray's attorneys in 1968–69. Stoner also had connections to James Venable and Joseph Milteer; some of the leading members of the White Knights of the Ku Klux Klan of Mississippi actively supported Stoner. Stoner was speaking to several White Knights on the evening of April 4, 1968, when MLK was killed.

JAMES VENABLE: Venable was the longtime leader of the National Knights of the Ku Klux Klan (NKKKK), the second-largest KKK group in America in the 1960s, headquartered in Stone Mountain, Georgia, with subordinate groups across the country as far as California. Venable shared a law office with J. B. Stoner in Atlanta, Georgia. Venable was suspected of plotting to kill Martin Luther King Jr., with Stoner, in 1965. Venable also knew Joseph Milteer and employed Floyd "Buddy" Ayers.

FLOYD "BUDDY" AYERS: An associate of James Venable, Ayers was, according to one witness, the bagman for the King murder, supplying money from Atlanta to Mississippi in connection with a bounty offer on Dr. King. Ayers gained national attention when he infiltrated King's funeral in 1968 and then later allegedly tried to kidnap King's father.

JOSEPH MILTEER: A rabid white supremacist, Joseph Milteer was an active supporter of the National States Rights Party, a devoted follower

of Wesley Swift, and the founder of his own independent (racist) political group, the Constitution Party. Independently wealthy, Milteer
traveled the country as a salesman, often meeting with other white
supremacists, such as James Venable. Milteer is famous for having been
secretly caught on tape, two weeks before the assassination of President John F. Kennedy, predicting the president would be shot with a
high-powered rifle from a high-story building. On that same tape, he
said that others were plotting to kill Martin Luther King Jr. Milteer
was in Atlanta, Georgia, when James Earl Ray fled to that city after
the murder of King. A confidential source of researcher Lamar Waldron says that Milteer secretly raised the money to kill King in 1968.

COLONEL WILLIAM POTTER GALE: Gale was a chief aide to
General Douglas MacArthur before returning to the United States
and becoming one of the leading white supremacists in the country.
He was a minister in the Church of Jesus Christ Christian and formed
his own paramilitary group, the California Rangers. In the 1970s,
Congress investigated Gale as a suspect in the King murder, connect-
ing him specifically to a King murder plot involving Admiral John
Crommelin, Noah Jefferson Carden, and Sidney Crockett Barnes.

ADMIRAL JOHN CROMMELIN: A WWII naval hero before entering civilian life and becoming one of the major voices of white supremacy in the nation, Crommelin was a leading member of the National
States Rights Party and ran on the party's ticket for vice president of
the United States of America in 1960. He was also a devoted follower
of Wesley Swift. He helped indoctrinate Thomas Tarrants into Swift's
worldview. Congress also investigated him as a suspect in the King
assassination in the late 1970s; he cooperated but denied he had any
involvement.

NOAH JEFFERSON CARDEN: A member of the White Citizens
Council of Mobile, Alabama, a group that led "formal" opposition
to the civil rights movement in that city, Carden was close to Sidney

Barnes and also knew Thomas Tarrants. Congress investigated him as a suspect in the King assassination.

SIDNEY CROCKETT BARNES: A white supremacist from Florida who was forced to flee to Mobile, Alabama, in the early 1960s because he was "too hot" for authorities, Barnes would later become a minister in Wesley Swift's church. He played tapes of Swift for anyone who would listen and helped indoctrinate many into Swift's cause, including a young Thomas Tarrants and Kathy Ainsworth, who became terrorists for Sam Bowers. Files show that Barnes plotted to kill Martin Luther King Jr. in 1963 and 1964. Congress investigated him as a suspect in the King assassination in the late 1970s; he openly refused to cooperate with the investigation. In 1968, he moved to Jackson, Mississippi, where he was closely associated with a number of men in the White Knights of the Ku Klux Klan of Mississippi, including Danny Joe Hawkins.

DANNY JOE HAWKINS: A militant member of the White Knights of Mississippi, Hawkins's entire family, especially his father, Joe Denver Hawkins, were known for their extreme hatred of blacks and Jews. Hawkins, along with Tommy Tarrants and Kathy Ainsworth, participated in a series of bombings from 1967 to 1968. On April 4, 1968, the day Rev. King died, Hawkins was arrested going the wrong way on a one-way street after attending J. B. Stoner's rally in the White Knights stronghold of Meridian, Mississippi.

KATHY AINSWORTH: A young Mississippi schoolteacher who led a double life as one of the chief terrorists of the White Knights in 1967 and 1968, Ainsworth was raised by her white supremacist mother, Margaret Capomacchia, to hate Jews and blacks. She was very close to Sidney Crockett Barnes, who gave her away at her wedding. Ainsworth joined Danny Joe Hawkins and Tommy Tarrants in a string of attacks against black and Jewish targets in 1967 and 1968. In one of those attacks, in Meridian, Mississippi, in June 1968, she replaced Danny Joe Hawkins as Tarrants's partner in crime, only to be shot and killed in a sting operation. Her mother would later relay supposed inside information related to the King murder and implicating Tommy Tarrants, to FBI informant Willie Somersett.

THOMAS ALBERT TARRANTS III, A.K.A. "TOMMY" OR "THE MAN": Tarrants was the self-described chief terrorist for the White Knights of the Ku Klux Klan of Mississippi in 1967 and 1968. Only in his twenties at the time, Tarrants was already closely affiliated with a number of white supremacist leaders, notably John Crommelin and Sidney Barnes. Having engaged in "petty" acts of racism from his high school days in 1963–66, Tarrants moved to Laurel, Mississippi, in 1967 and convinced Sam Bowers to use him in violent bombing operations directed at black and Jewish targets. He joined forces with Kathy Ainsworth and Danny Joe Hawkins. His participation was unknown to the FBI until late May 1968. In the week prior to King's murder, Tarrants went "underground" to launch a guerrilla campaign against the U.S. government. The reporter Jack Nelson includes references that suggest Tarrants may have been considering assassinating Rev. King, and he was a person of interest to the FBI in the immediate wake of King's murder. Tarrants was wounded in the June 1968 sting operation that killed Ainsworth. He was sentenced to thirty years in prison but was released early after he made a conversion to mainstream Christianity. He is now an active evangelical minister who has renounced his past views and ways. He denies any involvement in the King murder, and the authors believe efforts were made to frame him for the crime.

DONALD EUGENE SPARKS: A major criminal in the 1960s, Sparks was known for burglaries but was also a contract killer. His exploits eventually earned him a place on the FBI's Ten Most Wanted List. He was part of a gang of traveling criminals known as the new James gang, after its informal leader, Jerry Ray James. The group was concentrated in Oklahoma and included his close associate Rubie Charles

Jenkins, among others. Law enforcement would later consider the Jerry Ray James gang, and many others like it, a major criminal threat and label it the Dixie Mafia, even though these groups lacked the organization of the Sicilian Mafia and were not all concentrated in the Southeast. The so-called Dixie Mafia may have, however, been responsible for more killings than other organized crime groups in the 1970s. Separate reports say that the White Knights approached Sparks with an offer to kill Martin Luther King Jr. in 1964. A member of Sparks's criminal gang would later be connected with a bounty offer, also from the White Knights, in 1967.

LEROY McMANAMAN: Described by the FBI as a "big time criminal operator," McManaman was a career miscreant who was known for organizing a string of home burglaries in Kansas and for running an interstate car-theft ring with Rubie Charles Jenkins. Jenkins said that McManaman, who spent considerable time in Oklahoma, was a part of a gang with Jenkins and Sparks. McManaman is alleged to have approached a fellow, soon-to-be-released inmate, Donald Nissen, with a $100,000 bounty offer on MLK's life in 1967. Nissen reported that plot to the FBI, who superficially dismissed it.

GROUPS

THE CHURCH OF JESUS CHRIST CHRISTIAN (CJCC): This is the ministry Wesley Swift formed in 1946 that preached an extreme and violent form of Christian Identity beliefs. These included the ideas that Jews were the offspring of Satan and that other minorities were subhuman. A major tenet for the church was the idea that a race war would purify the world, especially of Jews. This ideology continues to have a powerful influence over white supremacists and racist groups to this day.

THE WHITE KNIGHTS OF THE KU KLUX KLAN OF MISSIS-
SIPPI (WKKKK): The most violent Klan group in America, led by
Samuel H. Bowers, its Imperial Wizard, the White Knights was
formed in December 1963 with members from the Original Knights
of the Ku Klux Klan (out of Louisiana) and others in Mississippi.
These men were disaffected with the lackluster response to integration in the South, and pushed for greater and bolder acts of violence.
At its peak from 1964 to 1965, the White Knights membership may
have had reached ten thousand, though by 1968 membership was less
than a few hundred. The FBI credits the group with over three hundred separate acts of violence; most notably, the White Knights are
credited with killing three civil rights workers in Neshoba County,
Mississippi (the Mississippi Burning murders), killing voting rights
activist Vernon Dahmer in 1966, and a wave of bombings against
black and Jewish targets from the fall of 1967 through the summer of
1968. Its most notable members, beyond Bowers, included Danny Joe
and Joe Denver Hawkins, Burris Dunn, Julius Harper, Alton Wayne
and Raymond Roberts, Byron de la Beckwith, Deavours Nix, and L.
E. Matthews. Kathy Ainsworth and Thomas Tarrants may have been
informal members of the group, as some documents describe them as
members of the "Swift Underground" who performed terrorist acts on
behalf of the White Knights.

THE NATIONAL STATES RIGHTS PARTY (NSRP): The NSPR
was the overt, political face of white supremacy in the 1960s, even as
it covertly recruited and inspired groups and individuals to perform
acts of extreme violence. Formed by J. B. Stoner and Edward Fields
in 1958, the group ran candidates for office, including vice president of
the United States, although they never received even a small fraction
of the national vote. On the other hand, the NSRP was actively involved in some of the most violent acts of resistance to integration in
America, acts so extreme that they even offended local Klan groups,
such as the United Klans of America in Alabama. The NSRP had

its headquarters in Atlanta, Georgia, and then in Birmingham, Alabama, and it focused its activities in the Southeast. Its major publication, *The Thunderbolt*, was a major source of information for racists across the nation.

THE NATIONAL KNIGHTS OF THE KU KLUX KLAN (NKKKK): This was, in the 1960s, the second-largest Klan organization in the United States, after the United Klans of America (UKA), in terms of membership. Headquartered in Stone Mountain, Georgia, the National Knights was led by Imperial Wizard James Venable. The NKKKK had affiliated groups and Klaverns across the country, including in Ohio and California. Notably, the California Knights of the Ku Klux Klan (CKKKK), formed in 1966 and led by Wesley Swift minister William V. Fowler, were an offshoot of the NKKKK. James Venable spoke to the California Knights on several occasions in 1967.

THE "TRAVELING CRIMINALS" OR "CROSSROADERS" OR "DIXIE MAFIA": These were loosely knit groups of outlaws willing to commit crimes, especially robbery and theft, across long distances. More of a phenomenon than an official organization, career criminals would join forces in decentralized gangs and work across state lines for major jobs. Primarily engaged in bootlegging across state lines, as some states remained "dry" after Prohibition was repealed in 1934, these criminals expanded their activities in the late 1950s and through the 1960s. This became more and more common as increasingly available phone communication and interstate travel, by plane or over the new interstate highway system, made cross-state activity more possible. The "traveling criminals" were especially active in two regions: the Southeast (stretching from the Mississippi Delta to Florida) and the Great Plains. Not to be confused with the Sicilian Mafia, these criminals lacked a hierarchy and were far less structured than conventional, organized crime syndicates. They were often, at the same time, more bold than the Sicilian Mafia, targeting even law enforcement officials (famously Sheriff Buford Pusser in Tennessee) and federal judges. By the 1970s, this loose-knit coalition was one of the major forces for criminal activity in the United States, with some crediting its members as having committed more actual killings than the Sicilian Mafia. In the late 1960s and early '70s, in response to this growing criminal gang, law enforcement began using the shorthand "Dixie Mafia," even though both terms are misnomers.

WHITE CITIZENS COUNCILS: These groups were formed, major city by major city, in the 1950s after the *Brown v. Board of Education* decision by the U.S. Supreme Court set the stage for ending segregation; their goal was to formally undermine integration. Often comprised of prominent business and civic leaders, they used their influence and resources to outwardly oppose the civil rights movement in a more "respectable" and legal way than that of the Ku Klux Klan. However, many White Citizens Council members were directly and indirectly tied to more violent groups, such as the NSRP and the KKK, even if those connections were often informal and covert. Joseph Milteer claimed to be an informal member of the Atlanta White Citizens Council, and Noah Jefferson Carden was a member of the Mobile White Citizens Council. Both men were connected with purported plots to kill Martin Luther King Jr.

AMERICANS FOR THE PRESERVATION OF THE WHITE RACE (APWR): Formed in the mid-1960s in Mississippi, this group was similar to the White Citizens Councils, in providing an outwardly "civil" response when undermining integration efforts. The group would, for instance, raise money for the defense funds for racists accused of hate crimes or publish newsletters opposing the integration of schools. However, the FBI recognized the APWR as a front for the White Knights, and its most prominent members and leaders were almost all, to a person, followers of Sam Bowers.

TIMELINE

1946	The Church of Jesus Christ Christian is founded by former Klan organizer Rev. Wesley Swift in Lancaster, California.
1957–58	Wave of bombings of Jewish synagogues across the Southeast; J. B. Stoner is suspected of planning the bombings, but he is never convicted for them.
1958	The National States Rights Party (NSRP) is formed in Tennessee; J. B. Stoner is its legal counsel. In Alabama, Stoner offers to plot the murder of several civil rights leaders, including Rev. King, for money.
September 1962	Riots at the University of Mississippi over the admission of its first black student, James Meredith, galvanize militant white supremacists across America.
May 1963	King's room at the Gaston Motel in Birmingham is destroyed by a bomb; almost simultaneously, the home of King's brother, A. D. King, is destroyed by a bomb.
June 1963	Assassination of Mississippi NAACP activist Medgar Evers by white supremacist Byron de la Beckwith; riots in Jackson, Mississippi, erupt following Evers's funeral.
September 1963	Former admiral John Crommelin, Noah Carden, Sidney Crockett Barnes, and former colonel William Potter Gale, all Swift followers, reportedly

plot a King assassination in Birmingham, Alabama. Bombing of the 16th Street Baptist Church in Birmingham, Alabama, by Klansmen kills four young girls; riots follow.

December 1963   The White Knights of the Ku Klux Klan of Mississippi is formed by disaffected Klan members in Louisiana and Mississippi; Sam Bowers is named their Imperial Wizard (leader).

1964   Reports say Carden, Crommelin, and Barnes continue to plot the murder of King. Reports say the White Knights are pursuing a contract-for-hire murder plot against King involving a criminal killer.

May 1964   In St. Augustine, Florida, the cottage where King was supposed to have been staying is the target of a machine-gun attack.

July 1964   The first of several major urban race riots breaks out in New York City. Sam Bowers inspires the murder of three civil rights activists in Neshoba County, Mississippi, in what will be known as the Mississippi Burning killings.

1965   The FBI receives informant reports that J. B. Stoner and National Knights of the Ku Klux Klan Imperial Wizard James Venable are plotting to murder Rev. King. Informant Delmar Dennis informs the FBI of a White Knights plot to assassinate King in Selma, Alabama.

February 1965   Swift follower Keith Gilbert plots to kill Rev. King in Los Angeles.

June 1965   National Knights–connected racist Daniel Wagner
                     says he was recruited into a failed plot to kill Mar-
                     tin Luther King Jr. in Ohio.

August 1965   Urban race riots in the Watts section of Los Ange-
                     les, California, receive national attention.

January 1966   Voting rights activist Vernon Dahmer dies in Mis-
                     sissippi as a result of a firebombing/shooting attack
                     plotted by the White Knights and Sam Bowers.

June 1966   On orders of Sam Bowers, innocent farmer Ben
                     Chester White is killed in hopes of luring Rev.
                     King into an ambush in Mississippi.

April 1967   James Earl Ray escapes from the Missouri State
                     Penitentiary in Jefferson City, Missouri.

May 1967   Soon-to-be released inmate Donald James Nissen
                     is approached by a fellow prisoner with a $100,000
                     bounty offer from the White Knights on the life of
                     Rev. King. James Earl Ray, now an escaped fugi-
                     tive, visits St. Louis and finds work in Illinois.

June 1967   Donald Nissen, released from Leavenworth Pen-
                     itentiary, reveals the $100,000 plot to the FBI.
                     Start of the "Long Hot Summer": urban race riots
                     erupt across America including in Atlanta, Geor-
                     gia; Boston, Massachusetts; and Tampa, Florida.
                     James Earl Ray flees to Canada in hopes of eventu-
                     ally escaping North America. Nissen is asked by a
                     Klan-connected acquaintance to deliver a package
                     to Jackson, Mississippi; he later learns the package
                     contained money for the King bounty.

July 1967	Race riots continue across the country.

August 1967   Failing to escape North America, James Earl Ray returns to the United States, specifically to Birmingham, Alabama. He assumes the false identity of Eric Starvo Galt and purchases a white Ford Mustang.

September 1967   Despite an FBI crackdown on its operations, the White Knights begin a months-long wave of bombings against black and Jewish targets; the bombings are later attributed to Thomas Albert Tarrants III.

October 1967   James Earl Ray moves from Birmingham, Alabama, to Mexico. Sam Bowers and six others are convicted for their roles in the Mississippi Burning murders; Bowers is sentenced to ten years but is released on appeal bond.

November 1967   James Earl Ray moves from Mexico to Los Angeles, California.

December 1967   James Earl Ray takes a trip to New Orleans, Louisiana, after visiting the California headquarters of segregationist third-party candidate and former Alabama governor George Wallace. Donald Nissen violates his parole and flees Atlanta, Georgia, after being threatened by a stranger for talking to authorities. Sam Bowers and Tommy Tarrants are arrested in Mississippi for reckless driving; Bowers is acquitted and Tarrants avoids trial.

January 1968   James Earl Ray moves to a run-down part of Los Angeles and stays in the St. Francis Hotel.

February 1968   James Earl Ray pursues the possibility of plastic surgery.

March 1968   According to the St. Francis Hotel manager, Allan O. Thompson, a mysterious visitor named James C. Hardin, who earlier had called James Earl Ray, visits Ray. Ray files a change-of-address card indicating he will move to Atlanta, Georgia, Martin Luther King Jr.'s hometown.

March 17, 1968   Per reporter Jack Nelson, Tommy Tarrants visits the Reverend Wesley Swift in California to get a rifle to kill King; Tarrants denies this in 2007.

March 18, 1968   MLK speaks at a rally for the Memphis Sanitation Workers Strike.

March 22, 1968   James Earl Ray shows up in Selma, Alabama, the same day King has a speaking engagement. Thomas Albert Tarrants III, the self-described chief terrorist for the White Knights, jumps bond and goes underground to wage guerrilla warfare against the U.S. government.

March 24, 1968   James Earl Ray arrives in Atlanta and rents a room in a rooming house on Peachtree Street.

March 28, 1968   Ray visits Birmingham, Alabama, and purchases a rifle; on this same day, King arrives to lead the Memphis sanitation workers in a protest march; the march turns violent, and King returns to Atlanta.

March 29, 1968   Rev. King announces he will return to Memphis the following week. Sam Bowers places a phone call to Birmingham, Alabama. In Birmingham, James Earl Ray purchases a .243 rifle.

March 30, 1968   James Earl Ray exchanges the .243 for a better, more expensive gun, the Remington Gamemaster .30-06 at the supposed suggestion of his "brother-in-law."

April 1, 1968   According to records and testimony, James Earl Ray returns to Atlanta, Georgia; Ray denies this.

April 2, 1968   James Earl Ray drives to Memphis, Tennessee.

April 3, 1968   King returns to Memphis to lead another protest march.

April 4, 1968   At 6:01 p.m., outside the Lorraine Motel in Memphis, Tennessee, a rifle bullet fatally wounds Martin Luther King Jr.

NOTES

CHAPTER 1: THE WARNING

1. Donald Nissen, in discussion with authors, November 9, 2009. The authors have had repeated conversations and interviews with Nissen over a period of years.

2. FBI, "Alleged Offer of $100,000 by White Knights of the Ku Klux Klan, Jackson, Mississippi, to Anyone Who Kills Martin Luther King." Main King File, file 100-1006671, section 73, at 207-210. In the authors' first contact interview, Nissen confirmed every detail in the June 1967 report without access to the document and without prompting by the authors—with one exception. The document claims that Nissen and McManaman were acquainted prior to going to prison. The FBI does not record and transcribe interviews with witnesses and does not directly quote them in reports. Instead, an agent reconstructs the interview from notes. The authors' experience, after reading thousands of such records in more than one case, is that the majority of details in an FBI report can be corroborated but agents are apt to misreport minor details. Rather than simply take Nissen's word for it, the authors compared Nissen's biography and prison/criminal records with McManaman's. There does not appear to be any overlap in their histories whereby the two could have developed a relationship. On this front, the FBI report appears to be wrong.

3. FBI, "Airtel from SAC Kansas City to Director, Re: Alleged Offer of $100,000 by White Knights of the Ku Klux Klan, Jackson, Mississippi, to Anyone Who Kills Martin Luther King; Serial: 157-472" (July 21, 1967). File obtained by the authors via Freedom of Information Act (FOIA).

4. FBI, "Airtel from SA Charles Kokes to SAC, Jackson, Re: Threat to Kill Martin Luther King 3/24/65; Serial: 157-2832" (April 6, 1965), and FBI, "Airtel from SAC, Kansas City to SAC, Jackson, Subject: MURKIN; Serial: 44-1917-SUB-E-6711." Two examples of this are the stories of Jack Maynard Ray and Carlos Lee Billings. In 1965, Ray, a former convict, told the FBI that a member of the Durham Citizens Council in North Carolina, George McLamb, approached him with a $5,000 offer to kill either James Farmer, the leader of the Congress of Racial

Equality, or Martin Luther King Jr. Ray, who has no relationship to James Earl
Ray, said the goal was to kill King in Alabama or Mississippi, where, McLamb
asserted, Ray could avoid prosecution. McLamb predictably denied this. Independently, and in that same year, Carlos Lee Billings, another individual with
a criminal background, told the FBI that two men involved him in a $50,000
bounty plot to kill King during the Selma voting protests. The purported attempt fell through, and Billings, who reasserted his claims years later, did not
know either man's last name, leaving the FBI with little to work with in confirming the claim. It is of course possible that one or both men made up the
story—which is the point: without the ability to corroborate the claims, the FBI
could not advance these and similar leads. It is worth noting that both plots, like
the Tampa plot discussed later in this chapter, originated in the Southeast.

5. FBI, "Airmail from SAC Tampa to Director" (July 4, 1974), MURKIN 44-
   38861, and Janet Upshaw, in discussion with the authors, December 15, 2010.
6. FBI, "Memo from Rosen to Deloach" (August 23, 1968), King Assassination
   FBI Central Headquarters File, MURKIN 44-38861-512, section 69, avail-
   able online at the Mary Ferrell Foundation, accessed September 15, 2010,
   www.maryferrell.org/mffweb/archive/viewer/showDoc.do?mode=search
   Result&absPageId=113185.
7. FBI, "Airtel from SAC Oklahoma City to Director re: Donald Eugene
   Sparks . . ." (April 24, 1968), King Assassination FBI Central Headquarters
   File, MURKIN 44-38861-2926; and FBI, "Airtel from Tampa to Director re:
   Donald Eugene Sparks . . ." (April 18, 1968), King Assassination FBI Central
   Headquarters File, MURKIN 44-38861-1331.
8. Bernie Ward, *Kansas Intelligence Report: The Dixie Mafia* (Topeka, KS: The Office of Attorney General Vern Miller, 1974).
9. "Fourth Suspected Robbery Gang Member Held," *Gadsden Times*, July 6, 1966.
10. Dee Cordry, "Dixie Mafia, Part 1," *The State Crime Bureau Journal* (blog), Oc-
    tober 11, 2009, statecrimebureau.wordpress.com/2009/10/21/dixie-mafia-part-1.
11. Faith Serafin, *Wicked Phenix City* (Charleston, SC: The History Press, 2014),
    107, 131.
12. "Biloxi's Tale of Murder, Extortion and Racy Photos," *New York Times*, De-
    cember 29, 1991.
13. Joe Shuras, post #27599 on "Buford Prusser," Topix, Selmer Forum, December
    20, 2013, www.topix.com/forum/city/selmer-tn/ToCBKHSBE7IASV4NG/p635;
    December 20, 2013, post #27599 by Veteran Cop-Joe Shuras.
14. Ward, *Kansas Intelligence Report*.
15. FBI, "Airtel from SAC Oklahoma City to Director re: Donald Eugene
    Sparks . . ." (April 24, 1968), King Assassination FBI Central Headquarters
    File, MURKIN 44-38861-2926; and FBI, "Airtel from Tampa to Director re:
    Donald Eugene Sparks . . ." (April 18, 1968), King Assassination FBI Central
    Headquarters File, MURKIN 44-38861-1331.
16. Michael Newton, *The Encyclopedia of Unsolved Crimes* (New York: Infobase
    Publishing, 2009), 199.
17. Nissen, in discussion with the authors, November 9, 2009.
18. Paul Hendrickson, "From the Fires of Hate, an Ember of Hope," *Washington Post*,
    July 22, 1998, www.washingtonpost.com/wp-srv/style/features/dahmer.htm.

CHAPTER 2: THE SPONSORS

1. Hendrickson, "From the Fires of Hate."
2. Jack Nelson, *Terror in the Night: The Klan's Campaign against the Jews* (New York: Simon & Schuster, 1993), 53–54, 103–104, 123.
3. Douglas O. Linder, "Mississippi Burning Trial (1967)." Famous Trials, accessed July 30, 2017, famous-trials.com/mississippi-burningtrial.
4. Charles Marsh, *God's Long Summer: Stories of Faith and Civil Rights* (Princeton, NJ: Princeton University Press, 1997), 50–53.
5. Hendrickson, "From the Fires of Hate."
6. *Activities of the Ku Klux Klan Organizations in the United States: Hearings Before the Comm. on Un-American Activities*, 89th Cong. 2936 (February 1 and 7–11, 1966), available online at the Internet Archive, www.archive.org/stream /activitiesofkuklo5unit/activitiesofkuklo5unit_djvu.txt.
7. Buckles made this claim while attempting to collect money to pay the ex-convict, who we believe to be Sparks. He told the audience that the "job would cost $1,200 with $400 upfront and $800 when the job was completed." One might assume that this is a different plot from the Sparks bounty because the dollar amounts are different. But it may be that they were attempting to raise part of the bounty when the rest of the money may have been coming from other sources, including the treasury of the group. An amount of $13,000 would be awfully high to Klan members when the White Knights had yet to prove themselves in any act of major violence. The Evers murder occurred before the group officially formed, and the Mississippi Burning murders were still two weeks away from the time of Buckles statement. The references to the Evers assassination and to the ex-convict are too reminiscent of the Sparks bounty to dismiss as a coincidence.
8. William H. McIlhany, *Klandestine: The Untold Story of Delmar Dennis and His Role in the FBI's War against the Ku Klux Klan* (New Rochelle, NY: Arlington House, 1975), 54.
9. Taylor Branch, *Pillar of Fire: America in the King Years* (New York: Simon & Schuster, 1998), 414, 498.
10. Gerald McKnight, *The Last Crusade: Martin Luther King Jr., the FBI, and the Poor People's Campaign* (Boulder, CO: Westview Press, 1998), 93.
11. Branch, *Pillar of Fire*, 414.
12. Jerry Mitchell, "KKK Killed Ben Chester White, Hoping to Lure and Kill MLK," *Clarion-Ledger*, June 10, 2014, www.clarionledger.com/story/journeyto justice/2014/06/10/ben-chester-white-kkk-mlk/10277551/.
13. Ibid.
14. Stuart Wexler, *America's Secret Jihad* (Berkeley, CA: Counterpoint Press, 2015), 143-45. This section, from "Bowers remained . . ." to ". . . White's homicide in Natchez" is taken almost verbatim, from Wexler's book.
15. Marsh, *God's Long Summer*, 64–66.
16. Ibid.
17. Ibid.
18. Rubie Jenkins, in discussion with the authors, March 18, 2010. Jenkins was elderly at the time of our conversation, but he was sharp. Jenkins was able, without prompting, to identify McManaman as a "redneck from Kansas." He acknowl-

edged that McManaman was "in our gang," referring to his group with Sparks. He denied knowing anything about the King assassination. We do not have any reason to believe Jenkins was ever in the loop from the available evidence.

19. "Pardon Recalls Famed Case Here," *Great Bend Daily Tribune*, August 23, 1957.

20. Leroy B. McManaman, Appellant, v. United States of America. 327 F.2d 21 (10th Cir. January 28, 1964).

21. FBI, "Re: Alleged Offer of $100,000 by the WKKKKOM to Anyone Who Kills Martin Luther King Jr. . . ." (July 24, 1967), Jackson Field Office File 157-7990. We obtained these files via the FOIA. They contain a number of key reports, including the prison records on Nissen and McManaman. These records confirm they worked at the same shoe factory. They confirm McManaman's desire to marry Sybil Eure. They also include a handful of informant reports, in which the FBI asked informants about a $100,000 bounty offer. These are notable for a few reasons. For one thing, they asked only a handful of informants, when the record indicates that they had dozens of them. Secondly, while none of the informants directly heard of a bounty, one informant said he heard that the White Knights were considering putting out flyers offering a $100,000 bounty on King's life. There is no evidence that any such flyers were ever printed. But this suggests that the White Knights had an expectation of having a large sum of money even when they supposedly were losing funds paying for legal defenses.

22. Ibid.

23. Ibid.

24. Nelson, *Terror in the Night*, 143–45.

25. FBI, "Sidney Crockette Barnes" (November 30, 1971), summary file, at 13. File obtained by the authors via FOIA.

CHAPTER 3: THE MOTIVE

1. FBI, "Summary Report of SA Samuel Jennings, White Knights of the Ku Klux Klan," FBI Jackson Field Office File 157-63, bureau file 157-1552, (February 24, 1969). Danny Joe Hawkins is also described as being a member of an "underground hit squad."

2. Michael Barkun, *Religion and the Racist Right: The Origins of the Christian Identity Movement* (Chapel Hill: University of North Carolina Press, 1994), 48–55.

3. Ibid., 23–28.

4. Ibid., 171–77.

5. Ibid., 104–11, 240.

6. Chester Quarles, *Christian Identity: The Aryan American Bloodline Religion* (Jefferson, NC: McFarland and Company, 2004), 180.

7. Wesley Swift, "Zero Hour, 2-4-62" (sermon), February 4, 1962, Dr. Wesley Swift Library, transcript, swift.christogenea.org/articles/ws1962.

8. Wright Thompson, "The Ghosts of Mississippi," ESPN: Outside the Lines, accessed April 16, 2015, sports.espn.go.com/espn/eticket/story?page=mississippi62.

9. Wesley Swift, "As in the Days of Noah, 9-30-62" (sermon), September 30, 1962, Dr. Wesley Swift Library, transcript, swift.christogenea.org/articles/days-noah-9-30-62.

10. Nelson, *Terror in the Night*.

11. "States Rights," OurCampaigns.com, accessed July 28, 2017, www.ourcam paigns.com/PartyDetail.html?PartyID=45.

12. Comm. on Un-American Activities, *Para-Military Organizations in California White Extremist Organizations, Part II: National States' Rights Party The Present-Day Ku Klux Klan Movement*, H.R. Rep., 90th Cong. 1st Sess. 63 (December 11, 1967).

13. Patsy Sims, *The Klan*, 2nd ed. (Lexington: University Press of Kentucky, 1996), 104.

14. Wexler, *America's Secret Jihad*, 1–13.

15. David Boylan, "A League of Their Own: A Look Inside the Christian Defense League," Cuban Information Archives, last modified March 17, 2006, accessed September 12, 2010, cuban-exile.com/doc_026-050/doc0046.html.

16. J. Harry Jones, *The Minutemen* (New York: Doubleday, 1968), 191.

17. James Aho, *The Politics of Righteousness: Idaho Christian Patriotism* (Seattle: University of Washington Press, 2014), 57.

18. Wikipedia, s.v. "Kenneth Goff," accessed August 3, 2017, en.wikipedia.org/wiki /Kenneth_Goff.

19. Eric Norden, "The Paramilitary Right," *Playboy* 16, no. 6 (1969), available online at the Harold Weisberg Archive at Hood College, accessed April 16, 2015, jfk .hood.edu/Collection/Weisberg%20Subject%20Index%20Files/M%20Disk /Minutemen/Item%20006.pdf.

20. Boylan, "A League of Their Own."

21. Wesley Swift, "Confusion Throughout the Land (10-9-67)" (sermon), October 9, 1967, Dr. Wesley Swift Library, transcript, swift.christogenea.org/articles /confusion-throughout-land-10-9-67.

22. Sims, *The Klan*, 135.

23. Norden, "The Paramilitary Right."

24. Ibid.

25. Thomas A. Tarrants, *The Conversion of a Klansman: The Story of a Former Ku Klux Klan Terrorist* (Garden City, NY: Doubleday, 1979), 50.

26. Diane McWhorter, *Carry Me Home: Birmingham, Alabama; The Climactic Battle of the Civil Rights Revolution* (New York: Simon & Schuster, 2001), 114–15.

27. Martin Luther King Jr., *Why We Can't Wait* (New York: Penguin, 2000), 96.

28. Ibid.

29. McWhorter, *Carry Me Home*, 341, 484, 495.

30. Ed King, in discussion with Stuart Wexler, September 25, 2014.

31. FBI, "Airtel from SAC Miami to FBI Director re: BAPBOMB, Sidney Crock-ette Barnes a.k.a. Racial Matters" (March 12, 1964), FBI file. The file contains two FBI follow-up interviews with Barnes pertaining to the 1963–64 reports. Barnes told the agents that he felt the 16th Street Baptist Church bombing had been done by "niggers," and that he had no personal knowledge of it, although if he had, he would never give it to government agents. He stated he had been playing golf at a local resort, with one of the other suspects (Noah Carden), on the date of the bombing. A separate report, from an FBI informant, reveals the informant's conversations with Barnes after the FBI interviews in which Barnes discussed how he had misdirected the FBI and his concern that the FBI apparently had identified or would shortly identify the men behind the bomb-ing because they already knew that Gale and Carden had been in Birmingham. Barnes also noted that when Carden was arrested on bootlegging charges, one

of a number of weapons taken into custody actually belonged to William Potter Gale of California; Carden was holding it for him at his home in Alabama. Carden's name will come up again in this book, associated with the Swift network and its members in North Carolina.

The informant reports also note a discussion in which Barnes states that because the primary target (designated as "Coon") had not shown up in Mobile, the point man from Alabama was unable to execute the plan. Barnes also stated that the FBI had way too much information about their plans for targeted Negro leaders and they were going to have to alter their plans.

32. Ed King, in discussion with Stuart Wexler, September 25, 2014.

33. FBI, "Airtel from SAC Miami to FBI Director re: BAPBOMB, Sidney Crockette Barnes a.k.a. Racial Matters" (March 12, 1964), FBI file.

34. *Activities of the Ku Klux Klan Organizations in the United States: Hearings Before the Comm. on Un-American Activities*, 89th Cong. 3428, 3441–42 (February 1, 7–11, 1966) (testimony of Daniel Wagner), available online at the Internet Archive, www.archive.org/stream/activitiesofkuklo4unit/activitiesofkuklo4unit_djvu .txt. While on the surface the purported assassination scheme seems fanciful— involving the murder of not only Dr. King but also the president of the United States and others—it does seem clear that at least Wagner was serious about the effort. Making the matter more confusing, and perhaps even more bizarre, is that the scheme included, among Witte's intended victims, her husband and NKKKK higher-up William Hugh Morris. Witte apparently wanted to shift allegiances to the Dixie Knights of the KKK and take the rest of the Ohio Klans (from the NKKKK) with her; killing Morris was part of this plan.

35. Ibid.

36. "The News of the Day," *Los Angeles Times*, May 20, 1964.

37. Keith Gilbert, email to authors, June 4, 2016.

38. Marsh, *God's Long Summer*, 54–66.

39. "The Klan Ledger," *Candy Brown Papers*, Wisconsin Historical Society: Freedom Summer Digital Collection, accessed April 16, 2015, cdm15932.contentdm .oclc.org/cdm/ref/collection/p15932coll2 /id/34854.

40. Marsh, *God's Long Summer*, 72.

41. McIlhany, *Klandestine*, 54.

42. Ibid.

43. Wesley Swift, "Confirmed of God In Christ, 2-6-67" (sermon), transcript, Dr. Wesley Swift Library, February 6, 1967, swift.christogenea.org/articles /confirmed-god-christ-2-6-67.

44. Neil Hamilton, *Militias in America: A Reference Book* (Santa Barbara: ABC-CliO, 1996), 63.

CHAPTER 4: THE TARGET

1. Large portions of this the text in this chapter and in the book as a whole have been taken verbatim from Stuart Wexler and Larry Hancock, *The Awful Grace of God* (Berkeley, CA: Counterpoint Press, 2013) and Stuart Wexler, *America's Secret Jihad: The Hidden History of Religious Terrorism in the United States* (Berkeley, CA: Counterpoint Press, 2015). The former is the original source for *Killing*

King and the latter includes several chapters devoted to the relevant topic.

2. Martin Luther King Jr., "I Have a Dream Speech" (speech), August 28, 1963, Lincoln Memorial, Washington, D.C., transcript, www.americanrhetoric.com /speeches/mlkihaveadream.htm.

3. Frank Newport, "Martin Luther King Jr.: Revered More After Death Than Before," *Gallup*, January 16, 2006, www.gallup.com/poll/20920/martin-luther-king-jr-revered-more-after-death-than-before.aspx.

4. David Bernstein, "The Longest March," *Chicago Magazine*, July 25, 2016, www .chicagomag.com/Chicago-Magazine/August-2016/Martin-Luther-King-Chicago-Freedom-Movement.

5. Martin Luther King Jr., "Nobel Lecture: The Quest for Peace and Justice" (speech), December 11, 1964, University of Oslo, Oslo, Norway, transcript and Adobe Flash audio, www.nobelprize.org/nobel_prizes/peace/laureates/1964 /king-lecture.html.

6. Malcolm X, "Message to the Grassroots" (speech), November 10, 1963, King Solomon Baptist Church, Detroit, Michigan, Michigan, teachingamerican history.org/library/document/message-to-grassroots.

7. "1964: Harlem Riots Flare Anew; 2 Negroes Shot," *New York Herald Tribune* (European Edition), July 21, 1964, iht-retrospective.blogs.nytimes.com/2014/07 /20/1964-harlem-riots-flare-anew-2-negroes-shot.

8. "WSB-TV newsfilm clip of Dr. Martin Luther King, Jr. speaking about recent race riots in New York State as well as the 1964 presidential election, New York, New York, 1964 July 27," WSB-TV newsfilm collection, reel 1188, 00:00/05:28, Walter J. Brown Media Archives and Peabody Awards Collection, the University of Georgia Libraries, Athens, Georgia, as presented in the Digital Library of Georgia, available online at the Civil Rights Digital Library, crdl.usg.edu /export/html/ugabma/wsbn/crdl_ugabma_wsbn_46952.html?Welcome.

9. Mitchell Lansberg and Valery Reitman, "From the Archives: Watts Riots, 40 Years Later," *Los Angeles Times*, August 11, 2005, www.latimes.com/local/la-me-watts-riots-40-years-later-20050811-htmlstory.html.

10. Martin Luther King Jr., "MLK Speaking to the People of Watts" (speech), August 19, 1965, Los Angeles, transcript, www.thekingcenter.org/archive /document/mlk-speaks-people-watts#.

11. Ibid.

12. Jim Vertuno, "LBJ Tapes Show MLK Feared 'Full Scale' Race War," *Associated Press*, April 11, 2002, www.myplainview.com/news/article/LBJ-tapes-show-MLK-feared-full-scale-race-war-8891725.php.

13. William J. Collins and Robert A. Margo, "The Economic Aftermath of the 1960s Riots in American Cities: Evidence from Property Values," National Bureau of Economic Research 10493 (May 2004); 22, Table 1.

14. Black Panther Party, "The Ten-Point Program," October 15, 1966, available online at the Marxist History Archive: History, www.marxists.org/history/usa /workers/black-panthers/1966/10/15.htm.

15. William M. King, "What Do We Want?" *Vietnam Generation Journal*, 4, no. 3–4 (November 1992), availabe online at The Sixties Project, accessed June 11, 2017, www2.iath.virginia.edu/sixties/HTML_docs/Texts/Narrative/King_What_ We_Want.html.

16. "Meet the Press: Civil Rights Special Featuring Black Leaders," *Meet the Press*, New York, NY: NBC Universal, August 21, 1966, transcript available online at NBC Learn, archives.nbclearn.com/portal/site/k-12/flatview?cuecard=48789.

17. Steve Chapman, "Political Violence Is as American as Apple Pie," *Chicago Tribune*, June 16, 2017, www.chicagotribune.com/news/opinion/chapman/ct-political-violence-america-history-perspec-chapman-20170616-column.html.

18. Martin Luther King Jr., "It Is Not Enough to Condemn Black Power . . ." October 1966, available online at the King Center, accessed June 11, 2017, www .thekingcenter.org/archive/document/it-not-enough-condemn-black-power#.

19. Allen D. Grimshaw, *A Social History of Racial Violence* (New Brunswick, NJ: 1969), 318, note 3. This poll focused on major cities. Polls of the entire country suggested less support for riots and violence in general.

20. Adam Fletcher Sasse, "A History of the North Omaha Riots," North Omaha History, accessed June 11, 2017, northomahahistory.com/2013/07/19/a-history-of-the-north-omaha-riots. Sasse includes a picture of a newspaper from the time period and this is the source for the direct quote. He does not provide a full enough picture to identify the original newspaper.

21. "Civil Disorder Chronology," s.v. "1967." In *CQ Almanac 2010*, 66th ed., edited by Jan Austin. Washington, D.C.: CQ-Roll Call Group, 2011. library.cqpress .com/cqalmanac/document.php?id=cqal67-1312893#H2_7.

22. Kirsten West Savali, "Martin Luther King Jr.: 'My Dream Has Turned into a Nightmare,'" *The Root*, January 16, 2017, www.theroot.com/dr-martin-luther-king-jr-my-dream-has-turned-into-a-1791257458.

23. "Civil Disorder Chronology."

24. Max Herman, "Newark (New Jersey) Riot of 1967." In *The Encyclopedia of American Race Riots*, vol. 2 edited by Walter C. Rucker and James N. Upton (Westport, CT: Greenwood, 2007), 452.

25. Sandra West, "Negro Reporter Tells Detroit Riot Story," *The Times-News*, July 24, 1967, news.google.com/newspapers?nid=1665&dat=19670724&id=T59 PAAAAIBAJ&sjid=ayQEAAAAIBAJ&pg=6942,1623294&hl=en. The passages from "In Newark . . ." to ". . . merchandise" were taken verbatim from Wexler, *America's Secret Jihad*, 131–32.

26. Collins and Margo, "The Economic Aftermath of the 1960s Riots."

27. Marquis Childs, "Guns Sales Mount as Tension Grows in This Strange Moment in History," *The Morning Record*, August 15, 1967, news.google.com /newspapers?nid=2512&dat=19670815&id=WiVIAAAAIBAJ&sjid=Xg ANAAAAIBAJ&pg=775,5019331&hl=en.

28. Martin Luther King Jr., "The Other America" (speech), March 14, 1968, Grosse Pointe High School, Grosse Pointe Farms, Michigan, transcript, www .gphistorical.org/mlk/mlkspeech/mlk-gp-speech.pdf.

29. Nate Jones, "Document Friday: 'Garden Plot': The Army's Emergency Plan to Restore 'Law and Order' to America," National Security Archive, accessed July 11, 2017, nsarchive.wordpress.com/2011/08/12/document-friday-garden-plot-the-armys-emergency-plan-to-restore-law-and-order-to-america.

30. U.S. Army Center for Military History, "US Department of the Army Civil Disturbance Plan 'GARDEN PLOT' 10-September-1968," National Security Archive, accessed July 11, 2017, nsarchive.files.wordpress.com/2010/09/garden-

plot.pdf. As we argue in the appendix to the book, the actions of the army in response to civil disturbances have been widely perceived as a sign that the national security state wanted to kill King—to prevent civil unrest. But as this chapter implies, anyone paying any attention to the conditions on the ground would realize that King was one of the only remaining voices of nonviolence with any influence left in the black community. Killing him would be more, not less likely to incite riots and unrest.

31. *U.S. News & World Report*, "Is Insurrection Brewing in the U.S.?" December 25, 1967, available online at the King Center, www.thekingcenter.org/archive /document/us-news-and-world-report-insurrection-brewing-us#.

CHAPTER 5: THE MONEY

1. Nissen, in discussion with Stuart Wexler, November 9, 2009.
2. FBI, "Re: Alleged Offer of $100,000 by the WKKKKOM to Anyone Who Kills Martin Luther King Jr.," July 24, 1967, File 157-7990, Jackson Field Office.
3. Nissen, in discussion with Wexler.
4. Chester L. Quarles, *The Ku Klux Klan and Related American Racialist and Antisemitic Organizations: A History and Analysis* (Jefferson, NC: McFarland and Co., 1999), 89.
5. Ibid.
6. "Transcript of the Milteer-Somersett tape," November 9, 1963, Mary Ferrell Foundation, accessed June 20, 2017, www.maryferrell.org/pages/Transcript_ of_Milteer-Somersett_Tape.html.
7. Lamar Waldron with Thom Hartmann, *Legacy of Secrecy: The Long Shadow of the JFK Assassination* (Berkeley, CA: Counterpoint, 2008), 604–605.
8. Ibid., 510–11.
9. Ibid., 511.
10. Chester Higgins, "Hair-Raising Experience: 'Kidnap' Try of King Sr. Foiled; Add More Police Protection," *Jet*, May 2, 1968, 14–19, books.google.com/books? id=UTgDAAAAMBAJ&pg=PA14&dq=hair-raising+experience+kidnap+ king&hl=en&sa=X&ei=9BpjUb_nDJC3oQHYtYCQDw&ved=0CDEQ6 AEwAA#v=onepage&q=hair-raising%20experience%20kidnap%20king& f=false.
11. Rev. John Ayers, interview with authors, November 16, 2010. Ayers had no information about any involvement in any plot by his brother to kill Dr. King, but he did not dismiss the idea out of hand, either. He added that his brother went to Alabama during the Selma voting rights protests, demonstrations that earned national attention for the level of violence, including killings, inflicted against nonviolent protestors. Rev. Ayers noted that his brother returned from Selma in a state of panic and even went into a brief period of hiding with another brother. The minister has always wondered if his brother participated in the Selma violence.
12. Higgins, "Hair-Raising Experience," 17. The article incudes an anecdote from civil rights activist Julian Bond. Bond described frequent and odd encounters with Floyd Ayers that both point to Ayers's eccentricity and paint a picture of a man with conflicted ideas of race relations. In terms of the latter, Bond described an instance in which Ayers arranged for Bond to jump a line to eat at a

restaurant. Bond did not know how Ayers had those connections. On the other hand, Ayers also told Bond that he worked for "the Ku Klux Klan, the FBI and the CIA," an unlikely story, for which there is no evidence.

13. "James Earl Ray: Selected Chronology," available online at the Harold Weisberg Archive at Hood College, accessed March 30, 2013, jfk.hood.edu/Collection /White%20Materials/White%20Assassination%20Clippings%20Folders /Miscellaneous%20Folders/Miscellaneous%20Study%20Groups/Misc-SG-109.pdf.

14. "Gaol Fugitive Sought Over King Murder," *Sydney Morning Herald*, April 22, 1968.

15. U.S. House Select Committee on Assassinations, *Investigation of the Assassination of Martin Luther King Jr.: Appendix to the Hearings Before the Select Comm. On Assassinations*, 95th Cong., 2nd Sess., vol. xiii, 267–74, available online at the Mary Ferrell Foundation, www.maryferrell.org/mffweb/archive/viewer /showDoc.do?docid=95664&relPageid=271.

16. FBI, "Memo from Rosen to Deloach" (August 23, 1968), King Assassination FBI Central Headquarters File, section 69, 58, available online at the Mary Ferrell Foundation, accessed March 30, 2013, www.maryferrell.org/mffweb/archive /viewer/showDoc.do?mode=searchResult&absPageid=1131852. It is important to point out that several prisoners told the FBI that they were not aware of any Cooley organization and that they had not overheard any bounty offers on King's life. Here one is faced with two issues. First, there is the classic argument from silence. The offers could easily have been floated to a select few people whom certain inmates could trust. To do otherwise would risk exposing the plot to prison authorities and snitches. Beyond that, many of these interviews were of people in prison. Any prisoner who knew of either the Cooley organization or plots against King would be risking retaliation from fellow inmates. The fact that Britton, Brown, and Louis Raymond Dowda (discussed later in this chapter) spoke of a prison bounty offer when they were out of prison, and confirmed parts or all of their statements years later, gives them an air of credibility one does not find in the other stories. As will become clear later on, Dowda appears to have had inside information that he withheld from investigators, that goes even further in explaining his insights about Ray looking for the "right price" to kill King. It is also worth pointing out that the authors dismissed the claim by another prisoner, Raymond Curtis, who clearly wanted to profit by creating an exaggerated story about insider information of a bounty on King.

17. W. Pate McMichael, "The Plot to Kill a King," *St. Louis Magazine*, September 17, 2009.

18. "James Earl Ray: Selected Chronology."

19. U.S. House Select Committee on Assassinations, *Investigation of the Assassination of Martin Luther King Jr.: Final Report*, 95th Cong., 2nd Sess., 360–64, available online at the Mary Ferrell Foundation, maryferrell.org/showDoc .html?docId=800&search=byers#relPageId=390&tab=page. Both attorneys and Byers confirmed the story to the committee, but Randall pointed out that Byers may have been inventing a King bounty story to smoke out the FBI informant. In this scenario, as envisioned by Randall, Byers would have harbored (apparently justifiable) suspicions about the informant; he would have given the King story to both attorneys in the presence of the informant in 1973 and then wait

to see if law enforcement would later confront him about the King bounty later. If they did, Byers would know who the snitch was by process of elimination. But the attorney admitted this was only speculation, and Weenick, the other attorney, asserted that "there seems to be no credible reason why he would have made it up and told it to me and Randall."

20. Ibid.

21. McMichael, *Klandestine*, 336.

22. Martin Hay, "Stuart Wexler & Larry Hancock, *The Awful Grace of God: Religious Terrorism, White Supremacy, and the Unsolved Murder of Martin Luther King, Jr.*" (review), Two Kennedys and A King, July 26, 2013, kennedysandking .com/martin-luther-king-reviews/wexler-stuart-and-larry-hancock-the-awful-grace-of-god-religious-terrorism-white-supremacy-and-the-unsolved-murder-of-martin-luther-king-jr. Hay's critical review of our earlier work is riddled with egregious errors that will be discussed in various endnotes and in the epilogue. The pull quote, at the beginning of the review for instance, claims that we "put Ray" at the Grapevine when we, in fact, never say that. Instead, we argue that Ray could have maintained some form of contact with the plotters by way of his brothers, who ran the bar. In the earlier book we say that Ray did not immediately pursue the plot after escaping prison; in this update we do. Hay goes on to claim that we have no credible evidence that Ray ever heard of a bounty. But to make this claim Hay dismisses the accounts of prisoners like Britton. He makes a blanket statement that all the prisoners who directly heard of Ray discussing a plot were looking for more lenient prison sentences and/or bounty rewards. But he has no actual evidence of this for any prisoner—Hay is the one speculating, not us. As a point of fact, Thomas Britton, who heard Ray discuss a $100,000 offer from a businessman's association, was not even in prison at the time he made his claim and expressly said he did *not* want a reward. Brown confirmed hearing Ray discuss a bounty years after the fact.

23. FBI, "Interview of Louis Raymond Dowda" (April 26, 1968), Memphis Murkin Field Office File. Sub K, vol. 2, serial 143A.

24. FBI, "Report of Alan G. Santanella" (May 17, 1968), Atlanta Murkin Field Office File 44-2386, at 29-41; and FBI, "Airtel, From SAC Los Angeles To Director, FBI, Re: Louis Raymond Dowda" (May 7, 1968), Memphis Murkin Field Office File. Sub E-686E. Dowda said that he stopped to visit a former prisoner in Kansas City, Paul Alvin Lail. Dowda said Lail would have known Ray but they were not especially close. He also stopped to visit a former prison guard from MSP, Pete Petrie, but Dowda claimed that they did not discuss Ray and that he did not even know, at that point—five months after the fact—that Ray had escaped. He also visited with the former supervisor of the kitchen at MSP, Lloyd Helt, and Jewell Rigger, someone he described as the wife of a former prisoner who worked at a California hospital. In other interviews, without mentioning his visit to Jewell, Dowda identified that inmate (the husband) as Donald Dean Rigger—one of the only other prisoners who had befriended James Earl Ray.

25. FBI, "Report of Alan G. Santanella," at 35-36.

26. Ibid.

27. FBI, "Airtel from SAC, Jacksonville to Director, FBI re: Airtel: 1-22-74" (February 8, 1974). The source claimed that Dowda referenced six businessmen who

helped sponsor the plot. He could not remember the first name of the GM executive, but thought the last name might be Collier. It is entirely possible, given the secondhand nature of the report, that the source accidentally confused the name of the GM executive with the man who owned the Bonanza Sirloin Pit, E. R. Collins. Either way, the reference to a GM executive is important confirmation of Lamar Waldron's anonymous source on the King bounty.

CHAPTER 6: DETOUR

1. Gerold Frank, *An American Death: The True Story of the Assassination of Dr. Martin Luther King, Jr., and the Greatest Manhunt of Our Time* (New York: Doubleday, 1972), 300–301. Frank has come under deserved criticism for working, behind the scenes, with the FBI on his King assassination book, as well as others. The authors only use him for basic information.

2. Ibid., 315. Ray's understanding was a common one for the time; in interviewing other convicts at Missouri State Penitentiary, the FBI determined that there was a general knowledge of how to get Canadian identification, and the descriptions were very much in line with the process Ray followed.

3. Ray would make a number of mistakes in acquiring his new identities including misspelling names.

4. Philip Melanson, *The Martin Luther King Assassination: New Revelations on the Conspiracy and Cover-Up* (New York: SPi Books, 1994), 42. Much of the controversy over Ray's aliases involves issues developed by Professor Melanson. Melanson points out, among other things, that Ray selected names of men who bore a resemblance to James Earl Ray and that Ray adjusted the spelling of their names at suspicious times in ways that reflect someone with ongoing knowledge of the men. This is most notable with the Galt alias. At one point, Ray adjusted his use of the Galt alias to include the middle name Starvo—Eric Starvo Galt. Melanson points out that this occurred at the same time that the real Eric Galt began to use the middle initials "St.V." The real Galt, Melanson notes, used rather large circles for periods, circles Melanson said could be confused with the letter "o." Hence Ray's use of Starvo, while initially a sign that he did not know what he was doing, becomes a shocking coincidence for Melanson—someone looking at St.V. on paper might read it as "StoVo" which is strikingly similar to "Starvo." The problem here, again, is from two closely related issues. The first is that Ray himself insisted he developed his aliases. Melanson believes this is a lie, and even Ray's last lawyer, William Pepper, doubted Ray's story. But then what is the motive for Ray's lie? If, as Melanson and Pepper imply, some intelligence agency (or someone like Raul) supplied Ray with the alias, why would he lie about it? Ray openly endorsed "the government did it theories" until he died. This gets to the second problem with Melanson's theory—the assumption that, even if Ray had help with his aliases, that help, even if it was ongoing, came from U.S. intelligence operatives. Criminals used Canada as one of the major pipelines to acquire fake identification and/or leave the country. Underworld figures developed sophisticated procedures to meet that demand. Criminal groups were just as capable of supplying Ray with fake credentials and just as capable of making sure (for instance, reading Galt's mail)

that their clients updated the identities when necessary. Throwing investigators off the scent of criminal accomplices is a much better explanation for Ray's lies, assuming they even were lies, than diverting them away from the kind of shady intelligence operatives Ray always was quick to scapegoat for his actions.

5. James Earl Ray, *Who Killed Martin Luther King Jr.? The True Story by the Alleged Assassin* (New York: Marlowe, 1997), 125; and William Pepper, *Act of State: The Execution of Martin Luther King* (London: Verso, 2003), 248.

6. Report on Salwyn, President John F. Kennedy—Murder of—Assistance to the F.B.I, HSCA Administrative Folder U9, RC MP, available online at the Mary Ferrell Foundation, accessed September 15, 2010, www.maryferrell.org/mffweb /archive/viewer/showDoc.do?docId=10097&relPageId=153. Information provided by Marcelle Mathieu of Montreal.

7. Ibid.; information provided by Lise Robilland of Montreal.

8. Philip H. Melanson, *The MURKIN Conspiracy: An Investigation into the Assassination of Dr. Martin Luther King Jr.* (New York: Praeger, 1989), 44–50.

9. Ibid.

10. John Nicol, "Was the King Assassination 'Triggered' in Canada?" *CBC News*, last modified January 7, 2009, accessed December 15, 2010, www.cbc.ca/world /story/2008/04/28/fray-hearings.html. Nicol also cites an HSCA staffer, Melvin Kriedman, as saying that Congress came to believe that Ray was recruited into the plot in Canada.

11. Sims, *The Klan*, 143.

12. Charles Faulkner, "Murdering Civil Rights: Martin Luther King Jr., White Supremacy, and New Facts Supporting the Guilt of James Earl Ray," March 2013, the Mary Ferrell Foundation, March 2013, www.maryferrell.org/wiki /index.php/Essay_-_Murdering_Civil_Rights.

13. David Randall Davids, *The Press and Race: Mississippi Journalists Confront the Movement* (Jackson: University Press of Mississippi, 2000), 195.

14. Gerald Posner, *Killing the Dream: James Earl Ray and the Assassination of Martin Luther King Jr.* (New York: Harcourt Brace and Co., 1998), 170–71.

CHAPTER 7: ON HOLD

1. Ray, *Who Killed Martin Luther King?*, 77–80.

2. Waldron and Hartmann, *Legacy of Secrecy*, 531–32.

3. John Larry Ray and Lyndon Barsten, *Truth at Last: The Untold Story of James Earl Ray and the Assassination of Martin Luther King Jr.* (Guilford, CT: Lyons Press, 2008), 98–100.

4. William Bradford Huie, *He Slew the Dreamer: My Search, with James Earl Ray, for the Truth about the Murder of Martin Luther King, Jr.* (Montgomery, AL: River City, 1997), 17–69.

5. Frank, *An American Death*, 303–305. Frank's book, on larger points, should be treated with some caution. Frank enjoyed a special relationship with the FBI, one that he did not disclose, but which gave him access to government information in exchange for friendly stories.

6. Ibid., 304–305. Frank provides additional details that portray the fight as being with a group of black men, Ray arming himself with his pistol and talking

of killing them. This is one of the items for which Frank provides no specific citation. Congress, through the House Select Committee on Assassinations (HSCA) pursued this incident, interviewing the woman. She confirmed that there were two black sailors in the bar and that one was drunk, stumbling and touching her as he passed by; she felt Ray had lost his temper because the man had touched her rather than because of his race. The HSCA accepted her statement rather than favor the racial angle to the fight.

7. Ibid, 306.
8. Ibid.
9. James Earl Ray, *Tennessee Waltz: The Making of a Political Prisoner* (Saint Andrews, TN: Saint Andrew's Press, 1987), 59.
10. Posner, *Killing the Dream*, 200.
11. Waldron and Hartmann, *Legacy of Secrecy*, 540.
12. FBI, "Interview with Marie Martin" (April 13, 1968), MurKIN 1051-1175, section 9, at 263.
13. Tarrants, *The Conversion of a Klansman*, 59.
14. Swift, "Confusion Throughout the Land."
15. Newton, *Encyclopedia of Unsolved Crimes*, 177–80.
16. FBI, "Memorandum from SAC Jackson to FBI director; Subj: Suspended Racial Informant on 6/2/68" (July 12, 1968), 157-3082-18. File obtained by the authors via FOIA.
17. Nelson, *Terror in the Night*, 134.

CHAPTER 8: BACK IN BUSINESS

1. FBI, "Airtel from St. Louis to Director" (August 12, 1968), FBI Central Headquarters File, section 69.
2. Nissen, in discussion with the authors, November 9, 2009. Nissen says he told the FBI about the car-shooting incident when he was interviewed in August 1968, but the available files do not reflect this. It is possible that Nissen either neglected to tell them and is misremembering it or that the FBI did not note it in their summary report. The FBI does not tape its interviews and relies on notes. It is possible Donald told them about the car and they did not transfer the information to their report. The authors' considerable experience with FBI documents suggests that the FBI can miss or misreport details in the transcription process. Specifically, Nissen may be confusing what he told the FBI in St. Louis with what he told a prison warden in 1969, when Nissen pushed for and received a transfer to a protection facility. In speaking to the FBI in August of 1968, Nissen could have been worried about an unidentified federal law enforcement official (referenced as a go-between for the King bounty by McManaman) and chosen to be coy with his interrogators.
3. Ibid.
4. Nissen, in discussion with the authors, July 25, 2016.
5. Jesse Sublett, *1960s Austin Gangsters: Organized Crime That Rocked the Capital* (Mt. Pleasant, SC: The History Press, 2015).
6. FBI, "Airtel from St. Louis to Director" (August 12, 1968), FBI Central Headquarters File, section 69.

7. FBI, "James Venable FBI Headquarters File" (1967). File 1165004-001, 157-HQ-1628, section 2, at 3.

8. FBI, "Memorandum from SA Richard F. Kilcourse to SAC Los Angeles" (April 23, 1968), 62-5101.

9. FBI, "James Venable FBI Headquarters File."

10. Ibid.

11. Ibid. In fact, Vernable made a number of trips to California and spoke at several meetings. The file shows he was there at least on February 19, April 1, April 20, and April 28–29, 1967.

12. Comm. On Un-American Activities, *Para-Military Organizations in California White Extremist Organizations, Part II: National States' Rights Party The Present Day Ku Klux Klan Movement,* H.R. Rep., 90th Cong. 1st Sess. (December 11, 1967).

13. Faulkner, "Murdering Civil Rights." Martin Hay, a critic of our work, implies that Stein and his sister both lied about the nature of the Wallace visit. Hay places his stock in James Earl Ray, who refused to acknowledge the visit and had it stricken from a fifty-six-page stipulation of facts during his trial. The problem here is that unlike Ray, who had a motive to lie—to hide his associations with racists from investigators—neither Charlie Stein nor his sister had an obvious motive to make the story up. What's more, Ray made documented and repeated calls to the Wallace campaign while in Los Angeles.

14. FBI, "TO: Director, Atlanta, Birmingham and Miami RE: Atlanta Tel May Two Four Last" (May 5, 1968), MURKIN 44-38861-3959.

15. Wexler and Hancock, *The Awful Grace of God,* 208–209.

16. Louis Lomax, "Call Made to N.O.: Phone Booth Located in King Slayer Search," *New Orleans States-Item,* April 30, 1968, available online at the Harold Weisberg Archive at Hood College, accessed March 23, 2017, jfk.hood.edu /Collection/White%20Materials/King%20Jr%20Martin%20Luther/MLK% 20103.pdf. It is worth noting that Kent Courtney, a right-wing media personality in New Orleans, secretly recorded James Earl Ray's brother Jerry in conversation about an industrialist several months after the assassination and after James Earl Ray had been arrested. Jerry Ray was trying to find out if Courtney knew how to contact this industrialist. But Jerry Ray did not know the person's name. It is always difficult to evaluate what Jerry Ray has said in reference to the King assassination, as he has blatantly contradicted himself on numerous occasions, claiming at times to have played games with reporters and investigators with his previous comments. In this instance, as in a handful of others, he is saying something in private. But his other claim in his recorded conversation with Courtney, that this industrialist somehow "employed" James Earl Ray since August of 1967, is nonsensical. James Earl Ray's documented activities render this impossible. What this suggests is that Jerry Ray may have been "fishing" for a way to contact potential bounty sponsors, in hopes of getting help (or possibly money) from the sponsors, but that Jerry did not have a clear idea of what he was looking for. Any direct communication with his brother about potential conspirators in New Orleans would have been monitored, so Jerry may have been investigating the news reports relaying information from Charles Stein on this "industrialist." In an odd way, it suggests that Jerry Ray, whom others have accused of complicity in the King murder, was not as

well-informed about his brother's conspiratorial activities as his critics suggest. It is also worth noting, however, that Jerry Ray sought out a well-connected right-wing segregationist, Courtney, to try to make contact with this supposed industrialist. In other words, Jerry Ray, who was close to his brother James, on some level believed the King murder was connected to right-wingers. For more, see Jeffrey Caulfield, *General Walker and the Murder of President Kennedy* (Moreland Hills, OH: Moreland Press, 2015).

17. Harold Weisberg, letter to Jim Lesar (December 15, 1976), available online at the Harold Weisberg Archive at Hood College, accessed March 29, 2017, jfk .hood.edu/Collection/Weisberg%20Subject%20Index%20Files/L%20Disk /Leads%20Louisana/Item%2015.pdf.

18. Harold Weisberg, letter to Mark Lynch (August 26, 1985), available online at the Harold Weisberg Archive at Hood College, accessed March 30, 2017, jfk.hood.edu/Collection/Weisberg%20Subject%20Index%20Files/A%20Disk /ACLU/ACLU%2008.pdf.

19. FBI, "Joe Daniel Hawkins" (July 28, 1970), report of Special Agent Samuel Jennings.

20. Harold Weisberg, "Chapter 26: Lingering Questions That Should X Must X Linger" from an unpublished manuscript available online at the Harold Weisberg Archive at Hood College, accessed May 18, 2017, at 426–28. jfk.hood.edu /Collection/Weisberg%20Subject%20Index%20Files/HW%20Manuscripts /Posner%20(MLK)/Posner26.doc. Weisberg was not one to speculate, but he came to strongly consider the possibility that James Earl Ray had criminal, conspiratorial connections to Edward G. Partin, a union leader out of Baton Rouge who eventually turned against Teamster leader Jimmy Hoffa. Particularly suspicious, to Weisberg and others, was a Baton Rouge number Ray provided to his King assassination defense team. Ray claimed this number belonged to someone in Baton Rouge, whom he did not know, but whom "Raul" claimed was some sort of go-between to relay information about where they could meet. Ray said he called that number on his way out of Birmingham in October of 1967, and the unidentified individual who picked up told Ray to go to Mexico. Ray told federal investigators that he found the name for the number after laboriously going through Louisiana phone books: Herman Thompson. Thompson was an East Baton Rouge law enforcement officer with purported ties to Partin. But authors uncovered material in which Ray attributes the finding to help from Z. T. Osborne, a Nashville attorney. Z. T. Osborne was one of Jimmy Hoffa's main attorneys. It seems likely that Ray was convinced, for whatever reason, to plant damning information about Hoffa's nemesis, Partin, in the media. One should therefore be suspicious of a number of supposed leads that point toward Partin.

21. Marsh, *God's Long Hot Summer*, 138.

22. Newton, *Encyclopedia of Unsolved Crimes*, 176, 178.

23. McWhorter, *Carry Me Home*, 572.

CHAPTER 9: IN WAITING

1. FBI. "Report of Joseph T. Boston Subj: Thomas Albert Tarrants, III" (August 26, 1968), Bureau file 157-519 at 4–5.

2. Tarrants, *The Conversion of a Klansman*, 59.
3. Newton, *Encyclopedia of Unsolved Crimes*, 180.
4. FBI, "Memo to SAC Jackson; Subj: J.B. Stoner," 157-3082-19.
5. Marsh, *God's Long Hot Summer*, 64–66.
6. Newton, *Encyclopedia of Unsolved Crimes*, 179–80.
7. W. O. Dillard, *The Final Curtain: Burning Mississippi by the FBI* (Denver, CO: Outskirts Press, 2007).
8. Nelson, *Terror in the Night*, 53–54, 103–104, 123.
9. FBI, "Samuel Holloway Bowers Jr." (August 9, 1968), bureau file 157-1654, section 23, at 15.
10. Newton, *Encyclopedia of Unsolved Crimes*, 180.
11. Taylor Branch, *At Canaan's Edge: America in the King Years, 1965–68* (New York: Simon & Schuster, 2006), 486.
12. Stokely Carmichael and Charles V. Hamilton, *Black Power: The Politics of Liberation in America* (New York: Vintage Books, 1967), 44, 46–47, 50–55.
13. McKnight, *The Last Crusade*, 144.
14. Martin Luther King Jr., "The Drum Major Instinct" (speech), February 4, 1968, Atlanta, Georgia, transcript and audio, 39:11, mlk-kpp01.stanford.edu/index .php/encyclopedia/documentsentry/doc_the_drum_major_instinct.
15. "James Earl Ray: Selected Chronology."
16. Posner, *Killing the Dream*, 213.
17. Wexler and Hancock, 213–15.
18. Wexler and Hancock, *The Awful Grace of God*, 213–15.
19. Department of Justice, FOIA Response to files on James Wilborn Ashmore/J.C. Hardin, 2011.

CHAPTER 10: STALKING

1. *King Encyclopedia*, s.v. "Memphis Sanitation Workers Strike (1968)," accessed March 30, 2013. mlk-kpp01.stanford.edu/index.php/encyclopedia /encyclopedia/enc_memphis_sanitation_workers_strike_1968.
2. Wesley Swift, "Children of the Spirit" (sermon), March 17, 1968, Dr. Wesley Swift Library, transcript, swift.christogenea.org/book/export/html/792.
3. Nelson, *Terror in the Night*, 140.
4. Jerry Mitchell, "Book Probes MLK Killing," *Clarion-Ledger*, January 3, 2008, www3.nd.edu/~newsinfo/pdf/2008_01_03_pdf/Book%20probes%20MLK%20 killing.pdf.
5. Ibid.
6. Jack Nelson. Transcript of interview with Thomas Albert Tarrants, III, June 20, 1991. Jack Nelson Collection, Manuscript Archive and Rare Book Library, Emory University. MSS 1237 Box 3. The authors have edited the written transcript to reflect what was said, verbatim, in the audio tapes. Thanks to Charles Faulkner for his help in obtaining this material.
7. U.S. House Select Committee on Assassinations, *Investigation of the Assassination of Martin Luther King Jr.: Final Report*, 297.
8. "James Earl Ray: Selected Chronology."
9. Waldron and Hartmann, *Legacy of Secrecy*, 444.

10. U.S. House Select Committee on Assassinations, *Investigation of the Assassination of Martin Luther King Jr.: Appendix to the Hearings Before the Select Comm. On Assassinations*, 95th Cong., 2nd Sess., vol. xiii, 214, available online at the Mary Ferrell Foundation www.maryferrell.org/mffweb/archive/viewer/show Doc.do?mode=searchResult&absPageId=999305.

11. FBI, "Alleged Offer of $100,000 by White Knights of the Ku Klux Klan, Jackson, Mississippi, to Anyone Who Kills Martin Luther King." Main King File, file 100-1006671, section 73, at 207–10.

12. Tarrants, *The Conversion of a Klansman*, 59–60.

13. U.S. House Select Committee on Assassinations, *Investigation of the Assassination of Martin Luther King, Jr.: Final Report*, 375–76, available online at the Mary Ferrell Foundation, maryferrell.org/showDoc.html?docId=800&search=depalma #relPageId=405&tab=page. The HSCA found reports from two Minutemen, Vincent DePalma and Earle Baumgartner, independently corroborating the potential assassination of King. They also said that the Minutemen hoped to start a civil war in the United States. Given the close connections between the Minutemen and Swift, this is noteworthy, as is the fact that Tarrants, who identified closely with the Minutemen, met with Dennis Mower, a senior figure in the group, when visiting Swift in California. Mower was one of Swift's closest aides, and if former Minuteman Keith Gilbert is correct, Mower was a key figure behind the 1965 attempt to kill King with dynamite at the Palladium. Several other Minutemen insisted that the accounts of strike teams were propaganda and meant to smoke out informants like DePalma and Baumgartner. DePugh and Payson testified to this effect to the HSCA. Interestingly, documents the authors obtained reveal another Minutemen source federal investigators contacted in 1968 in the wake of King's shooting. This source also dismissed the possibility that the Minutemen killed King but for a different reason: he believed the shooting would have been more professional if they were involved. But the source pointed to another right-wing group he once belonged to as strong candidates for King's murder. This group, he insisted, was determined to kill King. Who were they? The White Knights of the Ku Klux Klan of Mississippi. For this second account see FBI, "Re: Vincent DePalma at Asheville, North Carolina" MURKIN File 44-1987-Sub 39-A (April 18, 1968).

14. FBI, "Teletype To: New Orleans From: Jackson (157-9586) re: My Call This Date Re: Eugene Smith Mansfield AKA Sunset" (April 10, 1968), MURKIN File 44-1987-Sub E-196.

15. Nelson, *Terror in the Night*, 140.

16. Department of Justice, *Report of the Department of Justice Task Force to Review The FBI Martin Luther King Jr., Security and Assassination Investigations*, January 11, 1977, available online at the Harold Weisberg Archive at Hood College, accessed March 30, 2013, at 17–20. jfk.hood.edu/Collection/Weisberg%20 Subject%20Index%20Files/O%20Disk/Office%20of%20Professional%20Responsibility%20Report%20Appendix%20C/Item%2003A.pdf. This is an internal FBI assessment of their original MLK assassination investigation.

17. "James Earl Ray: Selected Chronology."

18. Jeffrey Cohen and David Lifton, "A Man He Calls Raoul." *New Times* (April 1, 1977), at 21-37, available online at the Harold Weisberg Archive at Hood Col-

lege, jfk.hood.edu/Collection/Weisberg%20Subject%20Index%20Files/C%20 Disk/Cohen%20Jeff/Item%2006.pdf.

19. Faulkner. "Murdering Civil Rights." Larson, who was Bowers's business partner at Sambo, was a senior officer in the military reserve. But we do not know if he made the call or if he had a connection to Alabama. The timing of the call still cries out for an explanation.

20. U.S. House Select Committee on Assassinations, *Investigation of the Assassination of Martin Luther King Jr.: Final Report*, 95th Cong., 2nd Sess., 297–99, available online at the Mary Ferrell Foundation, www.maryferrell.org/mffweb /archive/viewer/showDoc.do?mode=searchResult&absPageId=69366.

21. Weisberg letter to Mark Lynch (August 26, 1985).

22. Faulkner, "Murdering Civil Rights."

23. Martin Luther King Jr., "Remaining Awake Through a Great Revolution," available online at the Martin Luther King, Jr. Research and Education Institute, Stanford University, mlk-kpp01.stanford.edu/index.php/kingpapers /article/remaining_awake_through_a_great_revolution.

24. Ibid.

25. Wesley Swift, "Power in the Word" (sermon), March 31, 1968, Dr. Wesley Swift Library, transcript, swift.christogenea.org/book/export/html/794.

26. FBI, "Urgent Teletype from Dallas Field Office to Director, Memphis and Jackson" (April 23, 1968), MURKIN 44-38861-1836.

27. Department of Justice, *Report of the Department of Justice Task Force to Review The FBI Martin Luther King Jr., Security and Assassination Investigations.*

28. Martin Luther King Jr., "I've Been to the Mountaintop" (speech), April 3, 1968, Memphis, Tennessee, transcript, available online at mlk-kpp01.stanford.edu /index.php/encyclopedia/documentsentry/ive_been_to_the_mountaintop.

CHAPTER 11: ZERO HOUR

1. U.S. House Select Committee on Assassinations, *Investigation of the Assassination of Martin Luther King Jr.: Final Report*, 95th Cong. 2nd, Sess., available online at the Mary Ferrell Foundation, accessed April 16, 2015, www.maryferrell.org/ mffweb/archive/viewer/showDoc.do?mode=searchResult&absPageId=69366.

2. Melanson, *The Martin Luther King Assassination*, 87–90.

3. Ibid., 137.

4. Michael Honey, "King's Last Crusade," History News Network, George Mason University, accessed April 16, 2015, historynewsnetwork.org/article/37087.

5. McKnight, *The Last Crusade*, 79–81.

6. Ibid., 67.

7. Melanson, *The Martin Luther King Assassination*, 69–70.

8. McKnight, *The Last Crusade*, 77–78. Sen. McClellan continued the dirty tricks even after Dr. King's murder. A mere month after Dr. King's death, McClellan himself went to Director Hoover with an explosive story that black militants were planning to hijack the Poor People's March in Washington from the SCLC and unleash a "rein of rioting, looting, and armed insurrection." Hoover ordered a full-court FBI press on the intelligence from the senator's investigators (which McClellan claimed to be airtight). The massive FBI follow-up with

its own sources produced not the slightest corroboration, and after several weeks (during which McClellan "moved" the location of his key informant from Tennessee to Alabama and finally to Atlanta), the bureau finally managed to locate the source based on contacts within McClellan's committee. It turned out the source was in Mobile, Alabama, and the bureau determined that not only did he want money for his information, but also that he was "completely unreliable."

9. Mary Elizabeth Cronin, "Andrew Young Reflects on His Struggle in the Civil Rights Movement," *Seattle Times*, November 13, 1996, seattletimes.com/special /mlk/perspectives/reflections/pillow.html.

10. U.S. House Select Committee on Assassinations, *Investigation of the Assassination of Martin Luther King Jr.: Final Report*, 95th Cong. 2nd, Sess., available online at the Mary Ferrell Foundation, accessed April 16, 2015, hmaryferrell .org/showDoc.html?docId=800&search=%22spinal_column%22+%22 fractured+the+spine%22#relPageId=320&tab=page at 290.

11. FBI, "Report by SA Joe Hester, Memphis, 10 June 1968," available online at the Harold Weisberg Archive at Hood College, accessed March 29, 2013, jfk.hood .edu/Collection/Weisberg%20Subject%20Index%20Files/I%20Disk/Investigation%20King%20Martin%20Luther%20Jr%20Dr/Item%20080.pdf. Each of the two witnesses to the escaping man, Charles Stephens and William Anschutz, presents his own problems. Stephens was likely drunk at the time of the shooting and Anschutz said he did not get a good look at the man fleeing the building, even though he had a very brief verbal exchange with the man about whether the man had heard a nearby shot—the man had heard it. One should probably place weight only on the broad particulars: a man left Bessie Brewer's in a hurried state carrying a long package wrapped in a blanket.

12. Betty Nyagoni, "Washington (D.C.) Riot of 1968," in *The Encyclopedia of American Race Riots*, vol. 2, edited by Walter C. Rucker and James N. Upton (Westport, CT: Greenwood, 2007), 683–85.

13. Michael Honey, *Going Down Jericho Road: The Memphis Strike, Martin Luther King Jr.'s Last Campaign* (New York: W. W. Norton, 2007), 445–46.

14. Carol Dietrich, "King, Martin Luther King Jr. (Assassination of)," in *The Encyclopedia of American Race Riots*, vol. 2, edited by Walter C. Rucker and James N. Upton (Westport, CT: Greenwood, 2007), 341.

15. FBI, "Jesse B. Stoner" (April–May 1968.) 157-3082, Jackson Field Office.

16. Jack Nelson. Transcript of interview with unknown White Knight, 1969. Jack Nelson Collection, Manuscript Archive and Rare Book Library, Emory University. MSS 1237 Box 3.

17. Nelson, *Terror in the Night*, 139–41.

18. Wesley Swift, "4-24-68 Bible Study Q&A" (sermon), April 24, 1968, Dr. Wesley Swift Library, transcript, swift.christogenea.org/content/04-24-68-bible-study-qa.

19. FBI, "Urgent Teletype from Dallas Field Office to Director, Memphis and Jackson" (April 23, 1968), MURKIN 44-38861-1836.

20. FBI, "Samuel Holloway Bowers Jr." (August 9, 1968), Bureau File 157-1654, section 23, at 15. This is a summary file obtained by the authors via FOIA. The relevant excerpt from the document reads as follows: "On April 5, 1968, [Jackson Informant] T-2 advised that while in John's Cafe that morning, he saw Sam Bowers

and told him that he did a good job the previous night (making reference to the killing of MARTIN LUTHER KING Jr.). Sam Bowers remarked that he carried Billy Roy Pitts up to Memphis and that 'poor Billy Roy' did not know what they were up to, but they got King shot." At first glance, it seems like Sam Bowers must have been joking. Bowers himself had witnesses to place him in Mississippi when King was shot. Moreover, Pitts was a turncoat, who was cooperating with the FBI in their prosecutions of Bowers and other white Knights for the killing of activist Vernon Dahmer in 1966. On the other hand, there may have been more truth to the remark than was immediately apparent. In separate files related to the Dahmer case, other informants note that Bowers's underlings were still in contact with Billy Roy Pitts at the time of the King assassination. A "limited hangout" in which Bowers could implicate a White Knights deserter to throw suspicion off his involvement—and the involvement of anyone in his inner circle—would be consistent with what we think White Knights associates Sidney Barnes and Margaret Capomacchia were doing to Thomas Tarrants several months after the crime.

21. Dina Temple-Raston, "An FBI Man's Inside View of '60s America in Turmoil," *All Things Considered*, National Public Radio, August 7, 2009, www.npr.org /templates/story/story.php?storyId=111659247.

22. FBI, "Memo to SAC Jackson; Subj: J.B. Stoner" (August 6, 1968), 157-3082-19.

23. FBI, "Samuel Holloway Bowers Jr." (August 9, 1968), Bureau File 157-1654, section 23, at 15, 21.

24. U.S. House Select Committee on Assassinations, *Investigation of the Assassination of Martin Luther King Jr.: Final Report*, 95th Cong. 2nd, Sess., available online at the Mary Ferrell Foundation, accessed April 20, 2015, www.maryferrell .org/showDoc.html?docId=800&search=cb_AND+memphis+AND+%22final +report%22.#relPageId=413&tab=page.

25. *Activities of the Ku Klux Klan organizations in the United States: Hearings Before the Comm. on Un-American Activities*, 89th Cong. at 1532 (February 1, 7–11, 1966) (testimony of Earl Holcombe). Available online at the Internet Archive, accessed September 15, 2010, www.archive.org/stream/activitiesofkuklo5unit /activitiesofkuklo5unit_djvu.txt.

26. FBI, "Re: Suspects W. Davis, B. Chidlow, Vincent Walker, and Lawrence Rand," MURKIN 44-1987-Sub E-790, available online at the Harold Weisberg Archive at Hood College, jfk.hood.edu/Collection/Weisberg%20Subject%20 Index%20Files/W%20Disk/William%20Len%20Hotel/Item%2003.pdf.

27. The picture of the matchbook can be found here: register.shelby.tn.us/media/mlk /index.php?p=hotel+william+len+matchbook+front.jpg&album=Evidence+2.

CHAPTER 12: MANHUNT

1. U.S. House Select Committee on Assassinations, *Investigation of the Assassination of Martin Luther King Jr.: Appendix to Hearings Before the Select Comm. on Assassinations*, 95th Cong., 2nd Sess., vol. xii, 252, available online at Mary Ferrell Foundation, accessed December 11, 2010, www.maryferrell.org/mffweb /archive/viewer/showDoc.do?docId=95659&relPageId=392. In Los Angeles in December 1967, Ray wrote to the U.S.–South Africa Business Council requesting information about emigration to Rhodesia. His choice of destinations in Africa

is corroborated by a variety of his contacts in 1968, after he had successfully left Canada and traveled to Portugal, exploring possible mercenary jobs in Angola.

2. FBI, "Teletype: From Director to Birmingham, Memphis, Mobile, Los Angeles" (April 15, 1968), Memphis Field Office MURKIN 44-1987-SUB E-356.

3. U.S. House Select Committee on Assassinations, *Summary of Findings and Recommendations*, H.R. Rep., section 6, Evidence of a Conspiracy in St. Louis, 377, available online at the National Archives, accessed December 11, 2010, www .archives.gov/research/jfk/select-committee-report/part-2c.html#klan. 20; also FBI, "Airtel from SAC Miami to FBI Director re: BAPBOMB, Sidney Crockette Barnes a.k.a. Racial Matters" (March 12, 1964), FBI file.

4. *Activities of the Ku Klux Klan Organizations in the United States: Hearings Before the Comm. on Un-American Activities*, 89th Cong. 2936 (February 1, 7–11, 1966), available online at the Internet Archive, accessed September 15, 2010, www .archive.org/stream/activitiesofkuklo5unit/activitiesofkuklo5unit_djvu.txt.

5. FBI, "Airtel from SAC Oklahoma City to Director re: Donald Eugene Sparks . . ." (April 24, 1968), King Assassination FBI Central Headquarters File, MURKIN 44-38861-2926; and FBI, "Airtel from Tampa to Director re: Donald Eugene Sparks . . ." (April 18, 1968), King Assassination FBI Central Headquarters File, MURKIN 44-38861-1331.

6. Mitchell, "KKK Killed Ben Chester White."

7. Gerard Robinson, in discussion with the authors, September 29, 2011. Robinson knew of Tarrants from his time as a racist rabble-rouser at Murphy High School. It is worth noting that Robinson remembered the integration efforts in Mobile in 1963—and the response at local high schools—as being one of the few other occasions that he was asked to work in the city proper. In that instance, the small field office was stretched thin because of the sheer number of protests and counterdemonstrations at so many high schools. Robinson could not be positive that the search for Tarrants was the one in response to Tarrants jumping bond; however, the context of his comments/recollection made that obvious.

8. FBI, "BH 44-1740. Airtel: SAC Birmingham to Director," report by Special Agents Robert Barrett and William Saucier (April 8, 1968). The information was taken on April 6, 1968, and dictated on April 8, 1968. Under Tarrants's name, reference is made to a file 157-758, which turns out to be a Mobile field office file. The authors attempted to access this information via FOIA only to learn that Mobile 157-758 file had been destroyed in 1977. It is rare for the FBI to destroy a file while an individual (in this case, Tarrants) is still alive; it also came on the heels of Congress's new inquiry into Dr. King's murder, for which Tarrants's files were requested only a few months after this Mobile file had been destroyed.

9. FBI, "Teletype from Jackson To New Orleans" (April 10, 1968), Jackson Field Office MURKIN file 157-9586, CD-ROM 59161160, 147–149.

10. FBI, "Memorandum from SA Richard F. Kilcourse to SAC Los Angeles" (April 23, 1968), 62-5101.

11. Jim Ingram, in discussion with the authors, June 20, 2009.

12. Melanson, *The Martin Luther King Assassination*, 86–88.

13. FBI, "Urgent Teletype from Dallas Field Office to Director, Memphis and Jackson" (April 23, 1968), MURKIN 44-38861-1835.

14. FBI, "Samuel Holloway Bowers Jr." (August 9, 1968), Bureau File 157-1654, section 23, at 15.

15. Nelson, *Terror in the Night*, 140.

16. FBI, "Memo to SAC Jackson; Subj: J.B. Stoner" (August 6, 1968), 157-3082-19.

17. Waldron and Hartmann, *Legacy of Secrecy*, 504.

18. Ibid., 606.

19. Dan Christensen, "King Assassination: FBI Ignored Its Miami Informer," *Miami*, no. 12 (October 1976), 37–38, available online at Cuban Information Archives, last modified February 23, 2008, accessed September 15, 2010, cuban-exile.com/doc_101-125/doc0114.html.

20. "James Earl Ray: Selected Chronology."

21. John Nicol, "Canadian Connection to the Martin Luther King Assassination," CBC News, April 3, 1968, http://www.cbc.ca/news/world/canadian-connection-in-the-martin-luther-king-assassination-1.696100.

22. "James Earl Ray: Selected Chronology."

23. FBI, "Airtel from SAC, Newark to Director (Attn: FBI Identification Division)" (June 11, 1968), FBI Central Headquarters File, section 59, available online at Mary Ferrell Foundation, accessed September 15, 2010, www.mary ferrell.org/mffweb/archive/viewer/showDoc.do?docId=99876&relPageId=38. The authors obtained a copy with fewer redactions than the online version from the FBI MURKIN collection at the National Archives II, College Park. The releases include the names of the informants, which we have kept secret, as we do not know if they are alive or dead. Also, the MURKIN file number is hard to read, so we excluded it.

24. "James Earl Ray: Selected Chronology."

25. Wesley Swift, "Ye That Have Killed For Gold" (sermon), June 8, 1969, Dr. Wesley Swift Library, transcript, drwesleyswift.christsassembly.com/68-06-08.htm.html.

26. Huie, *He Slew the Dreamer*, 140–46.

27. U.S. House Select Committee on Assassinations, *Investigation of the Assassination of Martin Luther King Jr.: Hearings Before the Select Comm. on Assassinations*, 95th Cong., 2nd Session, vol. 8, 67, available online at the Mary Ferrell Foundation, maryferrell.org/showDoc.html?docId=95660&relPageId=71&search=%22fu_manchu%22. James Earl Ray wrote this to John Ray on July 15, 1968, under the alias "Lord Rolf Sneyd." Someone crossed out the paragraph that made reference to Fu Manchu and the Tongue. The FBI had to decipher the letter to make out the reference. John Ray claimed, under oath before the HSCA, that he did not know who these individuals were and he did not know who crossed out the paragraph.

28. Manuel Chait, "Brother Says Ray Told of Conspiracy," *St. Louis Post-Dispatch*, March 13, 1969, jfk.hood.edu/Collection/Weisberg%20Subject%20Index%20Files/R%20Disk/Ray%20John/Item%2008.pdf.

29. FBI, "From: SAC Miami to SAC: Jackson Re: Kathleen Madlyn Ainsworth, et al." (September 17, 1968), Jackson Field Office 157-51-62.

30. Nelson, *Terror in the Night*, 61.

31. Ibid., 192, 247.

32. Ibid., 217–39.

33. Ibid.

34. Ibid., 255.

35. FBI, "Summary Report of SA Samuel Jennings, White Knights of the Ku Klux Klan" (February 24, 1969), FBI Jackson Field Office File 157-63, bureau file 157-1552.

36. FBI, "Re: Alleged Offer of $100,000 by the WKKKKOM to Anyone Who Kills Martin Luther King, Jr . . ." (July 24, 1967), Jackson Field Office File 157-7990, 41. Leroy B. McManaman, Appellant, v. United States of America. 327 F.2d 21 (10th Cir. 1964).

37. FBI, "Airtel from St. Louis to Director" (August 12, 1968), FBI Central Headquarters File, section 69.

38. Higgins, "Hair-Raising Experience," 14–19. The article mentions Ayers's stay at a mental hospital. Ayers's brother says that this may have been connected to an impulsive, violent temper. "'Crashed' King Rites; Tries to 'See' LBJ; Quickly Arrested," *Jet* XXXIV (no. 7), May 23, 1968, 8-9.

39. Donald Nissen, interview with authors, November 2009.

40. Higgins, "Hair-Raising Experience."

41. onedrive.live.com/?cid=8A36D65B295B5998&id=8A36D65B295B5998%2123542&parId=8A36D65B295B5998%2123436&o=OneUp.

42. FBI, "Airtel from SAC Kansas City to Director re: Memphis Airtel to Kansas City 8-23-68" (September 10, 1968), MURKIN 44-38861-5161.

43. Ibid.

CHAPTER 13: MISDIRECTION

1. Ray, *Who Killed Martin Luther King Jr.?*, 127–30.

2. McMichael, *Klandestine*, 9.

3. Ibid., 232.

4. Waldron and Hartmann, *Legacy of Secrecy*, 497–501.

5. FBI, "Report of Leonard C. Peterson re: Ferris Wood Sullinger" (April 26, 1965), Miami Field Office File 157-1118.

6. Huie, *He Slew the Dreamer.*

7. Ibid., 110.

8. Ibid., 3.

9. House Select Committee on Assassinations, *Summary of Findings and Recommendations*, 1979, at 308, available online at the National Archives, accessed December 11, 2010, www.archives.gov/research/jfk/select-committee-report/part-2a.html#fingerprints.

10. FBI, "Airtel from Memphis to Director," section 72 (October 25, 1968), King Assasination FBI Central Headquarters File, MURKIN 44-38861-5328, available online at Mary Ferrell Foundation, accessed September 15, 2010, www.maryferrell.org/mffweb/archive/viewer/show-Doc.do?mode=searchResult&absPageId=1132538.

11. Susan Blakeney, email message to authors, March 12, 2010.

12. Jerry Ray letter to authors, April 2010. In his letter, Jerry Ray says that James became aware of Quinn via a fellow prisoner in Tennessee, after James Earl Ray's arrest. It is odd that Quinn, who seems to have had a low profile outside White Knights circles, was the attorney someone else referred to James Earl Ray, if indeed James told the truth on the matter. While some of Ray's earliest

attorneys (Arthur Hanes and J. B. Stoner) were, like Quinn, Klan-connected, they had much more obvious national reputations and profiles.

13. Peter Holley, "The 'Terrifying' Confederate Statue Some Tennesseans Want to Hide," *Washington Post*, June 25, 2015, www.washingtonpost.com/news /morning-mix/wp/2015/06/25/is-this-the-weirdest-confederate-statue-in-dixie.

14. Ray, *Who Killed Martin Luther King Jr.?*, 156.

15. Richard A. Price and J. David Woodward, *The Burden of Busing: The Politics of Desegregation in Nashville, Tennessee* (Knoxville: University of Tennessee Press, 1995), 56.

16. Waldron and Hartmann, *Legacy of Secrecy*, 690.

17. House Select Committee on Assassinations, *Summary of Findings and Recommendations*, 1979, at 377–82, available online at the National Archives, accessed December 11, 2010, www.archives.gov/research/jfk/select-committee-report /part-2c.html.

18. Marc Perrusquia, "Was James Earl Ray Paid to Kill MLK? Note Raises Question Anew," *Punxsutawney Hometown* 127 (May 2011), issuu.com/home townmagazine/docs/may2011/26.

19. House Select Committee on Assassinations, *Press Release*, November 30 and December 1, 1978, at 18, MLK Exhibit F-594, available online at the Mary Ferrell Foundation, maryferrell.org/showDoc.html?docId=145137&search=%22 jerry_ray%22+AND+stoner#relPageId=18&tab=page. This is a letter from Jerry Ray in support of J. B. Stoner's Senate campaign.

20. Harold Weisberg, letter to Phil Melanson (August 10, 1984), available at the Harold Weisberg Archive at Hood College, accessed May 29, 2017, jfk.hood .edu/Collection/Weisberg%20Subject%20Index%20Files/M%20Disk /Melanson%20Philip/Item%2036.pdf.

21. Peter Dale Scott, "Memo re: Milteer Int Review and HUAC Hearings On Ku Klux Klan (1966)" (July 9, 1974), available online at the Harold Weisberg Archive at Hood College, jfk.hood.edu/Collection/Weisberg%20Subject%20 Index%20Files/S%20Disk/Scott%20Peter%20Dale/Item%2022.pdf.

22. U.S. House Select Committee on Assassinations, *Investigation of the Assassination of Martin Luther King, Jr.: Hearings Before the Select Comm. on Assassinations*, 95th Cong., 2nd Session, vol. iii, at 178 (August 18, 1978), available online at the Mary Ferrell Foundation, maryferrell.org/showDoc.html?docId=95655&search=hobo _AND+raoul#relPageId=182&tab=page.

23. See the photo on page 235 for the comparison and judge for yourself.

24. Harold Weisberg, letter to Bud Fensterwald (August 14, 1969), available online at the Harold Weisberg Archive at Hood College, accessed May 24, 2017, jfk.hood.edu/Collection/Weisberg%20Subject%20Index%20Files/R%20 Disk/Ray%20James%20Earl%20King%20Martin%20Luther%20Jr%20 Suit%203-11-70/Item%2014.pdf.

25. Harold Weisberg, "Monograph: COINTELPRO LANE, or, CONGRESS INVESTIGATES ASSASSINATIONS," available online at Harold Weisberg Archive at Hood College, accessed May 24, 2017, jfk.hood.edu/Collection /Weisberg%20Subject%20Index%20Files/W%20Disk/Weisberg%20Harold /Cointelpro%20Lane%20Monograph/Item%2001.pdf.

26. Jefferson Cohen, "Ray Looks Guilty as Alibis Dissolve. But Was He Alone?" *In These Times*, September 5, 1978, available online at the Harold Weisberg Archive

at Hood College, jfk.hood.edu/Collection/White%20Materials/White%20
Assassination%20Clippings%20Folders/House%20Select%20Committee%20On
%20Assassinations%20Cips%20And%20Inventory/HSCA-MLK/HSCA-
MLK%2011.pdf.

27. Bruce Smith, "$11 Million Awarded in King Libel Suit," ABCNews, October 5,
1995, abcnews.go.com/US/story?id=95490.

28. William F. Pepper, "An Act of State: The Execution of Martin Luther King,
Jr." (talk), February 4, 2003, Modern Times Bookstore, San Francisco, California, transcript, www.ratical.org/ratville/JFK/WFP020403.html.

29. Coretta Scott King et al., *Plaintiffs, vs. Loyd Jowers, et al., Defendants*, Case
No. 97242, Shelby County, Tennessee District Court for the 13th District
at Memphis, December 8, 1999, available online at the King Center, www
.thekingcenter.org/sites/default/files/KING%20FAMILY%20TRIAL%20
TRANSCRIPT.pdf. One can simply do a CTRL+F for the words *objection* or
I object on this transcript and see that time and time again, Jowers's defense attorney, Lewis Garrison, turns down the opportunity to object. The only major
objections come from Tennessee's Assistant Attorney General at the time, Michael Myers, who was opposing Pepper's efforts to question a state undercover
drug investigator. Myers was not defending or representing Jowers in any way.

30. Sharon Rufo et al., *Plaintiffs, vs. Orenthal James Simpson, et al., Defendants*, Case
No. SC 031947, Superior Court of the State of California for the County of Los
Angeles, available online at simpson.walraven.org/oct23-96.html. Again, by
searching just this one day of civil trial testimony in the wrongful death lawsuit
filed against O. J. Simpson by the family of murder victim Ronald Goldman,
one can see over two dozen objections just during opening statements!

31. Martin Hay, "William F. Pepper, The Plot to Kill King: The Truth Behind
the Assassination of Martin Luther King Jr." (review), Kennedys and King,
August 1, 2016, accessed August 15, 2017, kennedysandking.com/martin-luther-
king-reviews/pepper-william-f-the-plot-to-kill-king-the-truth-behind-the-
assassination-of-martin-luther-king-jr.

32. Bill Curry, "Ray's Escape Raises a Question: Why Was It So Easy?" *Washington Post*, June 13, 1977, www.washingtonpost.com/archive/politics/1977/06/13
/rays-escape-raises-a-question-why-was-it-so-easy/4eebd5c2-b751-4765-af1b-
2a48ac69d139.

33. Jerry Mitchell, "Ex-wife: James Earl Ray 'Didn't Do Anything for Free,'"
Journey to Justice (blog), *Clarion-Ledger*, April 1, 2010, blogs.clarionledger.com
/jmitchell/2010/04/01/ex-wife-james-earl-ray-didnt-do-anything-for-free.

34. FBI, "FBI Miami Field Office Urgent Teletype from Miami to Director, Jackson, Memphis" (August 2, 1968), Memphis 44-1987.

35. FBI, "FBI Miami Field Office Urgent Teletype from Miami to Director, Jackson, Memphis," section 68 (August 6, 1968), FBI Central Headquarters File
MURKIN 44-58861-5021, available online at the Mary Ferrell Foundation, www
.maryferrell.org/mffweb/archive/viewer/showDoc.do?mode=searchResult
&absPageId=1131536.

36. FBI, "King Assassination FBI Central Headquarters File" (August 14, 1968),
MURKIN 44-38261-5051.

37. J. B. Stoner, letter to Fred Hockett (May 23, 1962), available online at the Harold

Weisberg Archive at Hood College, jfk.hood.edu/Collection/Weisberg%20
Subject%20Index%20Files/M%20Disk/Milteer%20J%20A/Item%2003.pdf.

38. FBI, "Airtel from SAC Miami to FBI Director re: BAPBOMB, Sidney Crockett Barnes a.k.a. Racial Matters" (March 12, 1964), FBI file.

CHAPTER 14: AFTERMATH

1. 18 USC §241, available online at the Legal Information Institute at Cornell Law School, www.law.cornell.edu/uscode/18/241.shtml. Indeed, when the FBI was gearing up for a possible federal prosecution of "Eric Galt"—before they had made the James Earl Ray connection—they prepared an indictment using this section of the federal code. Obviously, the case was never tried on a federal level, only locally in Memphis, Tennessee.

2. Waldron and Hartmann, *Legacy of Secrecy*, 571.

3. Department of Justice/Civil Rights Division Referrals; Affidavits, June 1968, available online at Mary Ferrell Foundation, accessed September 15, 2010, www.maryferrell.org/mffweb/archive/viewer/showDoc.do?mode=searchResult&absPageId=106673. See affidavit of John Webster DeShazo, a gun store regular who interacted with Ray.

4. Our work with another individual, Jason Kull, using reverse phone and public records searches, places the phone within five to ten minutes' driving distance from the gun store.

5. Curt Gentry, *J. Edgar Hoover: The Man and the Secrets* (New York: W. W. Norton, 2001), 662.

6. House Select Committee on Assassinations, *MLK Report Volume 13*, H.R. Rep., section C: Personal relations between the Department and the Bureau, 1979, at 174–75, available online at the Mary Farrell Foundation, accessed December 11, 2010, www.maryferrell.org/mffweb/archive/viewer/showDoc.do?mode=searchResult&absPageId=1004327.

7. House Select Committee on Assassinations, *Summary of Findings and Recommendations*, 1979, at 381–82, available online at the National Archives, accessed December 11, 2010, www.archives.gov/research/jfk/select-committee-report/part-2c.html.

8. Ibid., 377–78.

9. House Select Committee on Assassinations, *Summary of Findings and Recommendations*, 1979, at 451, available online at the National Archives, accessed December 11, 2010, www.archives.gov/research/jfk/select-committee-report/part-2e.html.

10. House Select Committee on Assassinations, *Summary of Findings and Recommendations*, 1979, at 377–78, available online at the National Archives, accessed December 11, 2010, www.archives.gov/research/jfk/select-committee-report/part-2c.html.

11. Ibid., 382. Ray initially stalled on executing the waiver for Arthur Hanes as well but relented. He never waived this protection for Stoner, however.

12. Ibid., 402. This claim came from Sapp and not from Somersett. Sapp correctly reported that Somersett had heard other rumors, notably a threat by union officials against King owing to King's connection to labor union strikes (e.g. what

he was doing in Memphis). Having looked at the available documentation from Somersett to the Miami PD, we agree with the HSCA that it is unlikely he told this story to law enforcement before the assassination. Lieutenant Sapp likely just misremembered a story Somersett reported later. Again, it is important to note that Somersett was an informant who simply reported everything he heard, regardless of whether the source for the information was exaggerating or lying or telling the truth.

13. Christensen, "King Assassination."

14. Ibid.. See the latter for the redacted names.

15. FBI File No. 62-117290: section 10, at 16, available online at Mary Ferrell Foundation, accessed September 15, 2010, www.maryferrell.org/mffweb/archive/viewer/showDoc.do?docId=146430&relPageId=14. The HSCA requested all relevant material on Tarrants (and others) in January 1978. The FBI, in their FOIA response to us, said they had routinely destroyed the relevant file, Mobile Field Office File 157-758, in 1977.

16. Jerry Mitchell, "Murder of Martin Luther King Jr.; Did Klan Have a role?" *Clarion-Ledger*, December 30, 2007. 39. FBI, "SA Ronald Johnson and SA Lester Amann Interviews with Sidney C. Barnes" (September 30, 1968), Jackson Field Office File 157-51. 40. FBI, "Sidney Crockette Barnes," summary file, at 13 (November 30, 1971).

17. FBI, "SA Ronald Johnson and SA Lester Amann interviews with Sidney C. Barnes" (September 30, 1968), Jackson Field Office File 157-51.

18. FBI, "Sidney Crockette Barnes" (November 30, 1971), summary file, at 13. File obtained by the authors via FOIA.

19. House Select Committee on Assassinations, *Summary of Findings and Recommendations*, 1979, at 377, available online at the National Archives, accessed December 11, 2010, www.archives.gov/research/jfk/select-committee-report/part-2c.html.

20. Ibid., 378. One wonders if the sources on Barnes and the source on the White Knights are one and the same. There is an example of at least one person who had connections to all the relevant parties (e.g., Barnes, Carden, and the White Knights).

21. FBI, "Information concerning individuals who were formerly associated with the WKKKKOM, Jones Co., Miss." (November 15, 1970), Jackson Report of SA Samuel Jennings, serial 809, at 31–32.

22. Mitchell, "Murder of Martin Luther King Jr."

23. Bruce Hoffman, *Holy Terror: The Implications of Terrorism Motivated by a Religious Imperative* (Santa Monica, CA: RAND Corporation, 1993), www.public good.org/reports/holywar3.htm.

24. Ibid.

25. Stanley Nelson, *Devil's Walking: Klan Murders Along the Mississippi in the 1960s* (Baton Rouge, LA: LSU Press, 2016), 67.

26. Bruce Hoffman, *Holy Terror*.

27. Ibid.

28. Taylor Branch, *Canaan's Edge*, 486.

INDEX

Page references for illustrations appear in *italics*.

Denver, Joe, 98
DePugh, Robert, 34, 131–32
DeShazo, John, 135
DeSoto Motel, 136–37
Detroit, Michigan, 56, 221
Dietrich, Carol E., 148–49
Dillard, Chet, 115–16
Dixie Klans, 65
Dixie Mafia: and bounty for King murder,
x–xi, 6, 9, 20, 62, 99, 101, 103, 123, 130, 137,
155–56, 182, 183, 194, 211; criminal activities
and murders, 6–8, 9–10, 73, 103, 110, 244,
246–47; and murder of Pauline Pusser,
6–7; and murders of Vincent and Margaret
Sherry, 7–8, 10
Dowda, Louis Raymond, 72–76, 205; and
James Earl Ray, 105–7
Dunn, Burris, 42, 112, 217, 245
Dunn, Dennis, 140

Edmondson, George, 169
Eidson, Billy Ray, 195
Eisenhower, Dwight, 33
Emory University, 126
Eure, Sybil, 21, 22–23, 61, 62, 101, 105, 174–75,
179
Evers, Medgar, ix, 13, 15, 18, 48, 63, 164,
220–21
Expo 67, 79, 81

Faulkner, Charles, 86, 108, 136, 138
FBI: and bounty offers for King
murder, xi, xii, 4–5, 8–10, 11, 14–21,
61–66; Counterintelligence Program
(COINTELPRO), 112; Integrated
Automated Fingerprints Identification
System (IAFIS), 224; investigations into
King murder, 11, 68, 70, 73–75, 135, 138, 140,
151, 152–57, 222, 224; and J. Edgar Hoover,
16, 57, 118, 194; manhunts, 161–80; and
murders of civil rights activists, 13–14, 42;
MURKIN (King murder) records, 109,
130, 207, 209, 217; prosecutions/convictions
of King murder and plots, 41, 203–18;
surveillance by, 20–21, 23–24, 65, 87, 88,
98–99, 131; and White Knights of the Ku
Klux Klan of Mississippi (WKKKKOM),
115–16, 214
Federal Communications Commission, 155
Fensterwald, Bud, 190, 193
Fields, Ed: and National States Rights Party
(NSRP), 32–33, 38, 88, 245

Fitzgerald, Harold, 101
Flamingo Hotel, 129
Ford, Henry, 26
Foreman, Percy, 181, 184, 185, 187
Forrest County, Mississippi, 12–13
Fort Payne, Alabama, 6, 9
Fowler, William V., 103, 105, 246
Frank, Gerald, 121; An American Death, 121
Frankhouser, Roy, 35, 150
Freedom Riders, 37
Freedom Summer (1964), 19, 22, 43
Friends of Rhodesia, 119
Fuller, Claude, 17–18
Fuller, Cliff, 130, 155–57

Gale, William Potter, 33, 123, 162, 210, 217,
218; and California Rangers, 34, 39, 108,
241
Galt, Eric (also Eric S. Galt, Eric Starvo
Galt). See Ray, James Earl
Galt, Eric St. Vincent, 80
Gandhi, Mahatma, 48
Gardner, Floyd, 22
Garrison, Jim, 193
Garrison, Lewis, 196, 197
General Motors, Lakeland factory, 65, 75, 167
Gentry, Curt, 208
Georgia, xi, 5, 63, 66, 76, 101, 105, 157, 177,
204
Gilbert, Keith, 40, 41, 132, 162
Goff, Kenneth, 34
Goldman, Ron, 197
Goodman, Andrew, 13, 19, 97
Gregory, Dick, 191
Griffith, D. W.: The Birth of a Nation, 26, 63

Hamilton, Neil, 45
Hancock, Larry: The Awful Grace of God:
Religious Terrorism, White Supremacy, and
the Unsolved Murder of Martin Luther King
Jr., x
Hanes, Arthur Sr., 183–84, 186, 188, 194
Hardin, J. C. See Ashmore, James Wilborn
Harlem, New York, 48–49
Harper, Julius, 245
Hawkins, Danny Joe, 96–97, 98, 99, 111, 116,
151–52, 172, 173, 242, 243, 245
Hawkins, Joe Denver, 242, 245
Hay, Martin, 197
Hebrew Benevolent Congregation, 104
Hendricks, Myrtis Ruth, 140, 151, 165–66,
207, 210, 214

ABOUT THE AUTHORS

STUART WEXLER has long been considered one of the top investigative researchers on domestic terrorism and radical religious activities. His books include *The Awful Grace of God* and *America's Secret Jihad*. His groundbreaking work on forensics and historical crimes has been featured on *NBC News* and in *The Boston Globe*, *Newsweek*, *The Daily Beast*, *USA Today*, and *The Clarion-Ledger*. He now lives and teaches in New Jersey, where he won the prestigious James Madison Teaching Fellowship in 2010.

LARRY HANCOCK is considered one of the top investigative researchers on the areas of intelligence and national security. He is the author of six books, including *Shadow Warfare* and *Surprise Attack*. Hancock's books have received endorsements and praise from former House Select Committee on Investigations staff members and the former Joint Historian for the State Department and Central Intelligence Agency. He lives in Oklahoma.